The Networked Recluse

The Connected World of Emily Dickinson

The Networked Recluse

The Connected World of Emily Dickinson

Mike Kelly   Carolyn Vega
Marta Werner   Susan Howe
Richard Wilbur

Published to accompany the exhibit
I'm Nobody! Who are you?
The Life and Poetry of Emily Dickinson
The Morgan Library & Museum   New York, New York
January 20 – May 21, 2017

AMHERST COLLEGE PRESS   MMXVII

The Networked Recluse

The Connected World of Emily Dickinson

AMHERST COLLEGE PRESS
Robert Frost Library • Amherst, Massachusetts

The Archives and Special Collections of Amherst College, The Morgan Library & Museum, The Houghton Library of Harvard University, The Boston Public Library, The New York Public Library, and The Archives and Special Collections of Mount Holyoke College have kindly given permission for the inclusion of images of materials in their collections for inclusion in this volume, under terms consistent with the Creative Commons license under which this volume is published.

Set in Atma Serif 11/14

ISBN 978-1-943208-06-7 paperback
ISBN 978-1-943208-07-4 electronic book

Library of Congress Control Number: 2016963773

Contents

Foreword

In late 1950 the Morgan Library & Museum received a gift of five first editions of Emily Dickinson's poems and published letters; an autograph poem, "Distance – is not the Realm of Fox"; and an autograph letter to Dickinson's cousin Perez Cowan. These books and manuscripts formed a compelling foundation to build a small but potent Dickinson collection at the Morgan.

Dickinson's powerful voice radiates through her original manuscripts. The letter to Cowan, written around February 1873, after a break in their correspondence, warmly notes that "much may have happened to both, but that is the rarest Book which opened at whatever page, equally enchants us." In addition to expressing her happiness at being in touch once again with Cowan, Dickinson breezily discusses his wife, his sister's marriage, their shared cousins, and a clergyman friend and thanks him for sending a paper he had edited. The letter exemplifies Dickinson's rich relationships with friends, family, and the world — networks explored in detail in the essays that follow and in the related exhibition *I'm Nobody! Who are you? The Life and Poetry of Emily Dickinson*.

Dickinson's earliest editors emphasized the poet's reclusiveness, and this reputation has endured. But "silence is all we dread," she wrote, and, although she withdrew from public life beginning in the 1860s, she maintained many connections throughout her life and was always a lively correspondent.

A desire to explore these connections led to a collaboration between the Morgan and Amherst College, which holds some 1,200 of Dickinson's manuscripts and letters. Also drawing on the unparalleled collections of Houghton Library, Harvard University; Mount Holyoke College; the Boston Public Library; the Emily Dickinson Museum; and the New York Public Library, this publication and the exhibition it accompanies contextualize the poet within her personal and literary networks and trace the development of her writing.

This is the first time these collections have been brought together for a major biographical exhibition. The show makes a number of important connections: drafts are shown alongside finished poems; a lock of Dickinson's hair sent to a friend is on display; and all of the portraits of the poet created in her lifetime have been reunited, including a recently discovered daguerreotype, which has never before been exhibited.

I am grateful to curator Mike Kelly, head of Archives and Special Collections at Amherst College, and to Susan Howe, Marta Werner, and Carolyn Vega for their contributions to this book. I would also like to acknowledge the generous support of the Ricciardi Family Exhibition Fund, the Lohf Fund for Poetry, the Caroline Macomber Fund, and Rudy and Sally Ruggles along with the assistance from the Acriel Foundation and the Gladys Krieble Delmas Foundation that has made this exhibition possible.

❧

A global institution focused on the European and American traditions, the Morgan Library & Museum houses one of the world's foremost collections of manuscripts, rare books, music, drawings, and ancient and other works of art. These holdings, which represent the legacy of Pierpont Morgan and numerous later benefactors, comprise a unique and dynamic record of Western civilization as well as an incomparable repository of ideas and of the creative process. The mission of the Morgan is to preserve, build, study, present, and interpret a collection of extraordinary quality in order to stimulate enjoyment, excite the imagination, advance learning, and nurture creativity.

Colin B. Bailey
Director, The Morgan Library & Museum

Introduction

Mike Kelly

When Mabel Loomis Todd and Thomas Wentworth Higginson published *Poems: Second Series* in the fall of 1891, they included a four-page manuscript image, a "Fac-simile of 'Renunciation,' by Emily Dickinson," as the frontispiece to that volume. In their preface, Dickinson's editors write about the shifts in her handwriting and her non-standard punctuation, including her "numerous dashes," further cementing her reputation as an unorthodox poet. Interest in Dickinson's manuscripts and their idiosyncrasies has waxed and waned over the past century, limited by both the accessibility of the originals and the technologies of reproduction and distribution. During the near century between the "fac-simile" included in *Poems: Second Series* and the landmark facsimile reconstruction of *The Manuscript Books of Emily Dickinson* by Ralph Franklin in 1981, the majority of Dickinson's manuscripts came to rest at Amherst College, Harvard University, Boston Public Library, and other repositories.

Dickinson scholars were quick to appreciate the value of the World Wide Web and digitization as tools for manuscript studies; the first iteration of the Dickinson Electronic Archives under the editorial guidance of Martha Nell Smith was launched in 1994 and remains active today. Other projects followed as scholars grappled with editorial as well as technological challenges. As of late 2016, full-color, high resolution, digital facsimiles of Emily Dickinson's manuscripts are more widely available than ever before. Amherst College made scans of all of the Dickinson manuscripts held there freely available via Amherst College Digital Collections (acdc.amherst.edu); Harvard University assembled The Emily Dickinson Archive with selected manuscripts from Amherst, the Houghton Library at Harvard University, and others; and the Boston Public Library has made the Dickinson manuscripts in the Galatea Collection of Thomas W. Higginson available through Flickr.

Figure 1: Emily Dickinson, "I suppose the time will / come," poem written in 1876 on the verso of an invitation from George Gould dated 1850 (Catalogue 2.15, page 37).

Apart from the obvious boon to scholarship, these digital tools enable us to approach Dickinson's manuscripts in new ways. Users of Amherst College Digital Collections can scroll through thumbnail images of all 853 manuscript objects in Amherst's collection, taking in at a glance the wide range of Dickinson's writing surfaces from standard stationery to fragments of envelopes. The Emily Dickinson Archive enables users to easily view manuscript drafts held by multiple repositories accompanied by Franklin's editorial notes.

Yet in spite of these great advances in access and usability, it is important to bear in mind the limits of the digital. Digital surrogates almost always conceal the true size and scale of the original; when every object is scaled to fit the user's display, with the ability to zoom in and out at will, the actual size of the original becomes obscured. With the ability to instantly scroll through hundreds of manuscripts in an instant, we lose track of their status as individual pieces of paper that were marked, folded, corrected, mutilated, sent through the mails, sewn into booklets, or tucked between the pages of a book.

This exhibition at the Morgan Library & Museum is an attempt to bridge the gap between the facility of the digital and the physical limitations of the originals. We selected a small group of items from Dickinson's vast literary remains to demonstrate the complex ways in which these often humble objects came into conversation with other people, places, and events in the poet's life. How, for instance, does the meaning of "I suppose the time will come" change when we learn that Dickinson wrote it on the back of an invitation she received from a classmate of her brother in 1850 (see Figure 1, left, and Cat 2.15)? Does one's impression of the iconic daguerreotype portrait of Dickinson shift when you can see the original image—scratches and all—inside its small plush case, rather than as a heavily retouched enlargement on a poster or web site? Did Dickinson attend the 1873 organ recital by Howard Parkhurst herself, or did her sister Lavinia bring her the copy of the concert program on which the poet wrote "Of our deepest delights there is a solemn shyness"? If the digital allows us to safely view artifacts across time and distance, encountering the originals in an exhibition case reminds us that these pieces bear many marks of their journey from the desk of Emily Dickinson in Amherst, Massachusetts to the Murray Hill neighborhood of Manhattan.

Another goal of this exhibition is to remind everyone that the story of Dickinson's manuscripts, her life, and her work is still unfolding. While the image of Dickinson as the reclusive poet who dressed only in white remains a popular myth, details of the actual life of Emily Dickinson continue to emerge. Several items included here were not known to exist until the current century. The scrap of biographical intelligence recorded by Sarah Tuthill in a Mount Holyoke catalogue, or the concern about Dickinson's salvation expressed by Abby Wood in a private letter to Abiah Root, were acquired by Amherst College in the last fifteen years. What additional fragments of Dickinson's life and relationships remain to be uncovered and identified in the attics and basements of New England?

Running through all of these concerns is the larger question of how to weigh and sift the evidence available to us to move beyond two-dimensional summaries of the lives of writers and artists of the past. The items included here are just a small selection of letters, poems, photographs, and other ephemera that illuminate small moments in Dickinson's life; as archives, libraries, and museums make more material available online, how do we explore, study, and deploy those materials to tell and re-tell the stories of figures like Emily Dickinson? What new questions will emerge from new modes of access? What shifts will take place in our understanding of the past when we can view not only Dickinson's manuscripts, but those of her friends, neighbors, contemporaries, and editors within the wider context of her historical moment?

6

Emily E. Dickinson,   Amherst.
Louisa Dickinson,   North Amherst.
Sarah E. Elmer, *dead*   Morristown, N. J.
Caroline J. Estabrook,   Camden, Me.
Abby R. Fletcher,   Andover.
Lucretia Foster,   Fitchburg.
Hannah C. Gilman,   Lowell.
Laura H. Gifford,   Waterville, N. Y.
Eliza B. Gridley,   Granby.
Ellen M. Hart,   New Britain, Ct.
Clara J. Harwood,   Rushville, N. Y.
Mary A. Hartwell,   Lincoln.
Eliza J. Holmes,   Waterbury, Ct.
Esther S. Humiston,   Waterbury, Ct.
Amelia D. Jones,   Springfield.
Hannah Jones,   Ludlow.
Alice C. Kimball,   East Thomaston, Me.
Angeline H. Kidder,   New Alstead, N. H.
Abby T. Linsley,   Barre, N. Y.
Elizabeth W. Marsh,   Sandusky, O.
Maria E Mason,   Palmer.
Caroline H. Merrick,   Cortland, N. Y.
Hannah Millard,   Delhi, N. Y.
Sara Morrill,   Alexandria, Va.
Elizabeth S. Olmsted,   East Hartford Ct.
Eliza P. Otis,   Cleveland, O.
Clara S. Packard,   Spencer.
Jerusha Pitkin,   East Hartford, Ct.
Julia M. Putnam,   Middleborough.
Eliza S. Reed,   Montpelier, Vt.
Emily D. Reed,   Montpelier, Vt.
Elizabeth A. Rice,   Bridport, Vt.
Margaret Robertson,   Sherbrook, Canada East.
Emily Sanford,   New Haven, Ct.
Harriet N. Sanford,   Medway.
Cordelia Sargeant,   Manchester, Vt.
Malvina Stanton,   Manchester, N. H.
Lucy E. Stearns,   New Ipswich, N. H.
Mary E. Stone,   Danbury, Ct.
Clara E. Thomas,   Hardwick.
Sarah S. Tuthill,   Greenport, L. I.

Sarah Tuthill, a student at Mount Holyoke Female Seminary in 1847, pencils brief character sketches of her classmates, including this observation about Emily Dickinson: "She is ever fair, and never proud, / Hath tongue at will and yet is never loud." Amherst College Archives and Special Collections.

The Realm of Fox:
The Dispersal of Emily Dickinson's Manuscripts

Carolyn Vega

Readers outside Emily Dickinson's intimate circle of friends and correspondents first had the opportunity to see one of her manuscripts in 1891, five years after the poet's death, when a facsimile of one of her manuscripts was published in *Poems: Second Series*, the second published volume of Dickinson's poetry (see Catalogue 5.26, page 86). The facsimile, placed just before the book's title page, reproduces the four manuscript pages of Dickinson's poem "Renunciation" ("There came a day – at Summer's full – ").

Facsimiles of contemporary literary works were somewhat novel at this time. Historical documents, autographs, maps, and illustrations had been reproduced in facsimile, initially as engravings made from tracings of the original and later as offset lithographs as the process was developed in the first decades of the nineteenth century. But facsimiles of literary texts—poems, novel drafts, etc.—were much less common. No book-length literary manuscript was reproduced until 1886.

Dickinson's idiosyncratic punctuation stands out immediately in the facsimile: her famous mark, now typically represented in type by an en-dash (as in "There came a day – at Summer's full – ") appears no fewer than forty-seven times in the manuscript. Her exuberant crossing of "t"s and proclivity towards the majuscule "E" is also notable. An 1891 reader, if she paused with the volume open to these facsimile pages and puzzled over the marks, may have been at a loss: the title "Renunciation" appears nowhere in the poem, much less as a title, and the poem does not appear elsewhere in the volume. A note above the poem says simply:

Fac-simile of "Renunciation," by Emily Dickinson.

PRINTED IN THE FIRST VOLUME OF HER POEMS.

This "first volume" is the famed *Poems*, published by the small Boston firm Roberts Brothers in 1890. Edited by two of Dickinson's friends and published in an edition of five hundred copies, it was an immediate success, selling out in a day

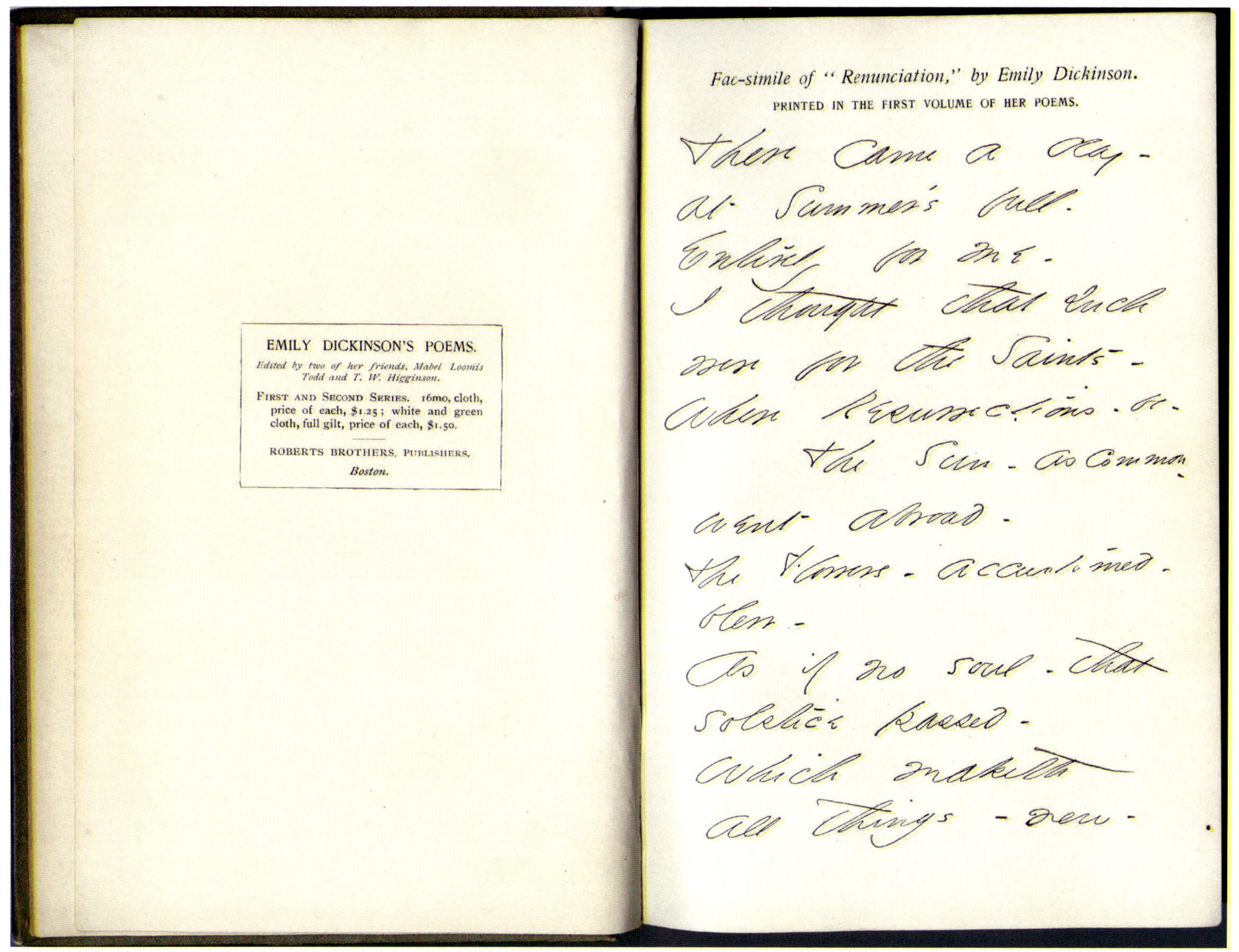

Figure 1: Emily Dickinson, *Poems: Second Series* (Boston: Roberts Brothers, 1891), frontispiece with facsimile of "There came a day – / at Summer's full – "; Amherst College Archive and Special Collections.

and being reprinted eleven times during the first year it was on sale.[1] In one of its earliest reviews, William Dean Howells proclaimed it the work of a "most singular and authentic spirit."[2]

The preface to *Poems: Second Series* remarks that the manuscript of "Renunciation" is a good example of Dickinson's handwriting at a transitional period, but there was something more at stake in the publication of the manuscript pages. As Millicent Todd Bingham—the daughter of Mabel Loomis Todd, one of the editors of the first several collections of Dickinson's poems and letters—explained in 1945, the facsimile was actually included as a way of showing flaws in the version of "Renunciation" published in an 1890 issue of *Scribner's Magazine*. By publishing the facsimile, Todd hoped to show that her interpretation of the poem (as it appeared in *Poems*) was the correct one. But the story is more complex still. The poem was in fact published in divergent versions in 1890 not just because different people

1. Lyndall Gordon, *Lives Like Loaded Guns* (New York: Penguin, 2010), 253.

2. William Dean Howells, "Editor's Study," *Harper's New Monthly Magazine*, January 1891, 319.

The Networked Recluse

edited the texts but also, as it happened, because editors were working from different manuscripts.

If a reader had been familiar with both appearances of the poem in print, she may have examined the facsimile pages with more interest than otherwise afforded such a curiosity: the manuscript text (although not the punctuation) corresponds to that in the 1890 book, while the *Scribner's* version "corrects" Dickinson's unusual lineation; prints "sail" for what appears in the seventh line to be "soul"; and omits entirely the fourth stanza, possibly, as Helen Vendler has noted, because editors found it blasphemous.[3]

A complex case, in other words, and one in which we can see, from the very beginning of the posthumous publication of Dickinson's poems, the huge importance of examining the work in manuscript.

❧

Emily Dickinson's manuscripts are famously challenging to interpret. She wrote nearly 1,800 poems, many in several drafts or variants.[4] Of these, only ten were published, all anonymously and likely without her consent, during her lifetime.

Dickinson's manuscripts fall into two broad categories: those retained by the poet and those sent or given to various friends and correspondents. The manuscripts were concentrated in two places when she died: in her bedroom (some believe the manuscripts were locked in a cherrywood chest), and in the possession of her sister-in-law and dear friend Susan Dickinson.

The manuscripts that Emily Dickinson retained included several booklets of poems, which had been created by sewing together folded sheets of stationery paper. In these booklets, commonly called fascicles, each poem is generally separated by a long dash, and Dickinson regularly employs idiosyncratic punctuation and capitalization. With one exception, the poems are untitled; several indicate alternate word or line choices in footnotes. For an author whose works only rarely appeared in print, scholars have considered the fascicles to be authoritative versions of the poems contained therein. The cache of manuscripts that Dickinson retained also included sheets that had been grouped together, but not sewn, as well as individual leaves and fragments.

Of those given or sent to friends, some are fluidly incorporated into the text of a letter, some carefully written out as fair copies on individual sheets. All—including the seemingly finalized fair copies—are challenging to interpret. Besides non-standard handwriting, experimental punctuation and poetics, and ambiguous word choice, readers must also consider for whom the poem was written (or copied). Dickinson regularly drafted multiple copies of the same poem for different friends;

---

3. Helen Vendler, *Dickinson: Selected Poems and Commentaries* (Cambridge, Mass.: The Belknap Press of Harvard University Press, 2010), 131.

4. Ralph W. Franklin, ed., *The Poems of Emily Dickinson* (Cambridge: Mass.: The Belknap Press of Harvard University Press, 1998) includes 1,789 poems represented in 2,500 individual manuscript texts.

in some cases changes might reflect a more final version, but in other cases it may
be the result of writing for a particular correspondent. Susan Dickinson was the
recipient of at least 252 poems, more than twice the amount sent to any other
person. At least thirty-seven other correspondents also received poems, and it
is clear that, although she did not publish her work, she regularly shared it with
friends and editors.

Shortly after Dickinson's death and the discovery of the manuscripts she retained,
Lavinia Dickinson, the poet's sister, asked Susan Dickinson to edit poems for
publication. Susan submitted a few poems to magazines, including, to *Scribner's*,
"Renunciation" ("There came a day – at Summer's full –"), which Susan prepared
from one of the four other complete drafts of the poem. According to later reports,
Lavinia objected to the publication of the poem and felt more generally that Susan
was taking too long in publishing the work, leading her to turn over manuscripts to
Susan's rival Mabel Loomis Todd, the much younger mistress of Susan's husband
Austin Dickinson, to continue publication. Todd set quickly to work, transcrib-
ing poems on a Hammond typewriter, a recent invention. Together with Thomas
Wentworth Higginson, one of the poet's literary mentors, she edited about 200
poems. They eventually persuaded Thomas Niles of Roberts Brothers to bring out
a small edition on a partial commission agreement in which Lavinia Dickinson
paid for the electrotypes.[5] This edition, which appeared in 1890 with the variant
"Renunciation," was a surprise to Susan Dickinson and instigated a battle between
Susan Dickinson and Mabel Loomis Todd for the control of Emily Dickinson's
literary legacy—and for her manuscripts.

Dickinson's manuscripts, split about evenly between Susan Dickinson and Mabel
Loomis Todd, were inherited through rival family lines until they were given in bulk
to Harvard University (Susan Dickinson's tranche, in 1950) and Amherst College
(Mabel Loomis Todd's, in 1956). It is remarkable that so few filtered out of either
Susan or Mabel's hands, or that the descendants did not sell the archive piecemeal
or at auction—particularly in view of the financial exigencies the heirs occasionally
faced. Dickinson's manuscripts have only infrequently appeared on the market,
chiefly because a significant share—some 1,873 poems and 650 letters—are held
by just two institutions.[6] A handful are scattered among other collections, including
the Morgan Library & Museum in New York.

Susan Dickinson occasionally gifted manuscripts, as did her daughter Martha
Dickinson Bianchi, and this is how some manuscripts eventually found their way
to the Morgan Library. At least two poems were given to Willard Wattles, a poet

---

5. Ralph W. Franklin, *The Editing of Emily Dickinson* (Madison: University of Wisconsin Press, 1967),
20.

6. Nine autograph poems have been sold at auction since May 1979: eleven have been offered, but
one was later discovered to be a forgery undertaken by Mark Hoffman, one was identified as a
transcript by Mabel Loomis Todd, and one—"She sped as Petals from a Rose"—was sold twice, first
in 1993 and again in 2013. Most recently, an undated note of a single line to an unidentified recipient
reading "No message is the utmost message for what we tell is done. Emily." sold at auction in New
York on December 9, 2015, for $20,000.

and professor of literature.[7] One was tipped into a first edition of Dickinson's *The Single Hound*, a volume brought forward by Martha Dickinson Bianchi in 1914, likely in a similar presentation to the "Renunciation" ("There came a Day – at Summer's full –") facsimile. The other, "The sun kept stooping – stooping – low–," was probably sent to Wattles loose, as it bears no marks of having been inserted into a volume.[8] This manuscript is marked with a penciled "x" on the verso, perhaps by Martha Dickinson Bianchi to identify it as one she would send to friends or collectors. Wattles kept both until his death in 1950. The Morgan acquired "The sun kept stooping – stooping low –" from his widow in 1953. It joined one other poem ("Distance – is not the Realm of Fox") already in the Morgan's collection; and in 1955 "Two – were immortal – twice –" was also added to the collection.[9] In that same year Thomas H. Johnson published the first complete edition of Dickinson's poetry.

All of the poems in the Morgan's collection were sent to Susan Dickinson. Two also appear in the fascicles; but one, written around 1866, exists in only the single copy. It reads:

> Distance – is not
> the Realm of Fox
> Nor by Relay of
> Bird
> Abated – Distance is
> Until thyself, Beloved.
> Emily.

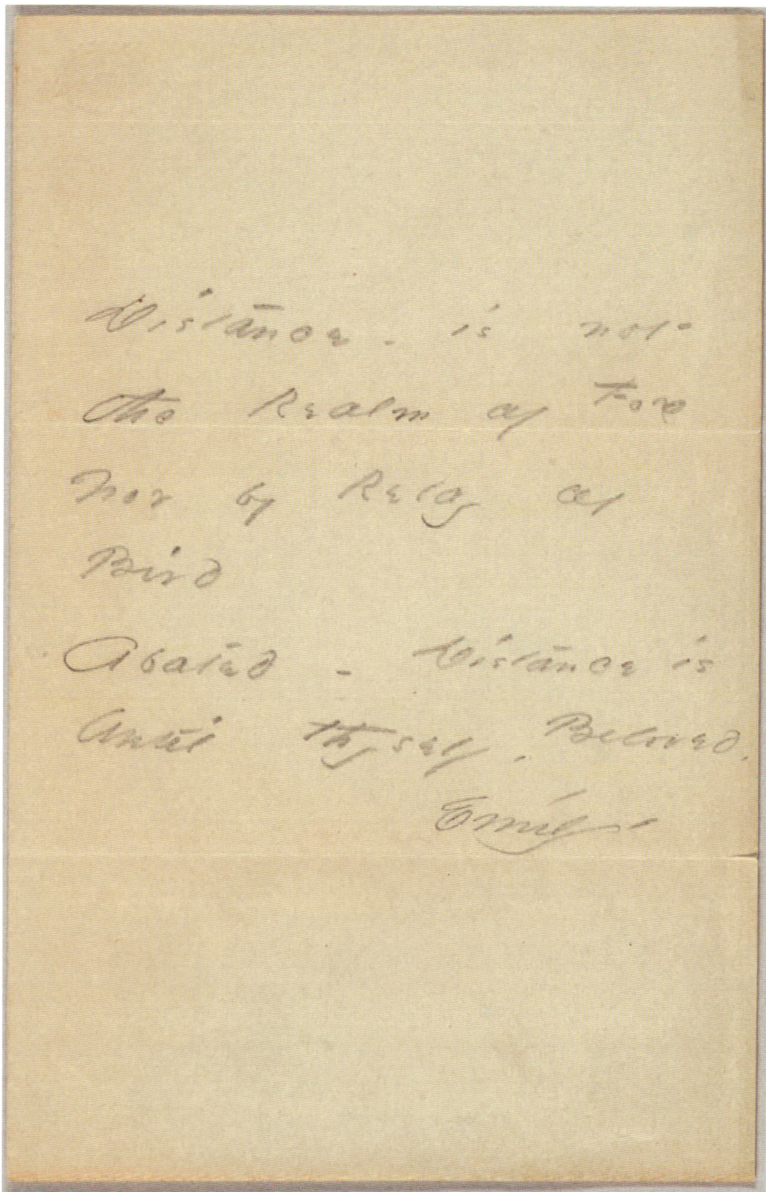

Figure 2: Emily Dickinson, "Distance – is not / the Realm of Fox" (Cat. 2.21), autograph poem signed and sent to Susan Dickinson ca. 1866. The Morgan Library & Museum, New York. Gift of Mrs. J. Ramsay Hunt, 1950. MA 1357.

---

7. "The sun kept stooping – stooping – low –," a fair copy of the poem sent to Susan Dickinson ca. summer 1860, was given to Willard Wattles by Martha Dickinson Bianchi; it is now in the Morgan's collection (MA 1488). "That Bells should ring, till all should know," one stanza of a longer poem sent to Susan Dickinson ca. 1871, was also given to Wattles by Martha Dickinson Bianchi in 1918; this manuscript was sold in New York on November 1, 2001.

8. Emily Dickinson, *The Single Hound: Poems of a Lifetime* (Boston, Little, Brown and Company, 1914); and Emily Dickinson, "The sun kept stooping – stooping – low –," fair copy of the poem sent to Susan Dickinson ca. summer 1860. The Morgan Library & Museum, New York. Purchased as the gift of William H. McCarthy, Jr. and F. B. Adams, Jr., 1953. MA 1488.

9. The Morgan's Emily Dickinson collection comprises the following manuscripts:
"The sun kept stooping – stooping – low –" (Franklin 182), autograph poem signed and sent to Susan Dickinson, ca. summer 1860. Purchased as the gift of William H. McCarthy, Jr. and F. B. Adams, Jr., 1953, MA 1488.
"Two – were immortal – twice –" (Franklin 855), autograph poem sent to Susan Dickinson, ca. early 1864. Gift of William H. McCarthy, Jr., 1955. MA 1641.
"Distance – is not the Realm of Fox" (Franklin 1128), autograph poem signed and sent to Susan Dickinson ca. 1866. Gift of Mrs. J. Ramsay Hunt, 1950. MA 1357.
Autograph letter to her cousin [Perez Dickinson Cowan], signed and dated ca. February 1873 (Johnson 386), on the marriage of his sister. Gift of William H. McCarthy, Jr. and F. B. Adams, Jr., 1951. MA 1358.
Autograph letter [to Adelaide Spencer Hills], signed and dated ca. summer 1874 (Johnson 417). Saying she believes "the sweetest thanks are inaudible" and remarking that flowers "are not quite earthly." Bequest of Gordon N. Ray, 1987. MA 4500.
Autograph letter to "Dear Girls" [Martha Dickinson and Sally Jenkins], signed and dated ca. 1883 (Johnson 845), concluding with the poem "Who has not found the heaven below" (Franklin 1609). Gift of William H. McCarthy, Jr. and F. B. Adams, Jr., 1954. MA 1556.

Her signature appears tucked up just under the last line, no farther apart than any of the other lines are from one another, almost incorporated into the poem itself, and underscoring the intimacy of the lines. The poem is written in pencil in Dickinson's distinctive handwriting of the mid-1860s. Although her handwriting changed over time, there is consistency within certain time frames and within genres or kinds of manuscripts. As a schoolgirl, she wrote in small cursive script typical of the nineteenth century; as an adult, she continued to write in ink but in a larger hand; but as she grew older, she began using pencil more frequently—eventually almost exclusively—and her handwriting transformed to include exaggerated and deliberate spaces between each letter, word, and line. Dickinson was treated by an ophthalmologist for several years, and trouble with her eyes may explain, at least partially, the drastic shift in her handwriting. Dickinson never dated her manuscripts, and this documented shift in her handwriting has helped scholars correctly place them.

For many neatly copied poems of the mid-1860s, such as "Distance – is not the Realm of Fox," Dickinson kept her letterforms distinct as if printed: her "e," for instance, never links to another letter and is—except for one case in this manuscript—transcribed as a small majuscule "E." In the text of the poem, there is economy in her small "E"s, but this becomes flourished in her signature.

There is a strong statement in her signature—it begins with the flourished E and ends in the unusually formed "y"—more like a long "s"—that underlines her name. The period and the dot of the "i" are similarly extravagant, overwhelming all other marks of punctuation on the page. Dickinson otherwise leaves clear spaces between each word and mark of punctuation. The finished poem was copied onto a sheet of standard stationery paper embossed "Paris" in the upper left corner. The poem is almost exactly centered on this page—there is only about a centimeter of difference between the upper and lower margins—and was written clearly out for presentation to Susan Dickinson.

Note the exactness and clarity with which Dickinson copied the text, along with the unusual punctuation and the comparatively flourished signature nestled almost within the body of the poem, which echoes the blank space three lines above. This verse appears nowhere else in Dickinson's manuscripts, which further frames the intimacy of the poem's theme: solitude is preferable to all company but the recipient's.

The complexity of interpreting Dickinson's manuscripts is heightened when examining unfinished or early-stage drafts, which defy straightforward reading. These drafts often include alternate words and lines. In some instances, scholars can infer Dickinson's decision by examining variant copies she sent to friends, but in many other cases the manuscript is a unique draft and her choice must remain ambiguous. Then there is the question of paper: some of the unfinished drafts are hastily penciled on odd-sized scraps, such as torn fragments or strips of wrapping paper. These may reflect the poet's immediate need to record a poem on whatever was at hand, but there are also nearly finished poems, or even some fair copies, written on unexpected kinds of paper: in one instance, Dickinson writes a poem about waiting for the inevitable on the back of an invitation sent by a young man some twenty-five years earlier; in another instance, she writes a poem about the intangibility of "the way hope builds his house" (see Catalogue 4.13, page 65) on an envelope cut, perhaps by Dickinson, in the shape of a house.

On the interior of a different envelope, this time cut into the shape of an arrow, she writes:

> A Pang is more
> conspicuous in Spring
> In contrast with the
> things that sing
> Not Birds entirely – but
> Minds –
> And Winds – Minute Effulgencies
> – When what they sung
> for is undone
> Who cares about
> a Blue Bird's Tune –
> Why, Resurrection
> had to wait
> Till they had moved
> a Stone –

In the manuscript, various elements are given dramatic emphasis: the pang acutely felt in the first line; the movement of the wind and minute effulgencies—small splendors—that fill out the point of the arrow; and the contraction to stillness while waiting for the resurrection are expressed in the shape of the page (see Catalogue 5.23, page 84). The performative aspect of the contours of this manuscript defied publishers until 2013, when Marta Werner and Jen Bervin included the poem in a new facsimile edition, *The Gorgeous Nothings*. This project followed the tradition established by the 1891 facsimile and continued by Ralph W. Franklin's 1981 *The Manuscript Books of Emily Dickinson*, but broke new ground by focusing on the so-called envelope poems, those written on non-standard sheets of paper. This was the first time that many readers were exposed to this aspect of Dickinson's manuscript practice.

Original manuscripts, when examined in facsimile or in person, give readers access to an author's creative process, otherwise obscured by the uniform language of type. This is especially important to acknowledge in Dickinson's case, since, with perhaps one exception, she did not authorize the publication of any of her poems. Working through folders of Dickinson poem after Dickinson poem is a rare experience. At the Morgan, one can examine the entire collection in a single sitting: there are just six manuscripts and about twenty-five books to look at. But at Amherst and Harvard there are dozens of archival boxes. Studying the manuscripts in these boxes is humbling—the entire œuvre of a very private person is at hand. The range of manuscripts includes everything from the fluid drafts and early sketches of poems to the seemingly finished fair copies that Dickinson might have shared with the public had she pursued publication more sedulously.

Her close friend Helen Hunt Jackson once told her: "You are a great poet—and it is wrong to the day you live in, that you will not sing aloud. When you are what men call dead, you will be sorry you were so stingy."[10] But although Dickinson did not publish, she did preserve her poems. Reading her vast body of work is challenging because even the most seemingly straightforward poems have elements buried beneath the surface. By encountering Emily Dickinson's poems in their original forms—in manuscript—we gain new tools to interpret her work.

---

10. Helen Hunt Jackson, Autograph letter to Emily Dickinson, signed and dated Colorado Springs, March 20, 1876 (Johnson 444a; Houghton Library, Harvard University).

I'm Nobody! Who are you?

The Life and Poetry of Emily Dickinson

Emily Dickinson, long acknowledged as one of the most important poets of the nineteenth century, remains an enigmatic figure. Well known as the reclusive "woman in the white dress" and as a solitary genius who penned some of the best-known American verse while in her bedroom, Dickinson was in fact deeply connected to her world. Her reputation for solitude stands in sharp contrast to the evidence of an extensive web of relationships to family, friends, and the literature and mass culture of her time.

She retained private copies of some 1,100 poems — most of which she carefully bound into hand-sewn booklets called "fascicles" — that were discovered after her death, but she also shared hundreds of poems with a wide network of correspondents. However, she saw essentially none of these poems to print: only ten were published during her lifetime, all anonymously and likely without her consent. Her unique process of composing manuscripts has challenged generations of editors, who have struggled to interpret and present her idiosyncratic punctuation, ambiguous word choice, and unusual use of paper.

Dickinson remains enigmatic, but a close examination of her original letters and poems illuminates the complexities of her relationships and the environment in which she lived and worked.

1.01   Otis Allen Bullard (1816–1853)
Emily Elizabeth, Austin, and Lavinia Dickinson
Oil on canvas, ca. 1840
Dickinson Room, Houghton Library, Harvard University

This portrait of Emily Dickinson (left) with her brother Austin (center) and sister Lavinia (right) was painted by Otis Allen Bullard in early 1840, when Emily was ten years old. Her short-cut auburn hair is striking, and it is fitting that this early image of the poet shows her holding a book and a flower, though it is unclear whether this is an illustrated publication or Dickinson's own album of pressed botanical specimens, which she had started the year before. The intimate bond between Dickinson and her siblings portrayed here is one that lasted until her death at age fifty-six in 1886.

The January 15, 1840 issue of *The Amherst Gazette* features an advertisement for Bullard's services, enabling us to date this portrait of the Dickinson children to early 1840.

1. Childhood

"I attend Singing School"

Emily Dickinson was born in 1830 into a tight-knit family that was at the social center of Amherst, a small college town in western Massachusetts. Her father was extremely protective of his children, but nevertheless encouraged them to pursue educational opportunities. Primary schooling for young women was not uncommon in Dickinson's time, and she formed many strong attachments to her schoolmates and instructors at Amherst Academy, where she was part of a close group of friends known as "the circle of five." Her exposure to poetry and keen use of language dates to her youth, as does her interest in the natural world and aesthetic presentation, evident in her herbarium, an album of carefully pressed botanical specimens.

   Dickinson lived almost her entire life in the shadow of Amherst College, which was co-founded by her grandfather and where her father served as treasurer between 1835 and 1873. Life in a small college town brought a steady stream of visitors from far and wide, and Dickinson lived within an intellectually stimulating environment that would later be reflected in her letters and poetry.

1.02   Charles Temple (1824–1906)
Emily Dickinson
Cut paper silhouette, 1845
Amherst College Archives and Special Collections,
1956.003

This silhouette portrait was cut by Charles Temple,
Dickinson's French instructor at Amherst Academy during
the 1842-43 academic year. Charles Temple and his older
brother Daniel were born on the island of Malta to American
missionary parents before relocating to Smyrna (now Izmir,
Turkey). It was a common practice for missionaries living
abroad to send their children to school in the United States,
resulting in a small but constant presence of international
students in the Amherst community. In this instance, we know
that Dickinson had ongoing contact with a young man with a
very different experience of life.

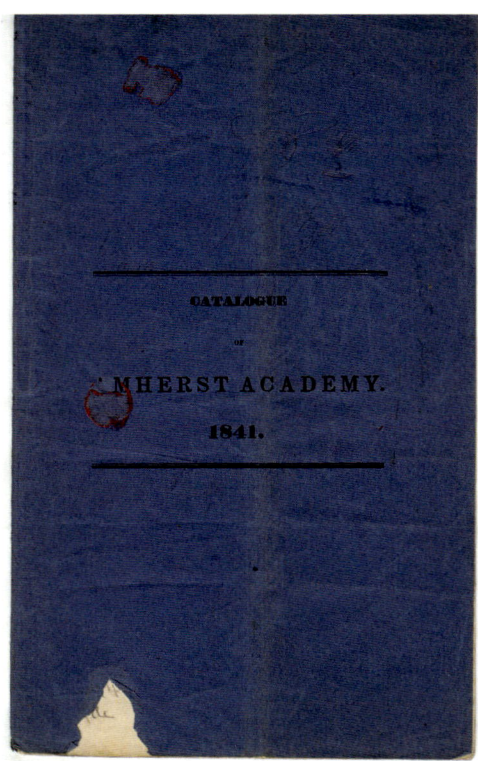

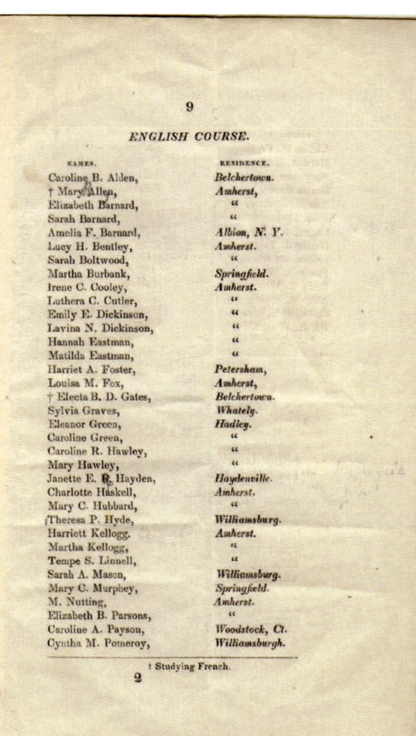

9

ENGLISH COURSE.

NAMES.	RESIDENCE.
Caroline B. Alden,	Belchertown.
† Mary Allen,	Amherst,
Elizabeth Barnard,	"
Sarah Barnard,	"
Amelia F. Barnard,	Albion, N. Y.
Lucy H. Bentley,	Amherst.
Sarah Boltwood,	"
Martha Burbank,	Springfield.
Irene C. Cooley,	Amherst.
Luthera C. Cutler,	"
Emily E. Dickinson,	"
Lavina N. Dickinson,	"
Hannah Eastman,	"
Matilda Eastman,	"
Harriet A. Foster,	Petersham,
Louisa M. Fox,	Amherst,
† Electa B. D. Gates,	Belchertown.
Sylvia Graves,	Whately.
Eleanor Green,	Hadley.
Caroline Green,	"
Caroline R. Hawley,	"
Mary Hawley,	"
Janette E. B. Hayden,	Haydenville.
Charlotte Haskell,	Amherst.
Mary C. Hubbard,	"
Theresa P. Hyde,	Williamsburg.
Harriett Kellogg.	Amherst.
Martha Kellogg,	"
Tempe S. Linnell,	"
Sarah A. Mason,	Williamsburg.
Mary C. Murphey,	Springfield.
M. Nutting,	Amherst.
Elizabeth B. Parsons,	"
Caroline A. Payson,	Woodstock, Ct.
Cyntha M. Pomeroy,	Williamsburgh.

† Studying French.

2

1.03   *Catalogue of the Trustees, Instructors, and Students of Amherst Academy: for the Year Ending July 1841*
Amherst: J. S. & C. Adams, 1841
Amherst College Archives and Special Collections, RBR WMA 194

Amherst Academy was founded in 1814 by Noah Webster, Samuel Fowler Dickinson (Dickinson's grandfather), and others; the same men would go on to establish Amherst College in 1821. These two printed catalogs contain a wealth of information about the primary school Dickinson attended, on and off, between fall 1840 and summer 1847. The catalog for her first year shows Dickinson and her sister Lavinia as members of the "English Course" in the "Female Department."

1.04   *Catalogue of the Trustees, Instructors, and Students of Amherst Academy: for the Academical Year Ending August, 1843*
Amherst: J. S. & C. Adams, 1841
Amherst College Archives and Special Collections, RBR WMA 214

In her third year at Amherst Academy, Dickinson advanced to the "Classical Course," which emphasized the study of Latin and Greek language and literature, as seen in this 1842–43 catalog. She was also marked as one of several students studying French under Charles Temple, a member of the Amherst College class of 1845. Her sister Lavinia is listed on the following page as a student in the "English Course" along with Abby Wood, one of Dickinson's closest companions in the 1840s.

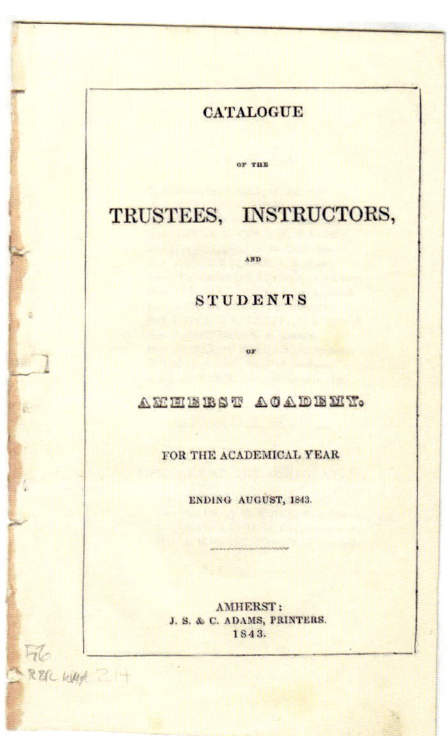

CATALOGUE

OF THE

TRUSTEES, INSTRUCTORS,

AND

STUDENTS

OF

AMHERST ACADEMY.

FOR THE ACADEMICAL YEAR

ENDING AUGUST, 1843.

AMHERST:
J. S. & C. ADAMS, PRINTERS.
1843.

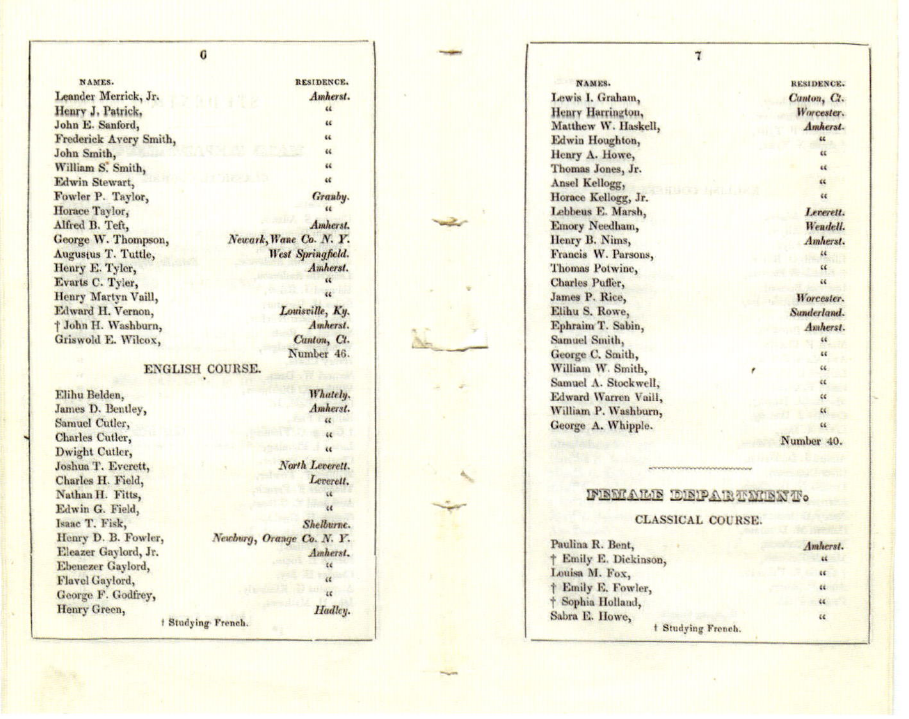

6

NAMES.	RESIDENCE.
Leander Merrick, Jr.	Amherst.
Henry J. Patrick,	"
John E. Sanford,	"
Frederick Avery Smith,	"
John Smith,	"
William S. Smith,	"
Edwin Stewart,	"
Fowler P. Taylor,	Granby.
Horace Taylor,	"
Alfred B. Teft,	Amherst.
George W. Thompson,	Newark, Wane Co. N. Y.
Augustus T. Tuttle,	West Springfield.
Henry E. Tyler,	Amherst.
Evarts C. Tyler,	"
Henry Martyn Vaill,	"
Edward H. Vernon,	Louisville, Ky.
† John H. Washburn,	Amherst.
Griswold E. Wilcox,	Canton, Ct.
	Number 46.

ENGLISH COURSE.

NAMES.	RESIDENCE.
Elihu Belden,	Whately.
James D. Bentley,	Amherst.
Samuel Cutler,	"
Charles Cutler,	"
Dwight Cutler,	"
Joshua T. Everett,	North Leverett.
Charles H. Field,	Leverett.
Nathan H. Fitts,	"
Edwin G. Field,	"
Isaac T. Fisk,	Shelburne.
Henry D. B. Fowler,	Newburg, Orange Co. N. Y.
Eleazer Gaylord, Jr.	Amherst.
Ebenezer Gaylord,	"
Flavel Gaylord,	"
George F. Godfrey,	"
Henry Green,	Hadley.

† Studying French.

7

NAMES.	RESIDENCE.
Lewis I. Graham,	Canton, Ct.
Henry Harrington,	Worcester.
Matthew W. Haskell,	Amherst.
Edwin Houghton,	"
Henry A. Howe,	"
Thomas Jones, Jr.	"
Ansel Kellogg,	"
Horace Kellogg, Jr.	"
Lebbeus E. Marsh,	Leverett.
Emory Needham,	Wendell.
Henry B. Nims,	Amherst.
Francis W. Parsons,	"
Thomas Potwine,	"
Charles Puffer,	"
James P. Rice,	Worcester.
Elihu S. Rowe,	Sunderland.
Ephraim T. Sabin,	Amherst.
Samuel Smith,	"
George C. Smith,	"
William W. Smith,	"
Samuel A. Stockwell,	"
Edward Warren Vaill,	"
William P. Washburn,	"
George A. Whipple.	"
	Number 40.

FEMALE DEPARTMENT.

CLASSICAL COURSE.

NAMES.	RESIDENCE.
Paulina R. Bent,	Amherst.
† Emily E. Dickinson,	"
Louisa M. Fox,	"
† Emily E. Fowler,	"
† Sophia Holland,	"
Sabra E. Howe,	"

† Studying French.

1.05   Orra White Hitchcock (1796–1863)

Amherst College in 1821

Ink and watercolor on paper, ca. 1845

Amherst College Archives and Special Collections,
Edward and Orra White Hitchcock Papers, MA.00027

These renderings of the Amherst College grounds show
how small the school was during Dickinson's lifetime. In
1821 (above), the year the college was founded, the campus
consisted of a single building and the nearby Congregational
Church. The student body doubled in the second year, and in
1823 (right) a second dormitory was completed. Dickinson
witnessed the growth of the college throughout her lifetime,
including the addition of Amherst's first Natural History
Museum—The Octagon—in 1847.

The drawing above was made by Orra White Hitchcock, wife
and collaborator of Edward Hitchcock, a geology professor and
later president of the college. She regularly created drawings
and paintings to accompany her husband's publications and
lectures. Their daughter, Mary, shared her mother's artistic
talents; she made the drawing at right.

1.06 Mary Hitchcock (1824–1899)
Amherst College in 1824 with the Bell Tower
Ink and ink wash on paper, ca. 1845
Amherst College Archives and Special Collections,
Edward and Orra White Hitchcock Papers, MA.00027

Probably sent
f. Easthampton
1845

William A. Dickinson

Lucy M. Baker

Monday A.M.

Dear brother Austin

As Mr Baker was going directly to where you are I thought I would write a line to inform you that if it is pleasant day after tomorrow we are all coming over to see you but you must not think so much of our coming as it may rain and spoil all our plans. however if it is not pleasant so that we do not come over

father says that you may come home on Saturday and if we do not come he will make some arrangement for you to come and write you what it. I attend singing school. Mr Woodman has a very fine one Saturday evenings and has quite a large school. I presume you will want to go when you return home. We had a very severe frost here last night and the ground was frozen hard. We all had our noses nipped a little. The Ladys Society meets over here tomorrow and I expect we shall have a very pleasant meeting. If you was at home it would be perfectly so. we wish much to hear from you. and if you have time I wish you would write a line and send by Mr Baker. Mattie wishes if you have stockings or any of them then that you should do them up in a little bundle I send them by Mr Baker. Accept much love from us all.

your affectionate sister E

If we dont come wednesday we may Thursday if not father will write you.

Opposite page:

1.07 Emily Dickinson (1830–1886)
Letter to her brother Austin, signed and dated Amherst,
autumn 1844
Amherst College Archives and Special Collections,
Emily Dickinson Collection, AC 550

1.08 Swinging seal
Richly chased gold, oval mount holds citrine gem,
"Emily" engraved in script; loop at one end for
suspending seal from chain.
English or American; circa 1850.
Gold, citrine; length: 1.9 cm
Dickinson Room, Houghton Library,
Harvard University

Dickinson's older brother Austin attended the Williston
Seminary in Easthampton, Massachusetts during the 1841-42
and 1844-45 academic years, just twelve miles away across
the Connecticut River. Whenever the brother and sister were
living apart, Dickinson maintained their close relationship
through frequent letters.

It was common to seal letters with wax pressed by a seal; this
one, engraved "Emily" in reverse, may have belonged to the
poet. The handwriting in this letter—in which she hopes to
visit the following day, tells him about her singing school, and
instructs him from their mother to look after his stockings in
the cold weather—is typical of Dickinson's early manuscripts;
over the next four decades, her handwriting would change
dramatically from this tidy script to the less orderly writing of
her late manuscripts.

Monday AM

Dear brother Austin

As Mr Baker was going directly to where you are I thought I would write a line to inform you that if it is pleasant day after to morrow we are all coming over to see you, but you must not think too much of our coming as it may rain and spoil all our plans. however if it is not pleasant so that we do not come over

Father says that you may come home on Saturday, and if we do not come he will make some arrangement for you to come and write you what it is. I attend Singing School. Mr. Woodman has a very fine one Sunday evenings and has quite a large school. I presume you will want to go when you return home. We had a very severe frost here last night and the ground was froz en-hard. We all had our noses nipped a little. The Ladys Society meets at our house tomorrow and I expect we shall have a very pleasant meeting If you was at home it

would be perfectly sure. we wish much to hear from you, and if you have time I wish you would write a line and send by Mr. Baker. Mother wishes if your stockings are any of them thin, that you should do them up in a little bundle & send them by Mr Baker. Accept much love from us all.

your affectionate sister E

If we don't come Wednesday, we may Thursday if not father will write you.

Autumn 1844. Letter composed in pencil by Dickinson to Austin Dickinson on two leaves (l = 12.3 x 10 cm) of one sheet of off-white, lightly ruled paper folded vertically in half and then horizontally into thirds. In lieu of an envelope, Dickinson addressed the letter on the outer fold to "William A Dickinson / per Mr. Baker." In 1844, Austin Dickinson was pursuing studies in Classics at Williston Seminary, in Easthampton, MA. Although a penciled note on letter reads, "Probably sent to Easthampton – 1845," Thomas H. Johnson dates the letter earlier based largely on Dickinson's internal reference to the frozen ground. This letter, though neatly executed, exhibits the irregular punctuation and capitalization typical of Dickinson's letters from this early period.

1.09 *The Holy Bible, Containing the Old and New Testaments:*
Translated Out of the Original Tongues
Philadelphia: J.B. Lippincott & Co., 1843
Emily Dickinson's copy
EDR 8, Houghton Library, Harvard University

Dickinson struggled with religious faith throughout her life, but she was intimately familiar with the Bible. This copy was given to Dickinson by her father and, in addition to her name stamped in gold on the green Morocco binding, it bears many marks of her use: Dickinson cut out individual words and portions of entire pages, folded down corners, and added botanical specimens. A clover flower that is believed to have been picked by the poet from her father's grave was once pressed between pages 286 and 287 in the first book of Samuel. See the manuscript of "Alone and in a circumstance" (Cat. 3.07, p. 51) for an example of Dickinson's use of text clippings as enhancements to her manuscripts.

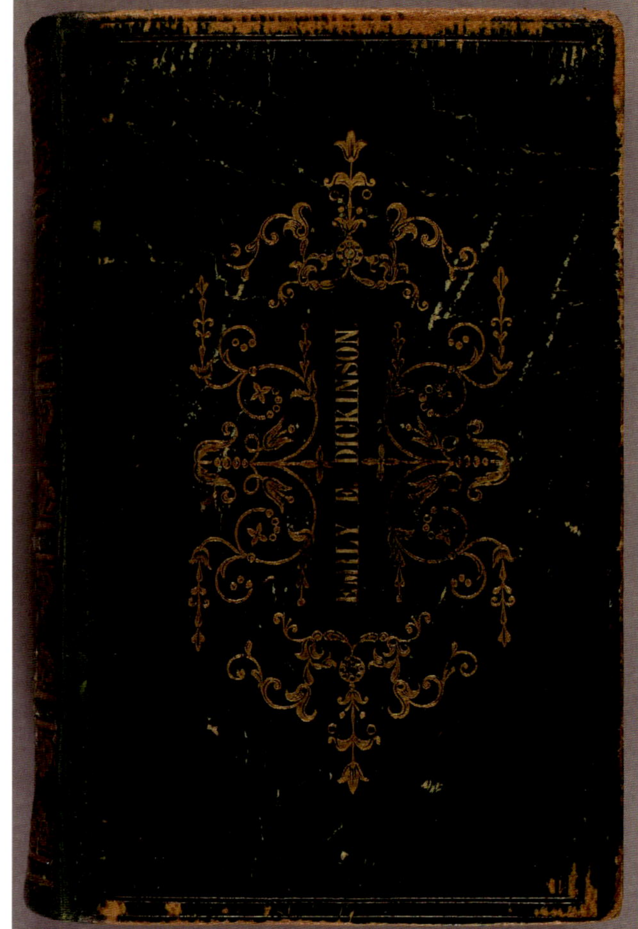

1.10 Clarissa Munger Badger (1806–1899)
Wild Flowers Drawn and Colored from Nature
New York and London: Charles Scribner;
Sampson Low, Son & Co., 1859
EDR 467, Houghton Library, Harvard University

Dickinson also received this book from her father as a New Year's gift for 1859. This book of hand-colored illustrations of flowers paired with verses by Mrs. Lydia Huntley Sigourney is exemplary of the sort of work Edward Dickinson found acceptable for his intellectual child. Sigourney lived in nearby Hartford, Connecticut and her conventional verse about nature and domestic themes was very popular during Dickinson's lifetime. This copy does not show any of the marks of use found in her Bible – no words or pictures have been cut out, and there appear to be no marks in pencil or ink other than her father's inscription at the front.

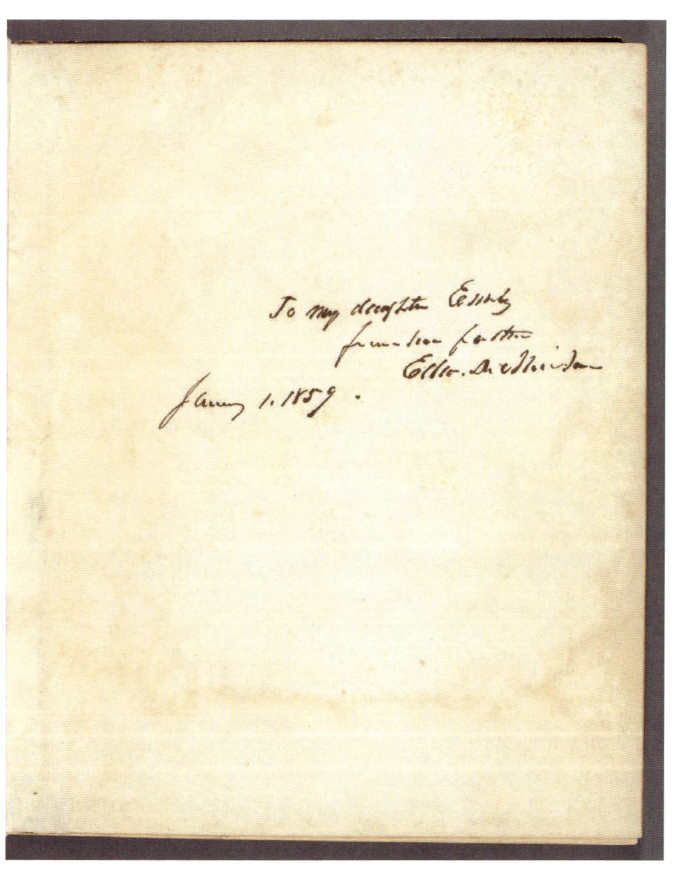

2. College & Friendships

A Year at Mount Holyoke

"Everything is pleasant & happy here"

At the age of sixteen, Emily Dickinson left home to study at
Mount Holyoke Female Seminary, a women's college, in nearby
South Hadley, Massachusetts. She tested into the first of three academic
levels, but was promoted to the second by mid-year, and took courses
in chemistry, logic, history and languages. She was roommates with her
cousin, Emily Norcross, and her time there is well documented in the
surviving letters she sent to her brother Austin and friend Abiah Root, one
of "the circle of five" friends from Amherst Academy. It was not unusual
for women to attend only a single year of higher education, and Dickinson
returned to Amherst at the end of the academic year.

2.01   Artist unknown

Mary Lyon

Ivory miniature made for Eunice Caldwell Cowles, 1832
Mount Holyoke College Archives and Special
Collections

Mary Lyon founded Mount Holyoke Female Seminary, a
women's college, in South Hadley, Massachusetts in 1837, and
she was principal of the school when Dickinson attended
ten years later. Before founding Mount Holyoke, she served
as the Principal of Byfield Seminary and became deeply
engaged with Congregationalist ministers such as Reverend
Joseph Emerson who advocated more academically rigorous
secondary education for women. The Mount Holyoke
curriculum served as an early model for women's colleges, and
was particularly notable for its strength in natural sciences.
Mary Lyon was also deeply concerned about spiritual welfare,
and Mount Holyoke students were pressured to make
confessions of faith. Dickinson was one of about thirty (from
a student body of more than 200) that declined to do so; Mary
Lyon regularly met with these students, whom she classified as
"No-Hopers."

Opposite page:

2.02   Knowlton Brothers, photographers

Mount Holyoke Seminary, South Hadley, Mass.

From *Connecticut Valley Views*
Stereoscope card
Northampton, Mass., ca. 1860

2.03   Photographer unknown

*Mount Holyoke Female Seminary students make doughnuts
and wash dishes in Domestic Hall*

Stereoscope card, ca. 1877

Mount Holyoke College Archives and Special
Collections

These images were made long after Dickinson's time at
Mount Holyoke, but she lived, studied, and socialized in
the Seminary Building pictured at top. The building housed
classrooms, parlors, bedrooms and a dining room in addition
to the college library and a periodical reading room. Students
did much of their own practical household management to
keep expenses low, including preparing meals and washing
floors and windows; when Dickinson was a student, she was
assigned the task of cleaning the knives. Mary Lyon was also
an advocate of physical fitness and exercise for young women,
requiring students take long walks and perform calisthenics.

KNOWLTON BROS., PHOTOGRAPHERS, NORTHAMPTON, MASS.
CONNECTICUT VALLEY VIEWS.
Mt. Holyoke Seminary, South Hadley Mass.

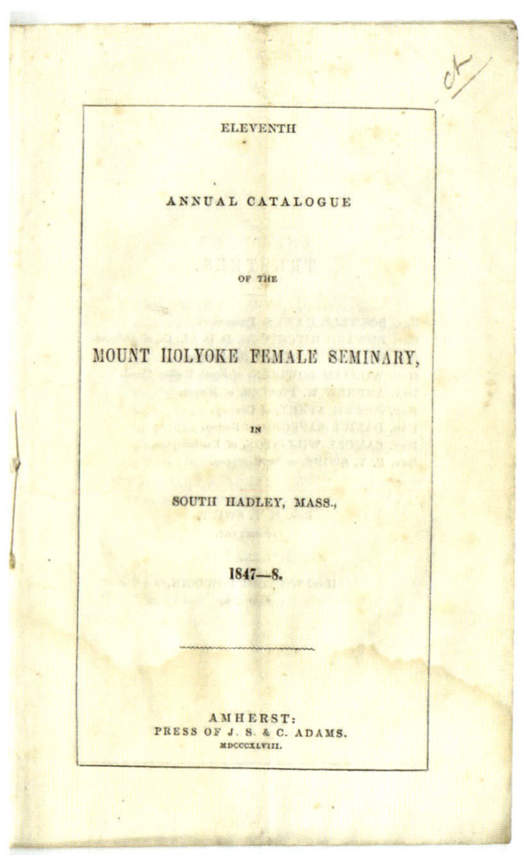

2.04 *Eleventh Annual Catalogue of the Mount Holyoke Female Seminary, in South Hadley, Mass., 1847–8.*
Amherst [Massachusetts]: Press of J.S. & C. Adams, 1848
Amherst College Archives and Special Collections, LD7088 .A2 1847/48

In the days before yearbooks were a common feature of American education, students often used copies of their school catalogues to record memories of their classmates and teachers. This copy of the Mount Holyoke catalogue for the year Dickinson attended is a rich source of information about her college experience. It belonged to Sarah Tuthill of Greenport, Long Island, who was a member of the "Middle Class" with Emily Dickinson. Although Tuthill's handwriting is very small and difficult to read, the lines written next to Dickinson's name have been deciphered: "She is ever fair, and never proud, Hath tongue at will and yet is never loud." Tuthill uses these lines from Shakespeare's *Othello* to describe impressions of her classmate.

Opposite page:

2.05 Amherst College
Exhibition of the Eclectic Society, Tuesday November 26, at 6 1-2 o'clock, P. M., 1850
Program with Emily Dickinson's notes
Amherst College Archives and Special Collections, Emily Dickinson Collection, AC 60

In November 1850, Dickinson attended a night of performances with her sister, Lavinia (here called "Vinnie"), and covered the program with notes. The writing on the cover is intriguing: "Vinnie & I sat together, Mr. Chapin her escort, Mr and Mrs Snell, mine. This night is long to be remembered. New things have happened. 'The crooked is made straight.' I am confided in by one — and despised by an other! And another still!" It is tempting to read romantic intrigue into these notes, but it is more likely that the "new things" Dickinson mentions are related to the ongoing religious revival.

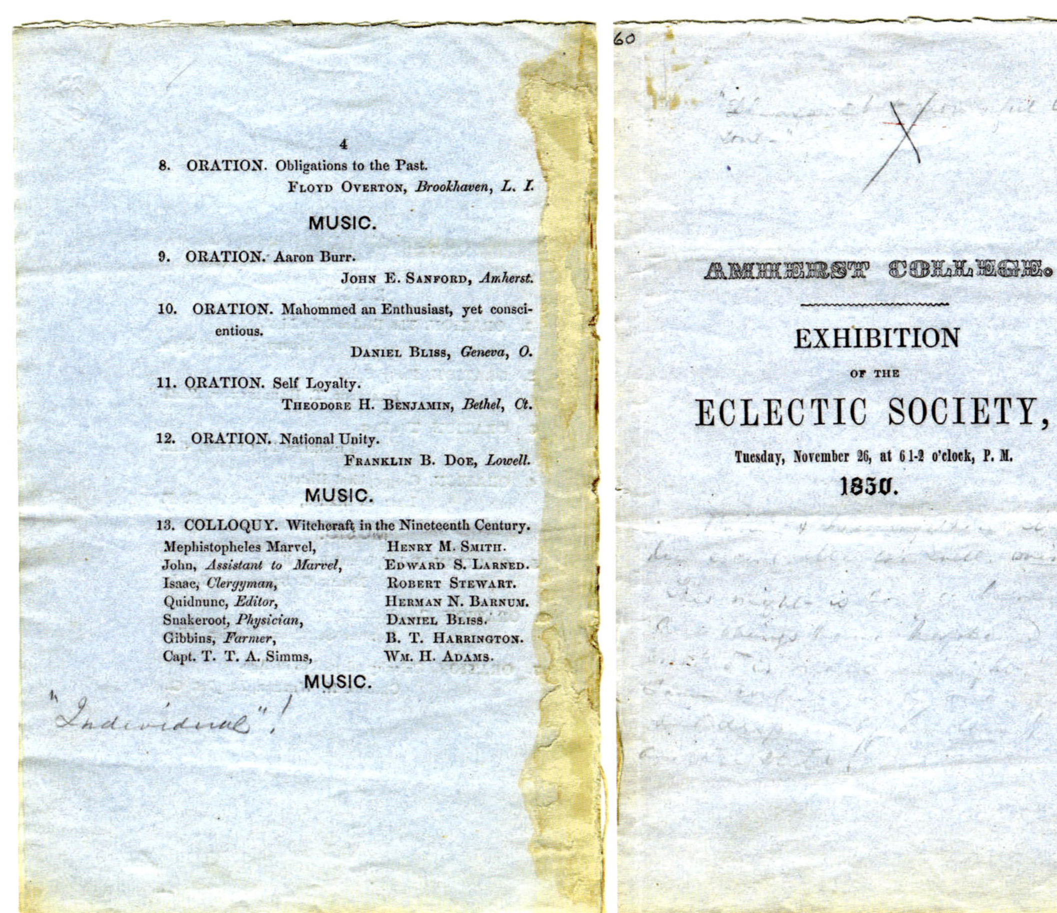

4

8. ORATION. Obligations to the Past.
    FLOYD OVERTON, *Brookhaven, L. I.*

MUSIC.

9. ORATION. Aaron Burr.
    JOHN E. SANFORD, *Amherst.*

10. ORATION. Mahommed an Enthusiast, yet conscientious.
    DANIEL BLISS, *Geneva, O.*

11. ORATION. Self Loyalty.
    THEODORE H. BENJAMIN, *Bethel, Ct.*

12. ORATION. National Unity.
    FRANKLIN B. DOE, *Lowell.*

MUSIC.

13. COLLOQUY. Witchcraft in the Nineteenth Century.

Mephistopheles Marvel,	HENRY M. SMITH.
John, *Assistant to Marvel,*	EDWARD S. LARNED.
Isaac, *Clergyman,*	ROBERT STEWART.
Quidnunc, *Editor,*	HERMAN N. BARNUM.
Snakeroot, *Physician,*	DANIEL BLISS.
Gibbins, *Farmer,*	B. T. HARRINGTON.
Capt. T. T. A. Simms,	WM. H. ADAMS.

MUSIC.

60

AMHERST COLLEGE.

EXHIBITION

OF THE

ECLECTIC SOCIETY,

Tuesday, November 26, at 6 1-2 o'clock, P. M.

1850.

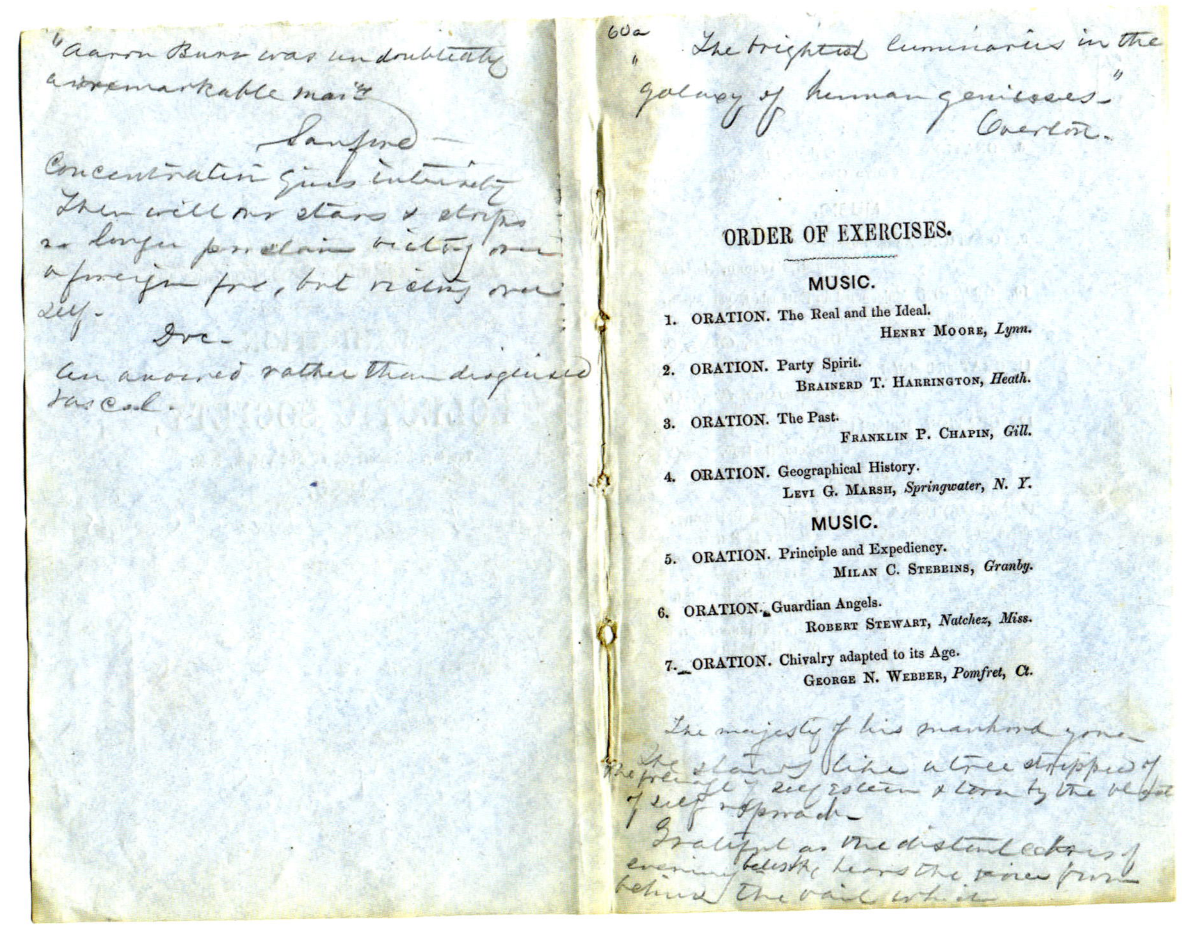

ORDER OF EXERCISES.

MUSIC.

1. ORATION. The Real and the Ideal.
    HENRY MOORE, *Lynn.*

2. ORATION. Party Spirit.
    BRAINERD T. HARRINGTON, *Heath.*

3. ORATION. The Past.
    FRANKLIN P. CHAPIN, *Gill.*

4. ORATION. Geographical History.
    LEVI G. MARSH, *Springwater, N. Y.*

MUSIC.

5. ORATION. Principle and Expediency.
    MILAN C. STEBBINS, *Granby.*

6. ORATION. Guardian Angels.
    ROBERT STEWART, *Natchez, Miss.*

7. ORATION. Chivalry adapted to its Age.
    GEORGE N. WEBBER, *Pomfret, Ct.*

2.06   Hannah Louisa Plimpton Peet Hartwell (1823–1908)
Herbarium, 1847-1868
Mount Holyoke College Archives and Special
Collections

This herbarium—an album of cut and pressed botanical
specimens—was compiled by Dickinson's classmate, Hannah
Louisa Plimpton. Most students at Mount Holyoke during this
period created their own herbaria, but Dickinson began work
on one of her own long before she attended Mount Holyoke. In
a letter to her friend Abiah Root in May 1845 Dickinson wrote:
"Have you made you an herbarium yet? I hope you will if you
have not, it would be such a treasure to you; 'most all the girls
are making one." Dickinson was as familiar with the botanical
details of the specimens she collected as she was with their
potential literary symbolism.

2.07   Emily Dickinson (1830–1886)
        Herbarium, ca. 1839–1846
        MS AM 1118.11, Houghton Library,
        Harvard University

Dickinson began compiling this herbarium around 1839, when she was just eight or nine years old, filling it with more than four hundred examples of plants and flowers from the fields and forests around her home. She compiled the cuttings with as much attention to aesthetic arrangement as to scientific classification. Dickinson also became an avid gardener, and the natural world would later figure prominently in her poetry.

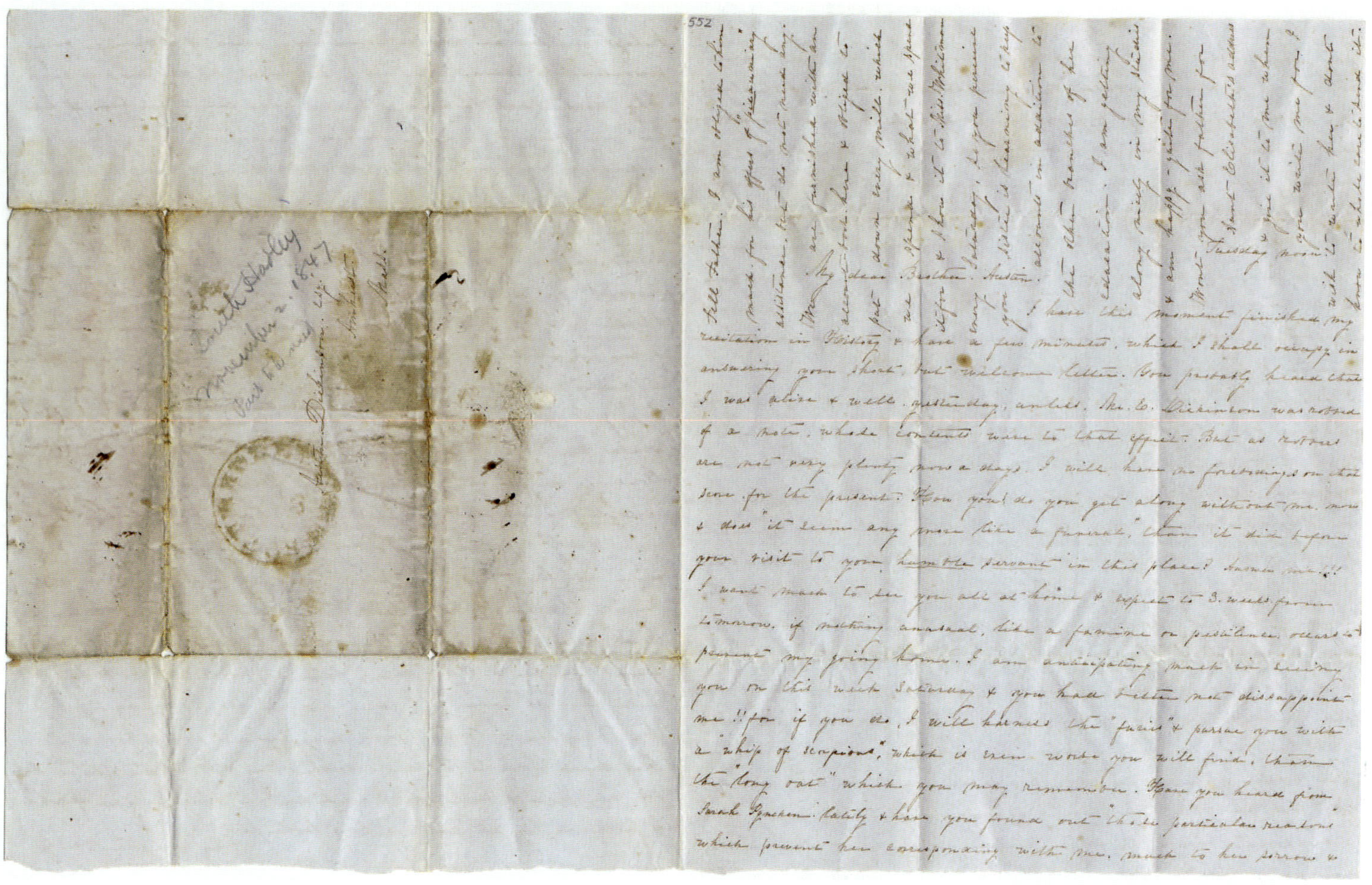

2.08 Emily Dickinson (1830–1886)

Letter to her brother Austin Dickinson, signed and
dated South Hadley, Mass., November 2, 1847
Amherst College Archives and Special Collections,
Emily Dickinson Collection, AC 552

Dickinson's primary concern in this letter to her brother while
she was at Mount Holyoke is the lack of letters received from
family and friends. She writes of Abby Wood: "I hear often
from Abby & think she has not forgotten me, though absent.
She is now my debtor to the amount of one long letter & I wish
you would inform her, if you have an opportunity, that I am
anxiously waiting to receive it." While Dickinson may have felt
this lack of letters from friends acutely during her year away
at school, it is a recurring complaint throughout her forty-odd
years of surviving correspondence.

The Networked Recluse

My dear Brother . Austin .

I have this moment finished my recitation in History & have a few minutes, which I shall occupy in answering your short, but welcome letter. You probably heard that I was alive & well – yesterday, unless, Mr. E. Dickinson was robbed of a note, whose contents were to that effect. But as robbers are not very plenty now a days, I will have no forebodings on that score, for the present. How you! do you get along without me, now & does "it seem any more like a funeral," than it did before your visit to your <u>humble</u> <u>servant</u> in this place? Answer me!!! I want much to see you all at home & expect to 3. weeks from tomorrow, if nothing unusual, like a famine or pestilence, occurs to prevent my going home. I am anticipating much in seeing you on this week Saturday & you had better not dissappoint me!! for if you do, I will harness the "furies" & pursue you with a "whip of scorpions," which is even worse you will find, than the "long oat" which you may remember. Have you heard from Sarah Pynchen lately & have you found out "those particular reasons" which   prevent her corresponding with me, much to her sorrow &

tell Father . I am obliged to him much . for his offers of "pecuniary" assistance, but do not need any – We are furnished with an account-book, here & obliged to put down every nickel, which we spend & what we spend & show it to Miss. Whitman every Saturday, so you perceive your sister is learning to keep accounts in addition to the other branches of her education. I am getting along nicely in my studies and am happy – quite for me. Wont you ask Father for Aunt Elisabeth's address & give it to me when you write me for I wish to write her & dont know to whose care to send it.

Tuesday noon.

November 2, 1847. Letter composed in ink by Dickinson to Austin Dickinson on two leaves of one folded sheet of wove, blue-gray stationery. In 1847, Dickinson was studying at Mary Lyon's Mount Holyoke Female Seminary, South Hadley, Mass. Dickinson addressed the letter herself, on the fold: "Austin Dickinson, Esq./Amherst./Mass. To save space, Dickinson has resorted to a modified form of cross-writing at the end of the letter, which appears on the opening leaf. A second sheet enclosed with the letter includes the South Hadley Seminary's "Bill of Fare."

Opposite page:

2.09   Photographer unknown
William Austin Dickinson
Daguerreotype
Amherst, Mass., ca. 1850
Amherst College Archives and Special Collections,
Amherst College Photograph Collection

Austin Dickinson graduated from Amherst College with the class of 1850. This daguerreotype portrait was likely made in the months immediately preceding commencement exercises, which were held on August 8, 1850. Even though the Dickinson home was just a short walk from the college, Austin lived on campus during his senior year.

Dickinson and her brother remained close until the end of her life, and it is through him that she made many important and lasting friendships.

2.09 Emily Dickinson (1830–1886)
Letter to Abiah Root, signed and dated
South Hadley, Mass., November 6, 1847
Mount Holyoke College Archives and Special
Collections

All of Dickinson's surviving letters from her year at Mount Holyoke are addressed either to her brother Austin or her friend Abiah Root. In this letter, Dickinson gives a long and detailed account of her journey from home, taking her entrance exams, her roommate, and a detailed report of her daily schedule and meals. In short, it sounds like a typical young person writing to a friend about her exciting first months of college. Dickinson's enthusiasm is unqualified: "Everything is pleasant & happy here & I think I could be no happier at any other school away from home."

Companions and Correspondents

"Meet me at sunrise, or sunset, or the new moon"

Amherst College was established in 1821 with the explicit goal of educating, in Noah Webster's phrase, "indigent young men of promising talents and hopeful piety" for the Christian ministry. After the Civil War, the college drifted away from this focus on missionary training, but during Dickinson's lifetime it was a hotbed for religious revivals. As the daughter of the college treasurer, Dickinson was expected to attend public events such as commencement and to assist with the annual trustee's reception hosted at her father's house.

Dickinson, who increasingly withdrew from society in the 1860s, led a socially active life when she was young. She attended performances, concerts, and lectures and remained close to friends she had made as a child at Amherst Academy. She also formed new relationships, often through her brother Austin. He introduced her to his friends—at least one with whom she had a flirtation—and Austin's wife, Susan, became one of the poet's dearest friends. Even as she became more reclusive, Dickinson maintained an active correspondence, penning more than 1,000 letters in her lifetime.

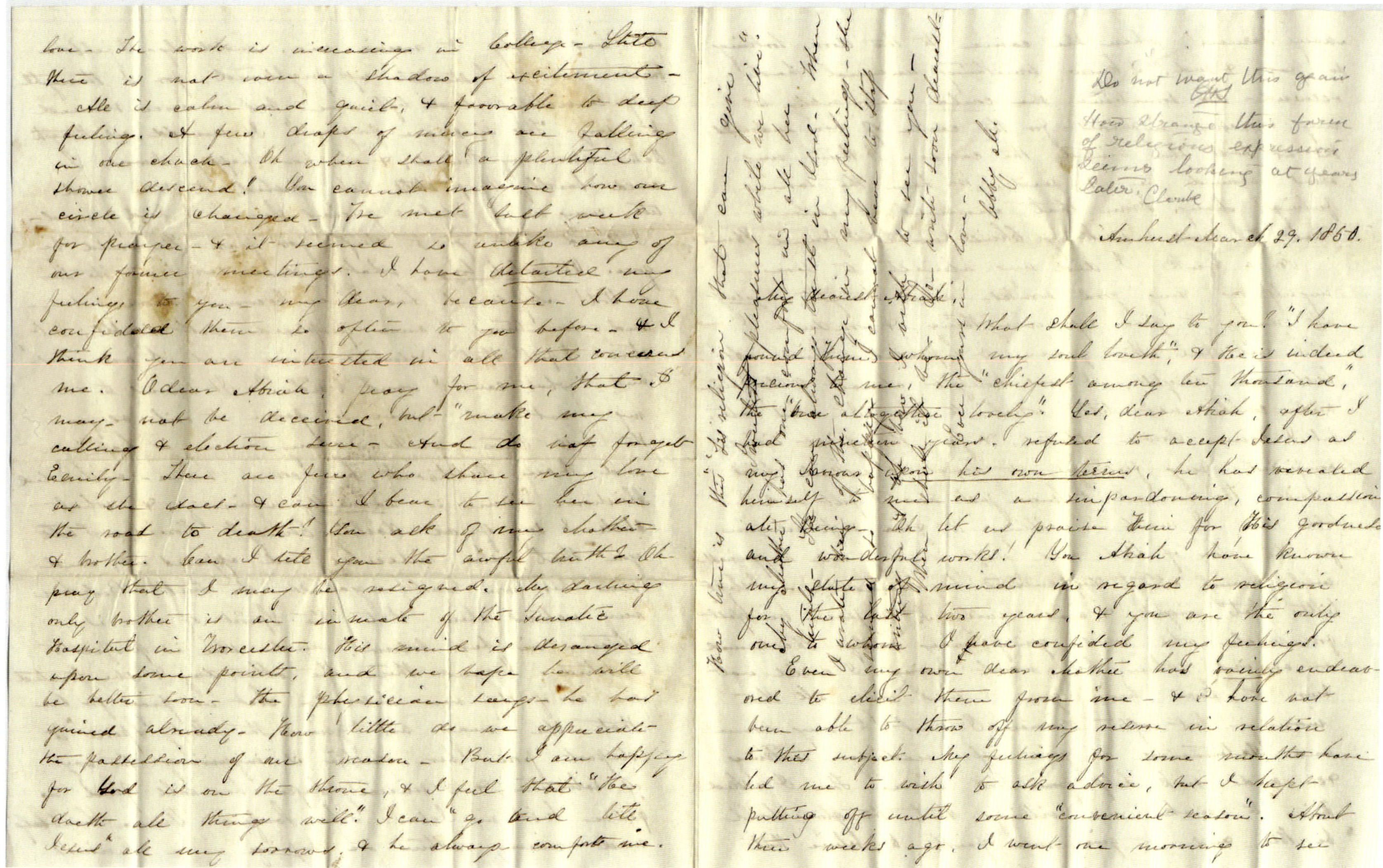

2.11   Abby Wood Bliss (1830–1915)
Letter to Abiah Root, signed and dated Amherst
[Massachusetts], March 29, 1850
Amherst College Archives and Special Collections,
2009.002

This previously unknown letter between two of "the circle of
five" friends from Dickinson's Amherst Academy days includes
a valuable report. A religious revival sprang up in Amherst in
1850; when Abby Wood visited Dickinson that spring, many
friends and family had recently made formal confessions of
faith. Dickinson resisted conversion since her days at Mount
Holyoke, and Wood writes of her visit: "…what shall I say of
our darling Emily? How can I tell you that she ridicules and
opposes us, and shuts her own heart against the truth …. I
went there the other day & she treated me as if she were insane
– Let us pray for her that she may not 'grieve the Holy Spirit' to
depart from her…"

Mary Warner, when she came to the door, looking so pale & sad. I knew something unusual had occurred. For some time she could not reply to my anxious inquiries - for the cause of her sadness, but at last she hinted the cause - I threw my arms around her & said, We have the same feelings Mary. From that moment, I resolved not to cease seeking Christ until I found Him.

For a week I did my utmost to save myself by my good works - and thought myself all ready to give up every thing, & wondered I did not feel the peace I expected to find. At last one night, I was brought almost to despair and could not tell what to do. It was late, but I came down stairs, & for the first time confided my feelings to uncle & asked his advice. He seemed to know just how I felt and told me I must be willing to give up religion for the glory of God and not for my own happiness and many other difficulties he removed - I slept little that night, & arose early to prepare breakfast for uncle who was going away early. He seemed so anxious when he went away I could not bear to have him go. I was busy all the morning, but after dinner I went to my room and determined to give up reading, talking &c - and seek help from God alone. Then I asked Him to make me willing that the glory should be His, and to give me faith to believe that

He was ready to receive me. Suddenly I felt a burden gone & I started up frightened, for I thought my convictions had left me, but a voice seemed to say - "Thy sins are forgiven." It seemed as though Jesus were my Friend, & oh how happy I was - I could hardly keep still but wished to run and tell every one - what a precious Saviour I had found - I dared not go to sleep for fear He would be gone. Oh what love, what condescension in the Son of God! My mind has since become more calm - and sometimes I am perplexed with doubts, but still I feel that "Jesus is mine and I am Thine" and "what can I want beside?" It seemed to me my heart was never so prone to evil as for the last three weeks. Mary Warner is hoping and Jane Hitchcock has come home - a decided Christian. Vinnie is earnestly inquiring - & what shall I say of our darling Emily! How can I tell you that she ridicules and opposes us, and steels her own heart against the truth. But her very actions shew that the Spirit of God is striving in her bosom, and she is perfectly wretched. I went there the other day & she treated me as if she were insane - Let us pray for her that she may not "grieve the Holy Spirit" to depart from her. Austin is inquiring the way of salvation, & I sincerely hope he will find no peace but in Jesus. John Sanford - Vinnie Humphrey and many others are hoping in a Saviour

Christian. Vinnie is earnestly inquiring - & what shall I say of our darling Emily! How can I tell you that she ridicules and opposes us, and steels her own heart against the truth. But her very actions shew that the Spirit of God is striving in her bosom, and she is perfectly wretched. I went there the other day & she treated me as if she were insane - Let us pray for her that she may not "grieve the Holy Spirit" to depart from her. Austin is inquiring the way of salvation, & I sincerely hope he will find no

2.12 Emily Dickinson (1830–1886)

Letter to Emily Fowler Ford, early 1850

Emily Fowler Ford papers,

Manuscripts and Archives Division

The New York Public Library, Astor, Lenox and Tilden

Foundations, MssCol 1038

Emily Fowler was another of Dickinson's friends who attended Amherst Academy in the 1840s. This letter was probably written in early 1850 just after Emily Fowler had returned from a trip. Dickinson longs to be reunited with her friend, remarking: "I wanted to write, and just tell you that me, and my spirit were fighting this morning…. I dreamed about you last night, and waked up putting on my shawl, and hood on to go and see you, but this wicked snow-storm looked in at my window, and told me I couldn't." In a later letter Dickinson enclosed a lock of her bright auburn hair (Cat. 2.30, p. 46).

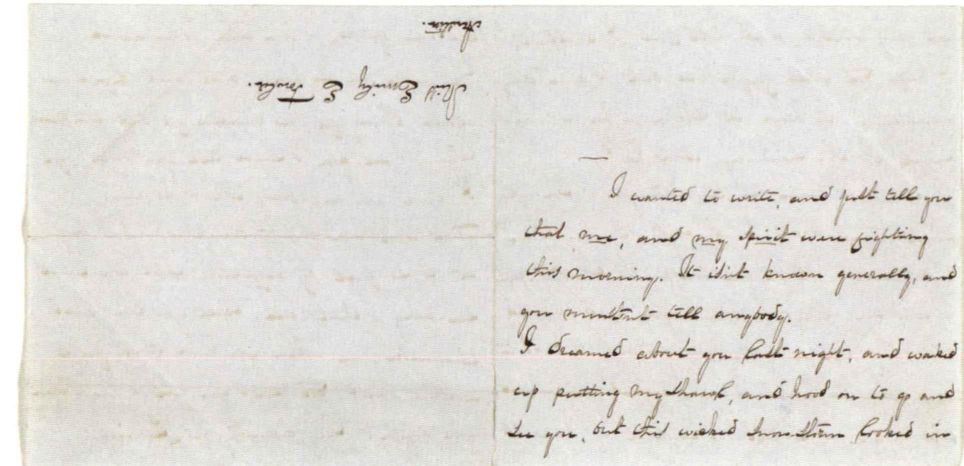

2.13 Photographer unknown

George Gould

Daguerreotype

Amherst, Mass., ca. 1850

Amherst College Archives and Special Collections,

Amherst College Photograph Collections

As a teenager, Dickinson met George Gould through her brother Austin. Gould came to Amherst from a nearby town and was dependent on the college's Charity Fund for his expenses. Many biographers suspect Gould wanted to marry Dickinson, but little evidence of their relationship remains. He stood six feet eight inches tall and asked her to accompany him on at least one outing; she saved that invitation for the rest of her life. Gould later became a successful minister and traveled widely.

2.14 *The Indicator: A Literary Periodical*
Conducted by Students of Amherst College
Vol. II, no. 7 (February 1850)
Amherst: Published by the Editors;
Printed by J. S. and C. Adams, 1850
Amherst College Archives and Special Collections,
LH 1 .A43 I52

Emily Dickinson's writing appeared in print for the first time in this literary magazine edited and published by Amherst College students. "Magnum Bonum" is her Valentine Eve invitation to an unknown suitor, likely George Gould, to "meet me at sunrise, or sunset, or the new moon – the place is immaterial. In gold, or in purple, or sackcloth—I look not upon the raiment. With sword, or with pen, or with plough—the weapons are less than the wielder. In coach, or in wagon, or walking, the equipage far from the man. With soul, or spirit, or body, they are all alike to me. With host or alone, in sunshine or storm, in heaven or earth, some how or no how—I propose, sir, to see you."

2.15 Emily Dickinson (1830–1886)
"I suppose the time will / come"
Poem written in 1876 on the verso of invitation from George Gould dated 1850
Amherst College Archives and Special Collections,
Emily Dickinson Collection, AC 240

On February 1, 1850, George Gould sent this invitation to a "Candy Pulling!!" to Miss Dickinson. We do not have any report of whether Dickinson accepted the invitation or what her feelings for Gould were, but we do know that she kept his invitation for the rest of her life. The lines on the back of the invitation were likely written in 1876, more than twenty-five years after she received it. An invitation from a time long past seems an appropriate sheet on which to write a poem about wanting to hinder and halt the inevitable march of time. (See also Figure 1, p. 2.)

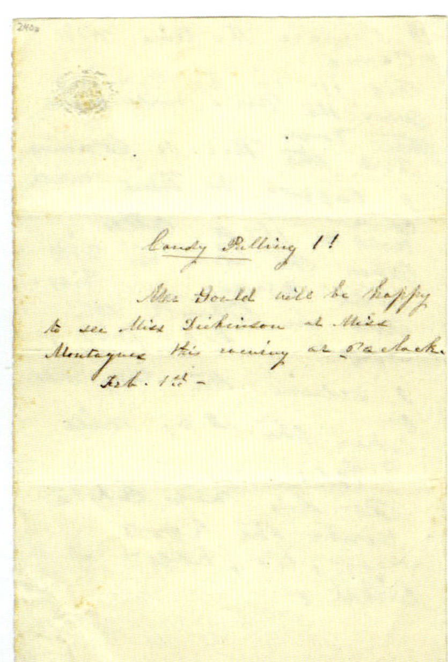

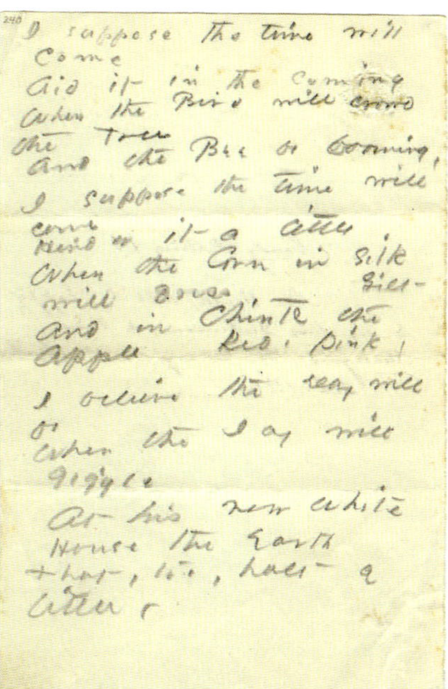

2.16 Emily Dickinson (1830–1886)
Retained draft of a letter to "Master," ca. 1858
Amherst College Archives and Special Collections,
Emily Dickinson Collection, AC 827

A group of three letters addressed only to "Master" remain one of the many mysteries that surround Dickinson. Discovered after her death, there is no way of knowing whether these letters were copied out and mailed, or if they never went beyond these private drafts. Dickinson's language is passionate, filled with concern for the health of someone distant. It was likely written in 1858, an important juncture in Dickinson's development as a poet: 1858 is the year she first bound together fair copies of her poems, an indication of a greater seriousness about her writing.

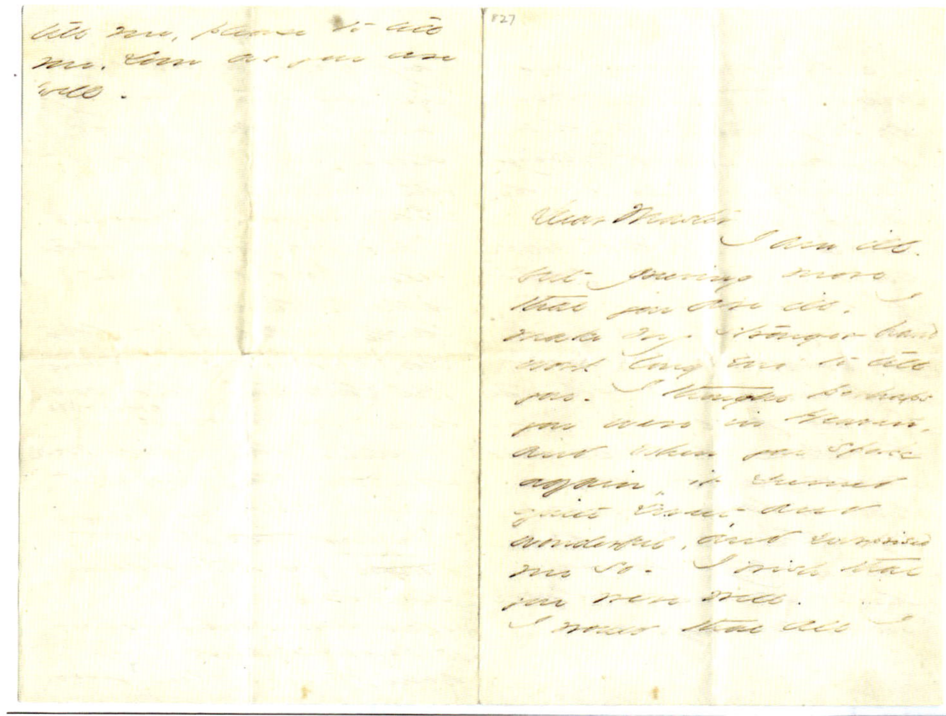

Opposite page:

2.17 Emily Dickinson (1830–1886)
Retained draft of a letter to Otis Lord (?), ca. 1880
Amherst College Archives and Special Collections,
Emily Dickinson Collection, AC 753

The only substantiated romantic relationship of Dickinson's life was with Otis Lord. He was her father's business partner, and became close to the poet in 1877, when she was in her late forties. They may have contemplated marrying, but Lord died in 1884.

This draft of a letter was likely intended for Lord. About halfway down the sheet, Dickinson writes: "It is strange that I miss you at night so much when I was never with you – but the punctual love invokes you soon as my eyes are shut – and I wake warm with the want sleep had almost fulfilled…"

When her letters were first published, this fragment was combined with five others and presented as a single letter. Examining the manuscript reveals more than even an accurate transcription: we see the jagged edge of the paper that Dickinson has turned sideways and passages fluidly crossed out. However, we may never know if any of these words were delivered to their intended recipient, and whether the intended recipient of this fragment was Judge Otis Lord or another.

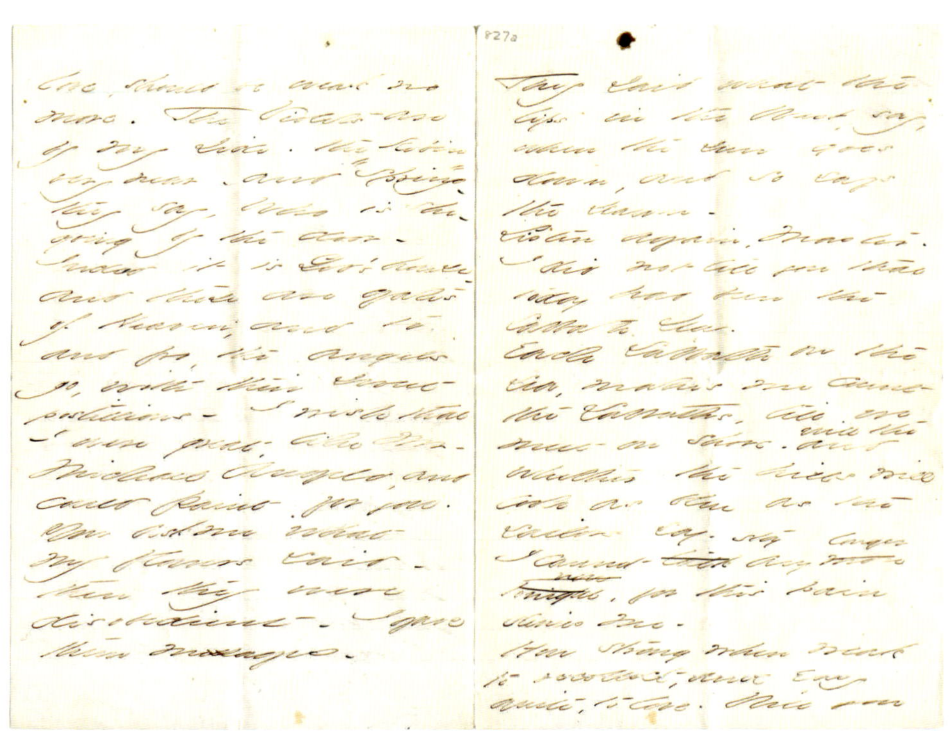

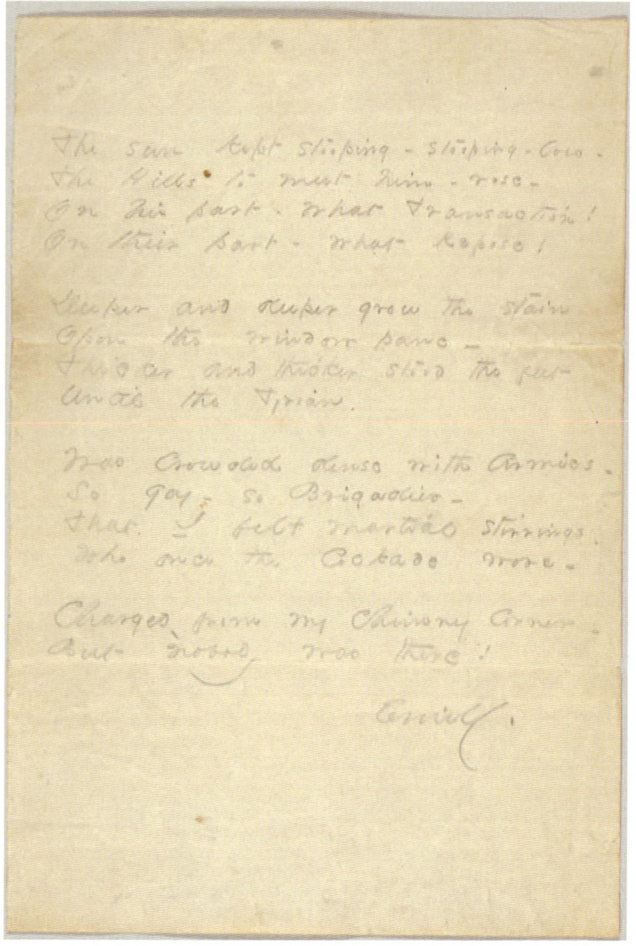

2.18   Photographer unknown
Susan Gilbert Dickinson
Daguerreotype ca. 1856
Courtesy of Emily Dickinson Museum,
Trustees of Amherst College

One of the most important friendships of Dickinson's creative life was her relationship with her sister in-law. Susan Gilbert became engaged to Austin Dickinson in 1853, and when they married in 1856 Dickinson's father built them a house—The Evergreens—just to the west of the Dickinson family home. The families frequently visited one another, and Susan also received at least 250 poems from Dickinson, more than any other person. Scholars continue to debate the nature of Dickinson's relationship with Susan, and the extent of her editorial input, but she played a unique and vital role in the poet's life.

Above right:

2.19   Emily Dickinson (1830-1886)
"The sun kept stooping – stooping – low "
Poem sent to Susan Dickinson, signed and dated ca. 1860
Morgan Library & Museum. Purchased as the gift of William H. McCarthy, Jr. and Frederick B. Adams, Jr., 1953, MA 1488

Next page:

2.20   Emily Dickinson (1830–1886)
"Two – were immortal – / twice – "
Poem sent to Susan Dickinson, ca. 1864
Morgan Library & Museum; Gift of William H. McCarthy, Jr., 1955, MA 1641

At page 9:

2.21   Emily Dickinson (1830–1886)
"Distance – is not / the Realm of fox"
Poem sent to Susan Dickinson, signed and dated ca. 1870
Morgan Library & Museum; Gift of Mrs. J. Ramsay Hunt, 1950, MA 1357

Two - were immortal -
twice -
the privilege of few -
to Eternity - obtained - in
time -

Reversed - Divinity -
that Our ignoble
Eyes
the Quality - perceive
Of Paradise Superlative
thro' their Comparative

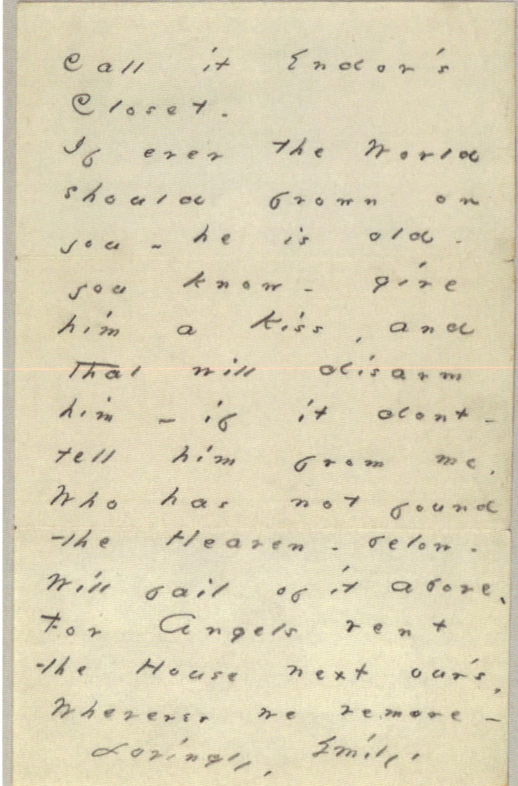

2.22 Emily Dickinson (1830–1886)
Letter to "Dear Girls" [Martha Dickinson and Sally Jenkins], signed and dated ca.1883
Morgan Library & Museum; Gift of William H. McCarthy, Jr. and Frederick B. Adams, Jr., 1954, MA 1556

Dickinson withdrew from society years before writing this letter, but remained deeply engaged with the lives of close friends and family until the end of her life. This letter from 1883 is addressed to "Dear Girls"—Dickinson's seventeen-year-old niece, Martha, and her friend Sally Jenkins— and is a clear expression of an aunt's playful love and devotion. A variant of the poem at the end of this letter was printed in 1896:

> Who has not found the heaven below
> Will fail of it above.
> God's residence is next to mine,
> His furniture is love.

Next page, above:

2.23 Emily Dickinson (1830–1886)
"The wind begun / to knead the / grass"
Poem sent to Elizabeth Holland, signed and dated 1864
Amherst College Archives and Special Collections, Emily Dickinson Collection, AC 814

2.24 Photographer unknown
Elizabeth Luna Chapin Holland
Carte de visite photograph, ca. 1878
Amherst College Archives and Special Collections, Emily Dickinson Collection

Next page, below:

2.25 Emily Dickinson (1830–1886)
"The day undressed / herself "
Poem sent to Elizabeth Holland, signed and dated ca. 1862
Amherst College Archives and Special Collections, Emily Dickinson Collection, AC 813

These two poems were also sent to Elizabeth and Josiah Holland. "The wind begun to knead the grass" (above) is an excellent example of Dickinson's habit of revising her work over several years. This is the earliest of five drafts; by the time she wrote the final draft in 1883, she changed the first line and made several alterations throughout.

"The day undressed herself" (below) also exists in variants: this fair copy and another retained copy. One unanswerable question about Dickinson's method is whether she sent the version she considered final, or whether the wording of this draft was selected with her intimate audience—the Hollands —in mind.

Dickinson corresponded with a wide network of friends and acquaintances, but only a handful received more than ten poems from her. Elizabeth Holland was one of these carefully chosen friends; she and her husband, Josiah, would receive more than ninety letters and thirty poems.

Dickinson met the Hollands in 1853 and quickly formed a lasting friendship. Elizabeth Holland was one of the few visitors Dickinson received at home after her withdrawal from public life in the 1860s, and their correspondence lasted until Dickinson's death. In a letter to Holland in 1878 Dickinson thanks her friend for sending this photograph: "Your sweet Face alighted in the Rain, with its Smile unharmed."

2.26 Emily Dickinson (1830–1886)

"Baffled for just a day or two "

Poem sent to Elizabeth Holland, signed "Emilie" and dated ca. spring 1859

MS Am 1118.2 (17a), Houghton Library, Harvard University

Dickinson rarely dated her manuscripts, but scholars have suggested this poem, with the neatly pinned rosebud in the upper margin, was likely written in the spring of 1859. It may have been accompanied by a short note (now lost) that reads in full: "Will someone lay this little flower on Mrs. Holland's pillow? Emilie." Elizabeth Holland gave birth to her third child in 1859; could motherhood be the "country I was never in!" that Dickinson references in the last line of the poem? Since it is now impossible to compare the two manuscripts to determine if details of the paper and handwriting match, we can only speculate.

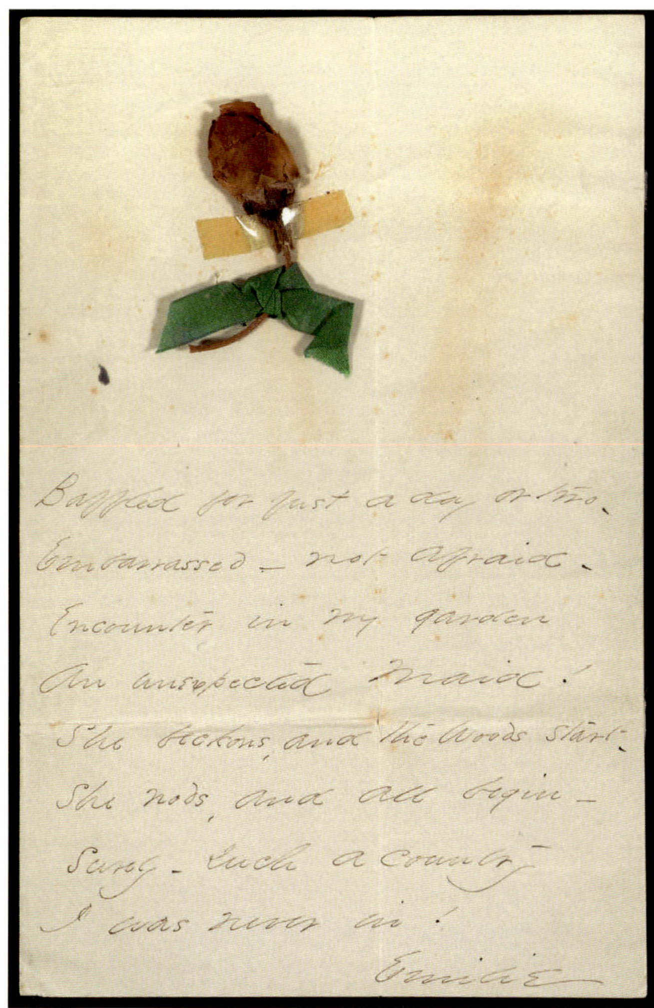

2.27 Emily Dickinson (1830–1886)

Transcription of a letter to Catherine Scott Turner, March 1859

Amherst College Archives and Special Collections, Emily Dickinson Collection, TR 60

Dickinson's relationship with Catherine Scott Turner, known as "Kate" to her friends, is another close bond that has invited speculation. Although the exact nature of their relationship is unknown, there is no denying that Dickinson formed a strong attachment to Turner, who met the poet in 1859. Only five letters from Dickinson to Turner are known, and only from the transcriptions Turner later prepared, but Dickinson's playful affection for her new friend is clear in this letter, in which she says "Stay! My heart votes for you, and what am I indeed to dispute her ballot –?"

A daguerreotype portrait of two women—perhaps Dickinson and Turner—is shown at 2.28.

2.28 Photographer unknown
Two Women
Daguerreotype ca. 1859
Private collection

This recently discovered daguerreotype of two women dates to about 1859. The woman on the left, with her arm gently placed around her companion, may be Emily Dickinson; the woman on the right, hands folded, is likely Kate Scott Turner, who Dickinson had met around this time through her sister-in-law, Susan. The two quickly formed a close bond and, although it will be difficult to prove the identities of these women beyond any doubt, the portrait is useful for its glimpse into female friendships in the mid-nineteenth century.

This is the first time the daguerreotype has been seen with the authenticated portrait below; compare the likenesses. Could this be Emily Dickinson?

2.29 Photographer unknown
Emily Dickinson
Daguerreotype
Amherst, Mass., ca. 1847
Amherst College Archives and Special Collections,
Emily Dickinson Collection, 1956.002

This iconic portrait of Emily Dickinson—with her steady forward gaze and dark hair—is the only authenticated photograph of the poet. It was likely made in Amherst between December 1846 and late March 1847, when Dickinson was sixteen years old. Dickinson's name was never inscribed on the daguerreotype, but its authenticity is based on the provenance of the item: Lavinia Dickinson gave the daguerreotype to a relative, Wallace Keep, and it remained in the family until 1956, when it was donated to Amherst College. It is not clear why Lavinia gave away such an important keepsake of her sister.

2.30 Lock of Emily Dickinson's hair
sent to Emily Fowler Ford, ca. 1853
Amherst College Archives and Special Collections,
Emily Dickinson Collection, 1983.005

The only authenticated photograph of Emily Dickinson (at
2.29) shows her with seemingly dark hair, but it was actually
bright auburn. She sent this lock to her friend Emily Fowler
with a note recalling: "I said when the Barber came, I would
save you a little ringlet, and fulfilling my promise, I send you
one today…"

In the nineteenth century, locks of hair were commonly
exchanged as keepsakes among friends and family. Compare
the color of this lock to the portrait of the young Dickinson
with her brother and sister (Cat. 1.01, page 14).

3. Literary Influences and Connections

"After long disuse of her eyes she read Shakespeare & thought Why is any other book needed?"

One benefit of life in a small college town is access to books, newspapers, and magazines that might not otherwise be readily available. The Dickinson family kept a respectable library in their home, and Dickinson also borrowed books from friends. In addition to her wide-ranging reading habits, she was personally acquainted with some major figures in the worlds of publishing and literature, chief among them the editors Samuel Bowles, Thomas Wentworth Higginson, and Thomas Niles, as well as the writer and activist Helen Hunt Jackson. Although Bowles and Higginson both championed women writers, their views were far from universal. Helen Hunt Jackson forged her own career as an author and urged Dickinson to publish her poetry, with one small success.

3.01 John Sartain (1808–1897), engraver
Mrs. E. Barrett Browning
Nineteenth century
Morgan Library & Museum
Bequest of Gordon N. Ray, 1987
MA 7346.5

Elizabeth Barrett Browning was one of Dickinson's favorite
poets; she hung an engraving, similar to this one, on the
wall of her bedroom. In addition to Browning's influence on
Dickinson's poetry, there were many similarities between
the women's lives. Both were raised by traditionally domestic
mothers and overbearing fathers; both were close to their
brothers; and both spent much of their lives withdrawn
from society. The major difference is that Browning actively
sought publication, starting with her first book at age 13, and
eventually reached an international audience with her most
popular books. Browning's death in 1861 was one of several
significant losses for Dickinson that year.

3.02 Elizabeth Barrett Browning (1806–1861)
Aurora Leigh: A Poem
New York, Boston: C. S. Francis & Co., 1859
Amherst College Archives and Special Collections,
Emily Dickinson Collection, PR4185.A1 1859

Dickinson wrote her name in the front of this copy of *Aurora
Leigh*, one of Browning's most popular books, and made several
marks throughout the text. The description of the narrator's
aunt near the beginning of the First Book of the poem has
several marks in Dickinson's hand: "She had lived we'll say, /
A quiet life, which was not life at all, / (But that, she had not
lived enough to know)." It is unsurprising that Browning's
book-length poem—and these lines in particular— about
the development of a woman writer would resonate with
Dickinson.

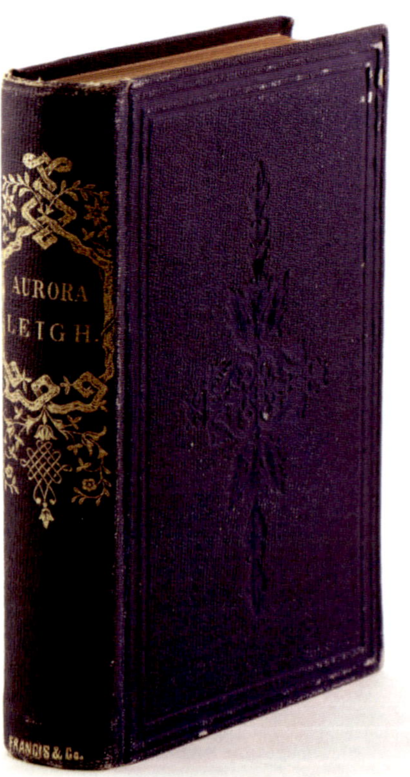

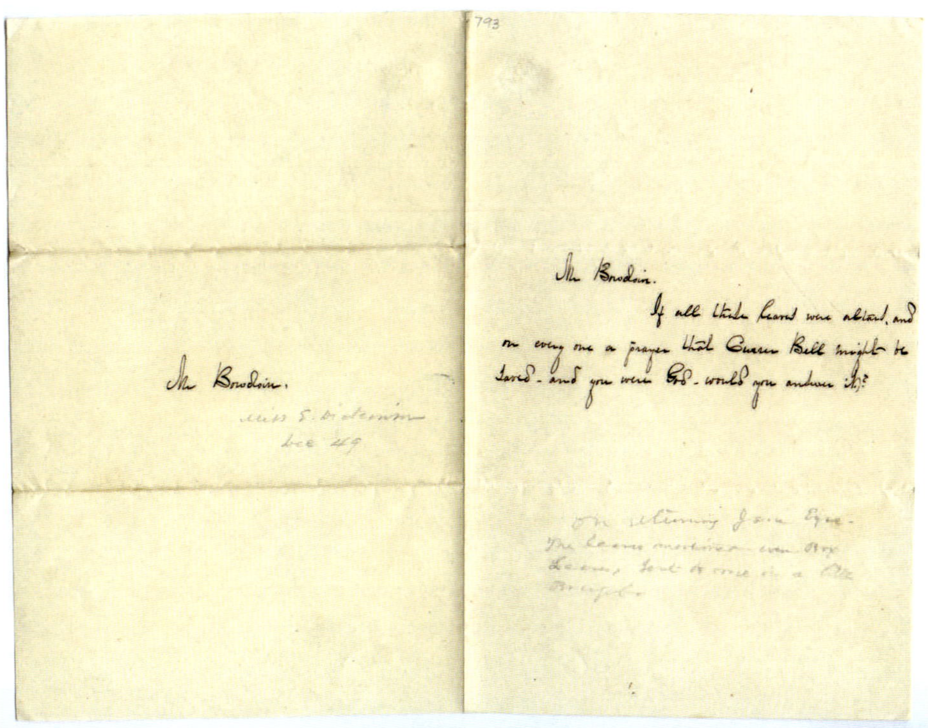

3.03 William Shakespeare (1564–1616)
Shakespeare's Plays
New York, Harper & Brothers, 1847 [i.e. 1844-1847]
Morgan Library & Museum
Purchased by Pierpont Morgan before 1913,
Bib 40992

The Dickinson family owned at least six different editions of books by and about William Shakespeare. The volume is typical of the wave of illustrated editions of his works published throughout the nineteenth century. Dickinson mentions Shakespeare by name in thirteen letters and one poem, but traces of his influence can be detected throughout her writing. Her friend and future editor Thomas Wentworth Higginson made a note after visiting Dickinson soon after she recovered from eye treatment in Cambridge in 1864: "After long disuse of her eyes she read Shakespeare & thought Why is any other book needed?"

Not shown:

3.04 Charlotte Bronte (1816–1855)
Jane Eyre: An Autobiography
New York: Harper and Brothers, 1848
Morgan Library & Museum
Bequest of Gordon N. Ray, 1987
PML 59976

3.05 Emily Dickinson (1830–1886)
Letter to Elbridge G. Bowdoin, ca. 1849
Amherst College Archives and Special Collections,
Emily Dickinson Collection, AC 793

Charlotte Brontë's first novel was first published in London in October of 1847, and became an international best seller. The first American editions were published in 1848. It is unknown which edition Dickinson read because she borrowed a copy from her father's business partner, Elbridge Bowdoin. She returned the book to him with this note: "If all these leaves were altars, and on every one a prayer that Currer Bell might be saved – and you were God – would you answer it?" Bowdoin helpfully notes in pencil that "the leaves mentioned were Box Leaves, sent to me in a little bouquet." Bowdoin regularly exchanged books with Dickinson by leaving them under the boughs of a boxwood bush in Dickinson's garden.

Opposite page:

3.06 Emily Dickinson (1830–1886)
"No 'sonnet' / had George Eliot"
Poem in a letter to Thomas Wentworth Higginson,
undated
Amherst College Archives and Special Collections,
Emily Dickinson Collection, AC 810

The May 1886 issue of *The Century Illustrated Magazine* included
a sonnet "To the Memory of H. H." by Thomas Wentworth
Higginson. "H. H." was Helen Hunt Jackson, who died in
August 1885. Dickinson and Higginson were deeply saddened
by that loss of their mutual friend. In this draft of a letter to
him, she acknowledges the poem by noting that no one had
written a sonnet for George Eliot after her death in 1880. In
the final version of the letter, Dickinson removed the mention
of George Eliot in favor of a more direct statement of her
appreciation: "The beautiful Sonnet confirms me – Thank you
for confiding it – "

3.07 Emily Dickinson (1830–1886)
"Alone and in a circumstance"
Poem with "George Sand" and "Mauprat" clipped from
Harper's Monthly pasted to sheet, ca. 1870
Amherst College Archives and Special Collections,
Emily Dickinson Collection, AC 129

This collage is one of Dickinson's most enigmatic manuscripts.
The two clippings tucked under the postage stamp were cut
from the May 1870 issue of *Harper's Monthly Magazine*, which
included a brief sketch of French novelist George Sand,
another of Dickinson's literary influences who wrote under a
male pseudonym. The article was prompted by the impending
publication of new translations of Sand's works by Roberts
Brothers—the publisher who would issue Dickinson's works
throughout the 1890s. Interpretations of this poem range
widely from playful verse about sitting in the outhouse to a
Freudian meditation on Dickinson's father, represented by the
locomotive on the stamp.

The Networked Recluse

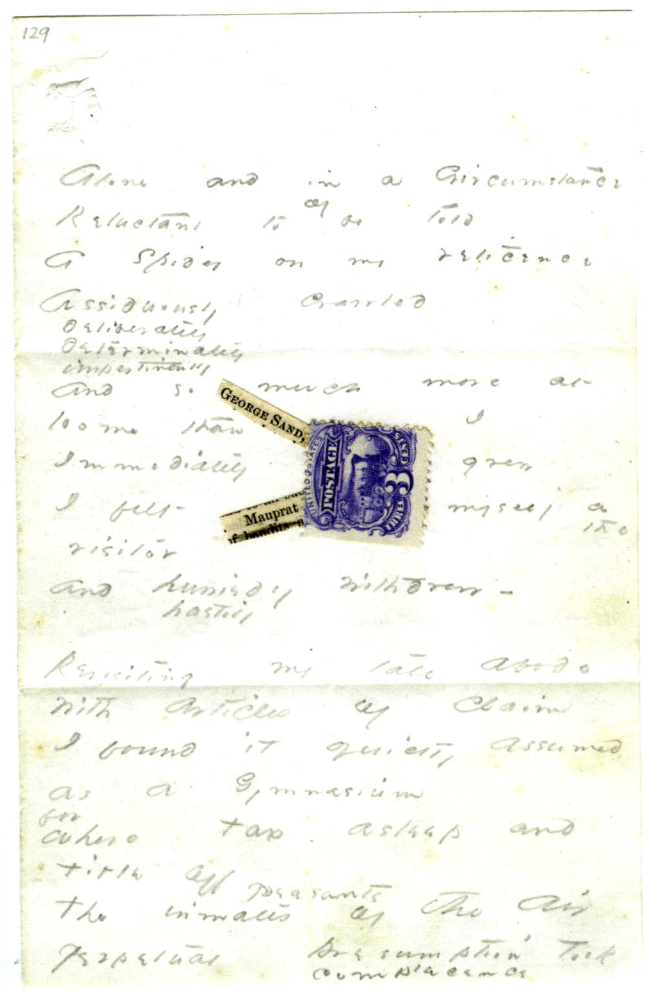

Alone and in a Circumstance
    of
Reluctant to be told
A Spider on my reticence
Assiduously   crawled
  deliberately
  determinately
  impertinently
And so much more at

Home than   I

Immediately   grew

I felt   myself a
               the
visitor

And hurriedly withdrew –
    hastily

Revisiting my late abode
with Articles of Claim
I found it quietly assumed
as a Gymnasium
for
where Tax asleep and
Title off
      peasants
The inmates   of the Air
Perpetual presumption took
    complacence

           lawful
As each were special
           only
Heir –
A If any strike me on
the street
I can return the Blow,
If any take my property
    seize
According to the Law
The Statute is my Learned
friend
But what redress can be
          nor
For an offence not here
          anywhere
nor e there
So not in   Equity –
That Larceny of time
and mind
The marrow of the
Day
By spider, or forbid
it Lord
That I should specify –

About 1870. Poem draft, with addenda, variants, and corrections, composed by Dickinson in pencil on both sides of one leaf (17.8 x 11.2 cm) of wove, off-white, faintly blue-ruled stationery embossed with a right-facing head, possibly representing Athena, in full profile. The manuscript has been folded horizontally into thirds. No other manuscript of the poem is known to be extant. Before composing the poem draft, Dickinson affixed a three-cent stamp (1869 issue) and two clippings from *Harper's Magazine* (May 1870) to the paper: the name "George Sand" and the title of Sand's novel "Mauprat." Here, variants and addenda seem to have occurred to Dickinson during the initial drafting process.

3.08 Emily Dickinson (1830–1886)

"Did you ever / read one of / her poems back/ward"
Manuscript fragment, undated
Amherst College Archives and Special Collections,
Emily Dickinson Collection, AC 851

Dickinson left behind dozens of scraps of paper that do not fit into the standard categories of "poems" or "letters." Dickinson may have been thinking of one of her favorite poets —Elizabeth Barrett Browning—when she put down these lines on a fragment of coarse wrapping paper. She writes:

Did   you   ever
read   one   of
her poems back-
ward, because
the   plunge   from
the   front   over-
turned   you?
I   sometimes
    often have —
  many times have –
A   something
overtakes   the
mind—

These lines are unique, and might never have been incorporated into a letter or poem.

3.09 Emily Dickinson (1830–1886)

Letter to Helen Hunt Jackson, about 1879
Amherst College Archives and Special Collections,
Emily Dickinson Collection, AC 816

Although Helen Hunt Jackson and Dickinson knew each other briefly during their days together at Amherst Academy in the 1840s, it was not until Thomas Wentworth Higginson reintroduced them as adults that a true friendship developed. Unlike most of Dickinson's incoming correspondence, several letters from Jackson have survived. In one 1879 letter Jackson wrote: "What should you think of trying your hand on the oriole? He will be along presently." Dickinson replied with one of four extant versions of "A Route of Evanescence" in this letter, introducing the poem:

Dear Friend,

     To the Oriole / you suggested / I add a Humming / Bird and hope / they are not untrue –

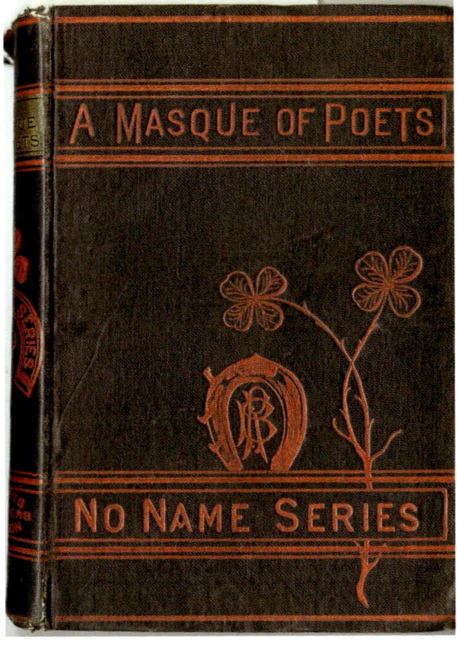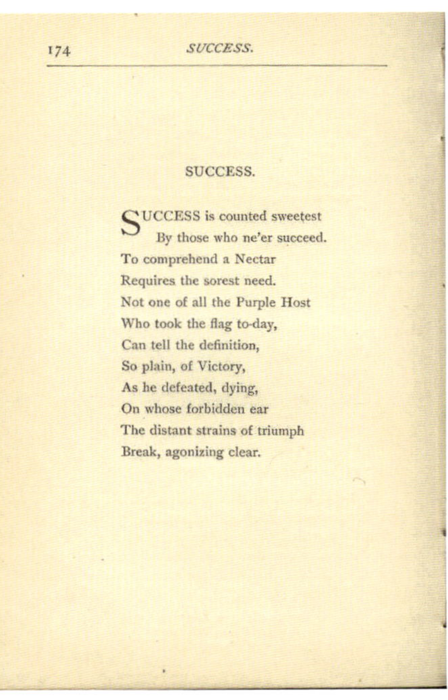

3.10 *A Masque of Poets Including Guy Vernon, a Novelette in Verse*
Boston: Roberts Brothers, 1878
Morgan Library & Museum
Bequest of Gordon N. Ray, 1987
PML 137103

Helen Hunt Jackson was a successful novelist, poet, and advocate for Native American rights, and she actively encouraged Dickinson to publish her poetry. She convinced Dickinson to contribute her poem "Success is counted sweetest" to this volume in the "No Name Series." The publisher, Roberts Brothers, advertised "a volume of anonymous poems from famous hands," which may have appealed to Dickinson. She could remain anonymous, yet be included among the most famous authors in the country. Thomas Niles, her editor at Roberts Brothers, later sent Dickinson a letter telling her many people guessed that her contribution was authored by Ralph Waldo Emerson.

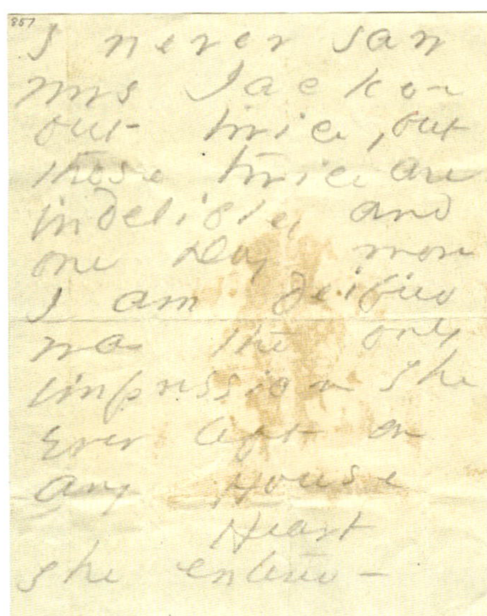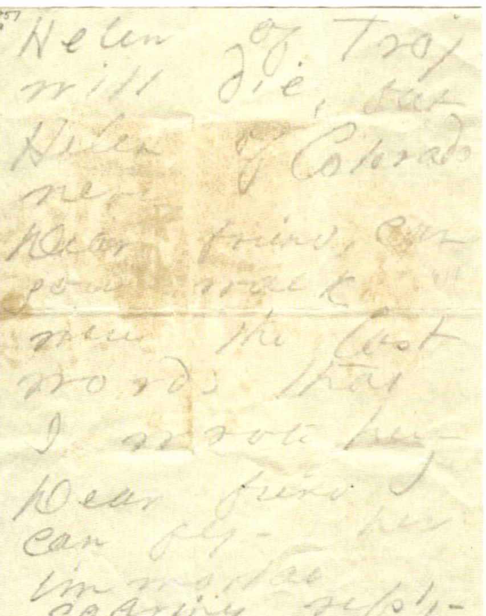

3.11 Emily Dickinson (1830–1886)
Retained draft of a letter to William Sharpless Jackson, ca. late 1885
Amherst College Archives and Special Collections, Emily Dickinson Collection, AC 857

Helen Hunt Jackson died of stomach cancer on August 12, 1885. Dickinson wrote to Jackson's husband in Colorado Springs to ask about her friend's final days; his response does not survive, but these two sheets of paper appear to be a draft of another letter Dickinson sent him. Dickinson's statement that "I never saw Mrs Jackson but twice" likely refers to the visits Jackson made to Amherst in October 1876 and October 1878, dismissing their childhood acquaintance at Amherst Academy. We will never know if Dickinson included this striking phrase, at the top of the second page, in her final letter to Mr. Jackson: "Helen of Troy will die, but Helen of Colorado, never."

4. Civil War Years

"I heard a Fly buzz – when I died – "

From the bombardment of Fort Sumter in April of 1861 until Robert E. Lee's
surrender to Ulysses S. Grant at Appomattox, Virginia on April 9, 1865, the
American Civil War profoundly influenced the lives of everyone living in the
United States. Massachusetts played an important role in the conflict, especially
after the destruction of the United States Armory and Arsenal at Harpers Ferry in
1861 briefly left the Springfield Armory as the sole government manufacturer of
muskets and other arms. Hundreds of Amherst residents, both white and African-
American, joined the Union Army, although Dickinson's brother Austin avoided
service. Students and faculty from Amherst College also joined the conflict, and
charity events related to the war became a regular feature of daily life.

Dickinson began collecting her rapidly increasing output of poems into hand-
sewn manuscript booklets, known as fascicles, as early as 1858, but the war years
saw a sharp increase in her output: thirty out of forty fascicles and at least five
unsewn sets of poems—each of which could include more than twenty unique
poems—date from the years 1861 to 1865. The majority of Dickinson's lifetime
appearances in print also date from this period.

4.01   "The Burnside Expedition—The Storming of Fort Thompson at New Bern, North Carolina, March 14, 1862"
Printed in *Harper's Weekly: A Journal of Civilization*
Vol. 6, no. 275 (April 5, 1862), 216 217
Amherst College Archives and Special Collections, AP2 .H32

Harper's Weekly was a major source for news of the war and was famous for its vivid illustrations published within weeks—sometimes days—of the events they depict. This two-page spread on the Battle of New Bern, North Carolina brought the conflict of 14 March 1862 into the homes of readers around the country, but news of this Union victory reached Amherst long before the illustration was published. The death of twenty-two-year-old First Lieutenant Frazar Stearns of the 21st Regiment Massachusetts Volunteer Infantry—the son of Amherst College president William Augustus Stearns—stunned the entire community.

4.02 Musket stamped "Amherst College Gymnasium"
Manufactured by the Springfield Armory,
Springfield, Mass., 1835
Amherst College Archives and Special Collections,
Objects Collection

When the Civil War began in 1861, Amherst College struggled to convince students to remain in school rather than enlist in the Union Army, although several students and faculty did. One strategy to keep students on campus was to add musket drills to the required physical education activities at the college, which explains why this musket has "Amherst College Gymnasium" stamped on the stock. The sound of students drilling was part of the soundscape of Dickinson's world throughout the Civil War years.

4.03 Photographer unknown
Frazar Stearns
Carte de visite photograph
Amherst, Massachusetts, 1861
Amherst College Archives and Special Collections,
Biographical Files

4.04 Emily Dickinson (1830–1886)
Letter to Samuel Bowles, dated March 1862
Amherst College Archives and Special Collections,
Emily Dickinson Collection, AC 680

Frazar Augustus Stearns was one of the Amherst College students who left school to enlist in the Union Army in 1861. This photograph of Stearns in his new uniform with an unidentified child—possibly his brother Winfred—was reproduced and widely distributed among the Amherst community after his death. In this letter to their mutual friend Samuel Bowles, Dickinson describes her brother Austin's reaction to the news of Stearns's death:

> Austin is chilled—by Frazer's murder—He says—his Brain keeps saying over "Frazer is killed"—"Frazer is killed," just as Father told it—to Him. Two or three words of lead – that dropped so deep, they keep weighing – Tell Austin – how to get over them!

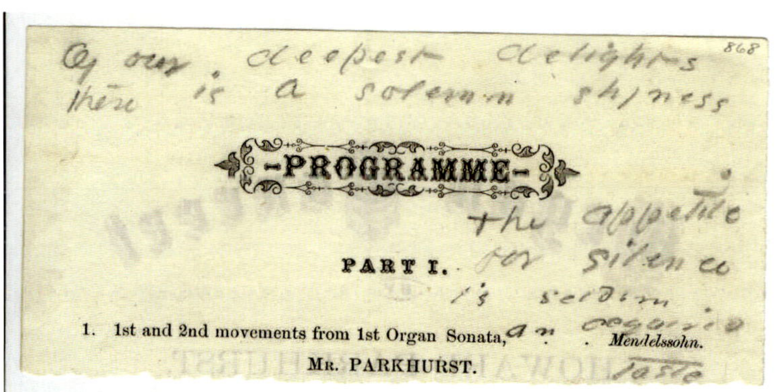

4.05 Emily Dickinson (1830–1886)
"A little madness / in the spring"
Poem, ca.1875
Amherst College Archives and Special Collections,
Emily Dickinson Collection, AC 106

At left:

4.06 Program for an Organ Concert by Howard Parkhurst,
June 27, 1873
With notes by Emily Dickinson
Amherst College Archives and Special Collections,
Emily Dickinson Collection, AC 868

Dickinson increasingly withdrew from public life during the
1860s, and her literary output slowed considerably after 1865.
Although she was writing fewer poems by the mid-1870s, she
maintained a practice of drafting several variants before
settling on a particular reading. In "A little madness / in the
spring," (left) she brainstorms potential adjectives: gay/bright,
quick/whole, swift/fleet, and includes an alternate line. She
also continued drafting lines on different kinds of paper,
such as this program (below). We do not know if she attended
the concert, or if she stayed at home and penciled these lines
reflecting on shyness and silence on a program her sister
Lavinia brought back.

4.07 Emily Dickinson (1830–1886)
      "Light is sufficient / to itself "
      Poem, dated 1863
      Amherst College Archives and Special Collections,
      Emily Dickinson Collection, AC 274

Pages 59–62:

4.08 Emily Dickinson (1830–1886)
      "I heard a fly buzz"
      Poem in Fascicle 84, dated 1863
      Amherst College Archives and Special Collections,
      Emily Dickinson Collection, AC 84

More than 900 of Dickinson's 1,789 extant poems were
written between 1860 and 1865, with 295 of those produced
in 1863 alone. "Light is sufficient to itself" (right) appears on
a loose sheet of stationery paper, whereas "I heard a fly buzz"
(in Fascicle 84, opposite page at *b*) was inserted, along with
twenty additional poems, into one of the hand-sewn fascicles.
Both are fair copies, with no corrections or deletions, but
the two other poems facing "I heard a fly buzz" are not: note
here Dickinson's habit of using small crosses to mark variants
where she had not yet made up her mind.

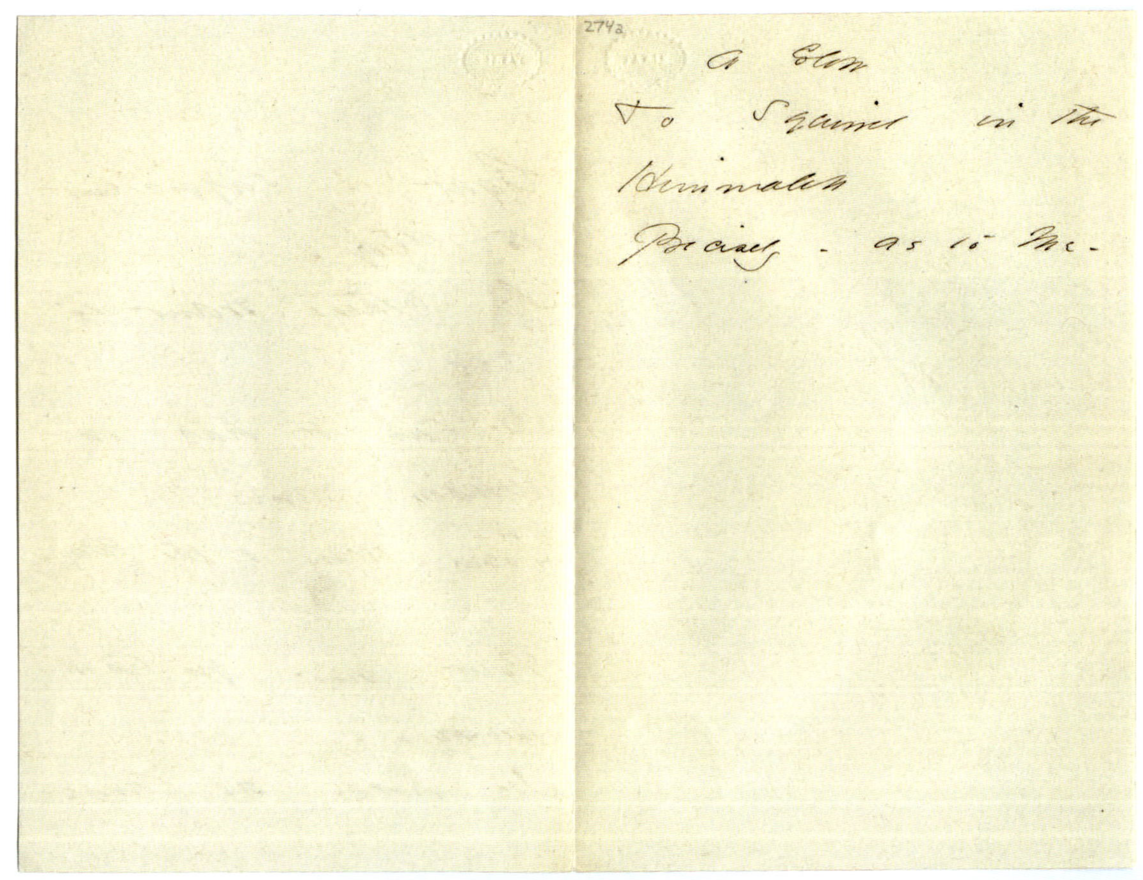

a.

b.

c.

d.

e.

h.

i.

f.

g.

j.

k.

I think the longest Hour
of all
Is when the Cars have
come —
And we are waiting for
the Coach —
It seems as though the
Time —
+ Amazed
+ Indignant — that the Joy
was come —
Did block the Gilded Hands
And would not let the Seconds
by —
But slowest instant — ends.

The Pendulum begins to Count —
Like little Scholars — loud —
The steps grow thicker — in
the Hall —
The Heart begins to crowd —

Then I — my timid service
done —
tho' service 'twas, of Love —
Take up my little Violin
And further North — remove.

So glad we are — a
Stranger'd deem
'Twas sorry — that we were —
For when the Holiday should
be —
There + publishes — a Tear.

Nor how Ourselves be justified
Since Grief and Joy are done
So similar — An Optizan
Could not — + Discern between —
+ Baffled but   + Conclude. Decide.

A Night — there lay
the Days between —
the Day that was Before —
And Day that was
Behind — were One —
And now — 'twas Night —
was here.

Slow — Night — that must
be watched away —
As Grains upon a shore —
Too imperceptible to note —
Till it be Night — no
more.

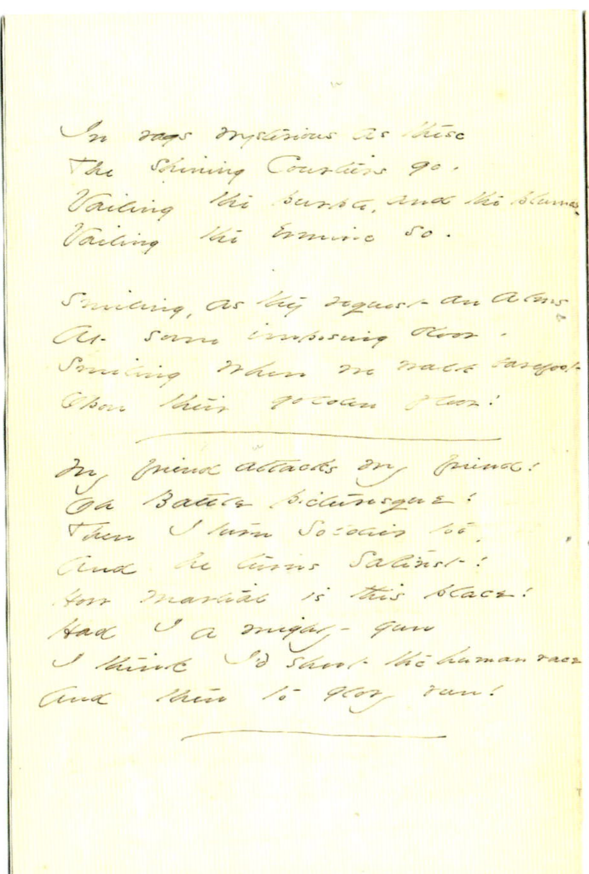

4.09 Emily Dickinson (1830–1886)
"Bless God, he went as soldiers"
Poem in Fascicle 80, dated ca. 1859
Amherst College Archives and Special Collections,
Emily Dickinson Collection, AC 80

4.10 Emily Dickinson (1830–1886)
"My friend attacks my friend!"
Poem in Fascicle 83, dated ca. 1859
Amherst College Archives and Special Collections,
Emily Dickinson Collection, AC 83

At first glance, "Bless God, he went as soldiers" (left) and "My friend attacks my friend" (right)—with language of soldiers, muskets, battles, and charges—could be read as Dickinson's reaction to the militarism that swept through her town during the Civil War, but both were likely written two years before the war began. Typical of the earliest fascicles, or hand-sewn manuscript booklets, there are no corrections or alternate readings. Although it is difficult to reconstruct the complete history of these manuscripts, the pencil markings were made by one of Dickinson's posthumous editors. Mabel Loomis Todd, one of the first editors, may have been responsible for the mutilation of the fascicle at left in an attempt to destroy the poem on the other side.

4.11   Emily Dickinson (1830–1886)
"I'm nobody! Who are you?"
Poem in Fascicle 11, ca. 1861
MS Am 1118.3 (35a), Houghton Library,
Harvard University

Dickinson included "I'm Nobody! Who are you?" in one of
her hand-sewn fascicles around six months after the outbreak
of the Civil War. She includes a crucial variant, underlined in
the right margin, but this is a unique composition: the poem
appears nowhere else in her manuscripts, so it is impossible
to know whether Dickinson would have chosen "banish"
or "advertise"—radically different possibilities—if she had
published it. Her earliest editors (who penciled "++3" in the
upper margin) selected "banish." This poem is often cited
as evidence for Dickinson's reluctance to publish her work,
despite the strong encouragement she received from friends.

4.12 Emily Dickinson (1830–1886)
"Soul, take thy risk"
Poem, undated
Amherst College Archives and Special Collections,
Emily Dickinson Collection, AC 357

4.13 Emily Dickinson (1830–1886)
"The way / hope builds his / house"
Poem, 1879
Amherst College Archives and Special Collections,
Emily Dickinson Collection, AC 450

Notions of house and home, as well as meditations on mortality, are major themes in Dickinson's writing. In one instance (below), she wrote a poem about a house on a piece of paper that looks like a house, a detail most editors fail to mention. The small slip of paper (above) with a few lines on one side and a tiny sketch of a gravestone on the other is another puzzle. The handwriting suggests a date of 1867, but the contrast between the handwriting and the neatness of the drawing is striking, and she may have drawn the gravestone years before adding her lines to the other side. When considering these unconventional manuscripts, it is essential to bear in mind that Dickinson had access to all the conventional writing paper she could ever need.

5. Lifetime Publications

"I had told you I did not print"

Closely examining Dickinson's unique manuscript practices provides a partial answer to the question of why she did not pursue publication. While Dickinson's social network included supporters of her writing and the work of women writers in general, there were equally strong voices arguing the opposite position. She regularly exchanged letters with influential editors such as Samuel Bowles and Thomas Niles, and literary mentors such as Thomas Wentworth Higginson. But, for all of their progressive views—Bowles, for instance, hired Fidelia Hayward Cooke as literary editor at *The Springfield Republican* in 1860—Dickinson was constrained by her father's disapproval and that of other figures she admired.

Ten of Dickinson's 1,789 poems were published during her lifetime, but always with added titles and altered punctuation. With one exception, the poems appeared in newspapers and periodicals on densely printed pages and surrounded by articles and advertisements, as was typical for the period. Dickinson is never credited—her poems all appear anonymously—and it is probable they were printed without her consent. At the same time, she did not shun publication absolutely, and submitted several poems to the editor that — although he never printed her poems while she was alive — would later publish the first three posthumous editions of her work, to great success.

4.11   Photographer unknown
Samuel Bowles
Daguerreotype
Springfield, Mass., ca. 1858
Amherst College Archives and Special Collections,
Bowles–Hoar Family Papers

This previously unknown daguerreotype of Samuel Bowles
was likely made in 1858, the year he became friends with the
Dickinsons. The poet once described him as "that Arabian
presence," and this portrait of the darkly handsome 32-year-
old Bowles stands in contrast to those taken later in life and
frequently reprinted in books about her. Bowles began his
career in the printing room of *The Springfield Republican*,
a weekly paper his father started in 1824. In 1844 Bowles
convinced his father to change to a daily format and was
named editor, a position he held until his death. Under his
direction, the *Republican* published seven of Dickinson's
poems.

5.02 Emily Dickinson (1830–1886)
"Blazing in gold and quenching in purple"
Here printed as "Sunset" in
The Springfield Daily Republican
Springfield, Mass., March 30, 1864
Amherst College Archives and Special Collections,
xxAN .D3

Dickinson's poem "Blazing in gold and quenching in purple" was published anonymously three times in early 1864: first in *The Drum Beat* for February 29, then in the March 30 issue of Samuel Bowles' *Springfield Daily Republican* (shown here), followed by the April 2 issue of the *Springfield Weekly Republican*. In this period, newspapers filled every available inch of the page with text; poetry was integrated closely with the surrounding stories and advertisements. Poems were always titled and appeared with conventional punctuation. When one compares Dickinson's idiosyncratic manuscripts to the dense pages of small print in her local paper, it is easy to imagine that this sort of publication would not appeal to her.

5.03 Emily Dickinson (1830–1886)
"A narrow fellow in the grass"
Here printed as "The Snake" in
The Springfield Daily Republican
Springfield, Mass., February 14, 1866
Amherst College Archives and Special Collections,
xx AN .D3

"A narrow fellow in the grass" was the last of Dickinson's poems printed in a newspaper. It appeared in the February 14, 1866 issue of *Springfield Daily Republican* (shown here) and, three days later, in the related weekly paper. In both instances, the poem appears under the title "The Snake."

It is assumed that Austin and Susan Dickinson were responsible for sending Dickinson's poems to Samuel Bowles for publication, and that her complaints about the printing of this poem—expressed in a letter to Thomas Wentworth Higginson (see Cat. 5.05, p. 70)—convinced the conspirators to end their program of involuntary publication.

in a sermon before. Much flattered, the young man asked what they were. "I heard the clock strike twice," was the reply.

"Father," said a little fellow, after having apparently reflected intently on something. "I shan't send you any of my wedding cake when I get married." "Why not, my son?" was the fond father's inquiry. "Because," answered the young hopeful, "you didn't send me any of yours!"

All Parisians have something of the woman in their composition. They are nervous, sensitive, (physically sensitive, the heart has nothing to do with it, a flood of tears relieves the nervous irritation instantly) of delicate tastes, gregarious, fond of dress, delight in show, love applause, and—abhor the country.

Somebody who knows, says that when two or more women, approaching you on a narrow walk, fall behind one another to enable you to pass, you may be sure they are ladies of uncommon politeness and consideration. The usual course pursued by women is to charge all abreast, sweeping everybody into the mud.

Praise is not worth much, and I always take care when I am its object to receive it as a pleasant sensation, as metal which has not been assayed, and, if I do not use caution, as very probably a source of injury. Praise should always be considered a free-will offering rather than as a deserved reward.—*German writer.*

A West Indian, who had a remarkably red nose, having fallen asleep in his chair, a negro boy who was in waiting observed a mosquito hovering round his face. Quashy eyed it very attentively; at last it lit upon his master's nose, and instantly flew off again. "Yah, yah," he exclaimed with great glee, "me berry glad to see you burn your fut."

SUNSET.

Blazing in gold, and quenching in purple,
  Leaping like leopards in the sky,
Then at the feet of the old horizon
  Laying her spotted face to die;
Stooping as low as the oriel window,
  Touching the roof, and tinting the barn,
Kissing her bonnet to the meadow—
  And the Juggler of Day is gone!

A soldier in the Armory square hospital, Washington, stone blind, was commiserated by a visitor. "Poor fellow," said he, "how sorry I am that he cannot see!" "See?" was the answer, "I can see. Unseen things that I never beheld until I was wounded are now visible to me, and I would not exchange these visions for all I ever saw before. They will never be lost sight of again! The things that are seen are temporal, but the things that are not seen are eternal!"

The happiness and unhappiness of a man's life depends upon the disposition with which he regards it. An unalloyed contentment of mind cannot be bought by man, it is the golden gift of heaven. But it is within the reach of all to soften to himself the rough shocks of life in this busy world. He may receive them courageously, sustain them patiently, and by his prudence alleviate or turn them aside; but even if his mind be unequal to these exertions, it need not, as is the case with too many, exert itself to annoy itself.
  William von Humboldt.

Not long since, an elderly woman entered a railroad car at one of the Ohio stations, and disturbed the passengers a good deal with complaints about a "most dreadful rheumatiz" that she was troubled with. A gentleman present, who had himself been a severe sufferer with the same complaint, said to her—"Did you ever try electricity, madam? I tried it, and in the course of a short time it completely cured me." "Electricity," exclaimed the old lady—"y-e-s, I've tried it to my satisfaction. I was struck with lightning about a year ago, but it didn't do me a mossel of good!"

York, Schermerhorn, Bancroft & Co.
The United States Service Magazine—February. New York, Charles B. Richardson.
The Stranger's Guide through Boston and Vicinity. Boston, Charles Thacher.
The Radical—February. Boston, A. Williams & Co.
The Home Monthly—February. Boston, C. H. Pearson & Co.
The New York Weekly Magazine—monthly part—January. New York, O. H. Bailey & Co.

THE SNAKE.

A narrow fellow in the grass
Occasionally rides;
You may have met him—did you not?
His notice instant is,
The grass divides as with a comb,
A spotted shaft is seen,
And then it closes at your feet,
And opens further on.

He likes a boggy acre,
A floor too cool for corn,
Yet when a boy and barefoot,
I more than once at noon
Have passed, I thought, a whip-lash,
Unbraiding in the sun,
When stooping to secure it,
It wrinkled and was gone.

Several of nature's people
I know, and they know me;
I feel for them a transport
Of cordiality.
Yet never met this fellow,
Attended or alone,
Without a tighter breathing,
And zero at the bone.

How to Use Chloroform.—The causes of

5.04 Emily Dickinson (1830–1886)
"A narrow fellow in / the grass"
Poem in Set 88, dated 1865
Amherst College Archives and Special Collections,
Emily Dickinson Collection, AC 88

Dickinson made at least one other copy of this poem, which
she sent in a letter to her sister-in-law, Susan, and which
later made its way to Samuel Bowles, who published it — with
alterations — in his *Springfield Republican*. This retained
draft of "A narrow fellow in the grass" is from approximately
1864 and shows the shift in Dickinson's practice away from
hand-sewing her manuscript booklets into fascicles. She began
instead to simply fold the sheets into sets. Fifteen such sets
are known to exist; the last dates from about 1877, when she
discontinued the practice of compiling poems into booklets.

 Emily Dickinson (1830–1886)
Autograph letter to Thomas Wentworth Higginson,
Boston Public Library, Ms. Am. 1093(23)

Dickinson expressed objections to the way her poem "A narrow fellow in the grass" appeared in the *Springfield Republican* without her consent in this letter to Thomas Wentworth Higginson, her friend and literary mentor: "Lest you meet my Snake and suppose I deceive it was robbed of me – defeated too of the third line by the punctuation. The third and fourth were one – I had told you I did not print – I feared you might think me ostensible. If I still entreat you to teach me, are you much displeased?"

Dickinson began corresponding with Higginson in 1862. Although they would not meet in person until 1871, she highly valued his opinion of her work.

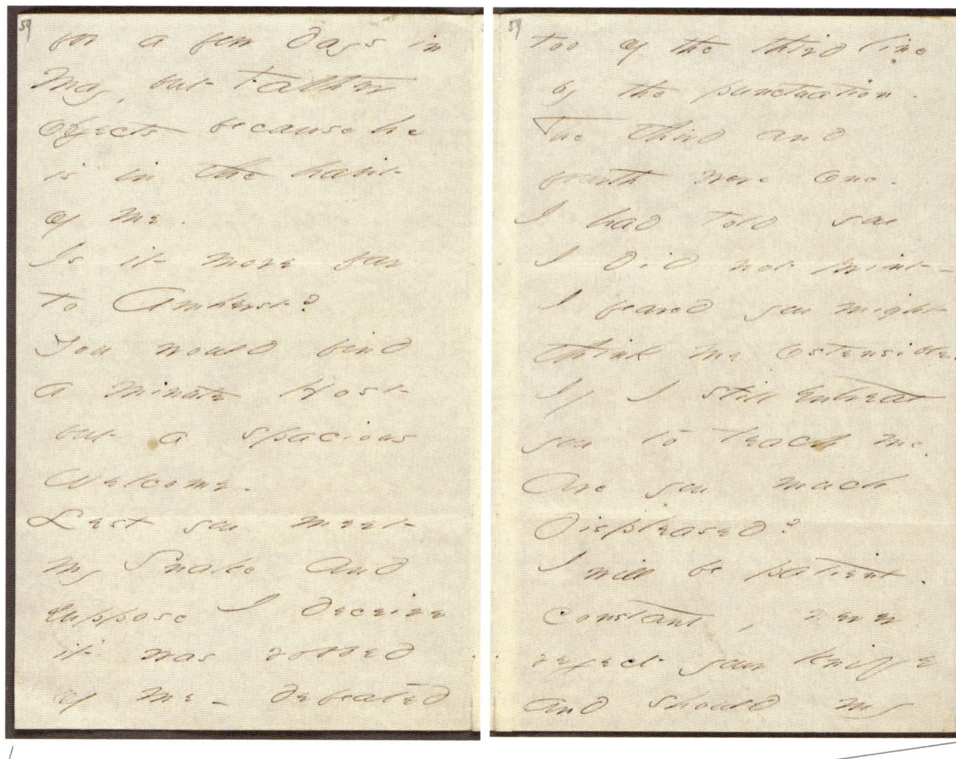

Amherst
Dear friend
          Whom
my Dog understood
could not elude
others –
I should be glad
to see you, but
think it an
apparitional pleasure –
not to be fulfilled –
I am uncertain of
Boston –
I had promised
to visit my Physician

for a few days in
May, but Father
objects because he
is in the habit
of   me –
Is   it   more far
to Amherst ?
You would find
a minute Host
but a spacious
Welcome –
Lest you   meet
my   Snake and
suppose I deceive
it   was   robbed
of me – defeated

too of the third line
by the punctuation –
The third and
fourth were one –
I had told you
I did not print –
I feared you might
think me ostensible –
If I still entreat
you to teach me –
are you   much
displeased?
I will be patient –
constant, never
reject your knife
and should my

my slowness goad
you, you knew before
myself that
Except the smaller
size
No lives are round –
These – hurry to a
sphere
And show and end –
The larger – slower
grow
And later hang –
The Summers of
Hesperides
are long –
          Dickinson

Early 1866. Letter from Dickinson to T. W. Higginson composed in ink on four leaves of wove, cream stationery folded horizontally into thirds for mailing. The poem beginning "Except the smaller size" and inscribed in the body of the letter exists in three variant forms: the earliest extant versions was copied into Fascicle 26 about summer 1863; a second copy containing only the opening two stanzas and variant in punctuation was sent to Susan Gilbert Dickinson in 1863; and, finally, this version sent to Higginson in 1866. The letter is accompanied by an envelope also addressed in ink by Dickinson to "Col. T. W. Higginson / Newport / Rhode Island." A three-cent stamp is affixed and marked "paid," and the envelope was postmarked in South Hadley on March 17.

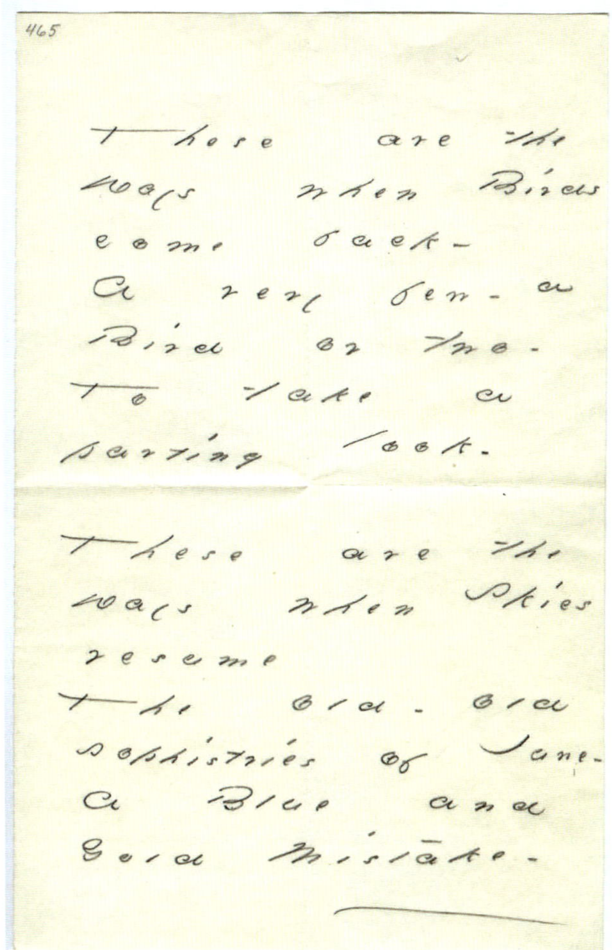

5.06 Emily Dickinson (1830–1886)
"These are the days when Birds come back"
Early draft of the poem, ca. autumn 1859
Amherst College Archives and Special Collections,
Emily Dickinson Collection, AC 654

5.07 Emily Dickinson (1830–1886)
"These are the / days when Birds / come back"
Fair copy of the poem, ca. 1883
Amherst College Archives and Special Collections,
Emily Dickinson Collection, AC 465

First published in *The Drum Beat*, "These are the days when Birds come back" is a poem Dickinson returned to several times. Three manuscripts of this poem exist, though Dickinson may have drafted as many as five. The draft (left) is the earliest, likely sent to Susan Dickinson in the autumn of 1859, and later given to Samuel Bowles possibly as a candidate for publication in *The Springfield Republican*. Nearly twenty-five years later, Dickinson returned to the poem, making the fair copy (right) around 1883. The increased space between each letter, word, and line is typical of Dickinson's handwriting in the last decade of her life.

5.08 Emily Dickinson (1830–1886)

"These are the days when birds come back "

Here printed as "October" in *The Drum Beat*

Brooklyn: Published by the Brooklyn and Long Island
Fair, for the Benefit of the U. S. Sanitary Commission,
March 11, 1864

Amherst College Archives and Special Collections,
Emily Dickinson Collection

During the Civil War, fundraising fairs were held in cities around the country to support the United States Sanitary Commission, a relief organization established in 1861 to assist sick and wounded Union soldiers. One fair, held in Brooklyn, was accompanied by a daily paper. *The Drum Beat*, edited by Dickinson family friend and Amherst College alumnus Richard Salter Storrs, Jr., was published during the duration of the fair, with an extra issue a week after the fair ended. Three of Dickinson's poems appeared in these pages, including "These are the days when birds come back," seen here under the title "October."

POPULAR SIMILIES.

As wet as a fish—as dry as a bone;
As bright as a bird—as crazed as a loon;
As plump as a partridge—as poor as a rat;
As strong as a horse—as weak as a cat;
As hard as a flint—as soft as a mole;
As white as a lily—as black as a coal;
As plain as a pikestaff—as rough as a bear;
As tight as a drum—as free as the air;
As heavy as lead—as light as a feather;
As steady as time—as uncertain as weather;
As hot as an oven—as cold as a frog;
As gay as a lark—as sick as a dog;
As slow as a tortoise—as swift as the wind;
As true as the Gospel—as false as mankind;
As thin as a herring—as fat as a pig;
As proud as a peacock—as blue as a grig;
As savage as a tiger—as mild as a dove;
As stiff as a poker—as limp as a glove;
As blind as a bat—as deaf as a post;
As cold as a cucumber—as warm as a toast;
As red as a cherry—as pale as a ghost.

OCTOBER.

These are the days when birds come back,
A very few, a bird or two,
To take a backward look.

These are the days when skies resume
The old, old sophistries of June,—
A blue and gold mistake.

Oh, fraud that cannot cheat the bee
Almost thy plausibility
Induces my belief,

Till banks of seeds their witness bear,
And softly, through the altered air,
Hurries a timid leaf.

Oh, sacrament of summer days,
Oh last communion in the haze,
Permit a child to join!

Thy sacred emblems to partake,
Thy consecrated bread to take,
And thine immortal wine!

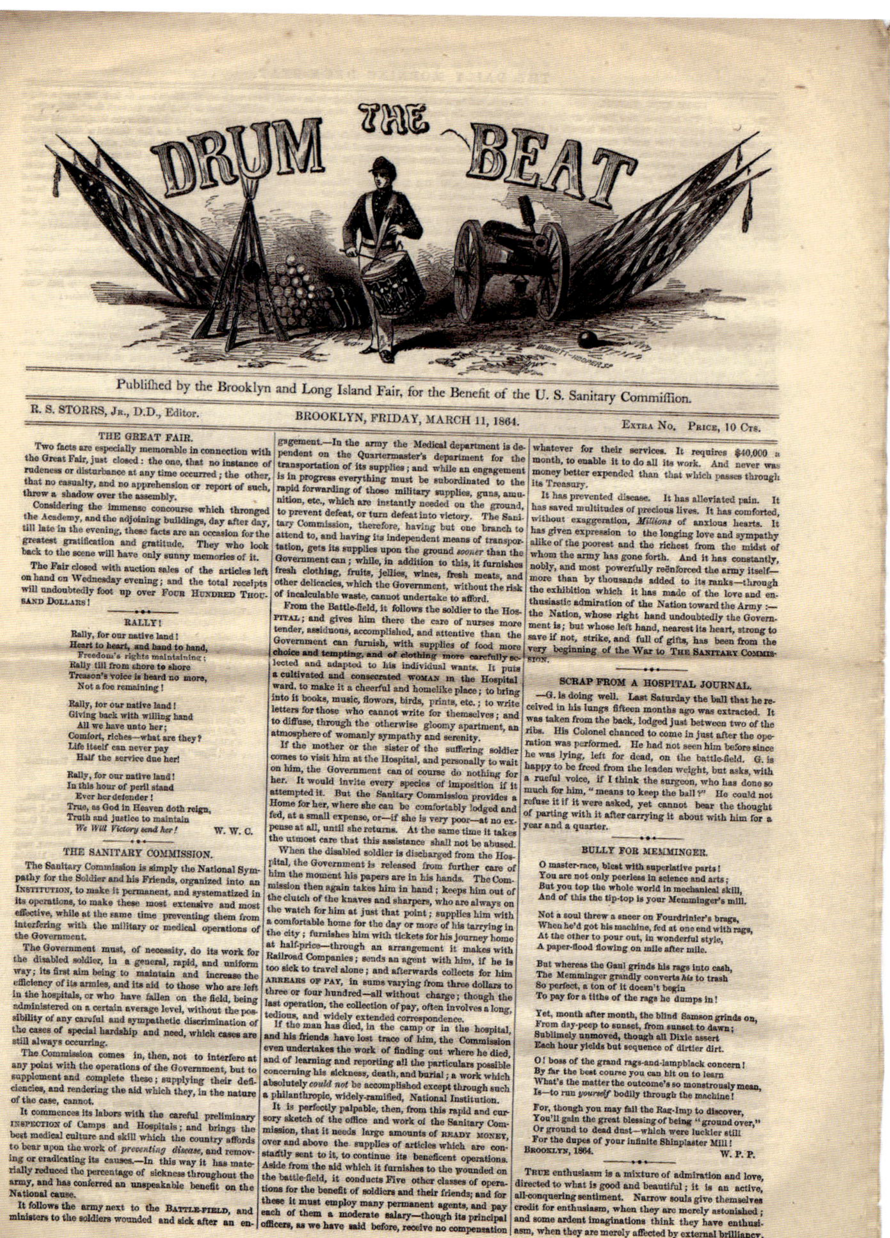

Published by the Brooklyn and Long Island Fair, for the Benefit of the U. S. Sanitary Commission.

R. S. STORRS, JR., D.D., Editor. BROOKLYN, FRIDAY, MARCH 11, 1864. EXTRA NO. PRICE, 10 CTS.

THE GREAT FAIR.

Two facts are especially memorable in connection with the Great Fair, just closed: the one, that no instance of rudeness or disturbance at any time occurred; the other, that no casualty, and no apprehension or report of such, threw a shadow over the assembly.

Considering the immense concourse which thronged the Academy, and the adjoining buildings, day after day, till late in the evening, these facts are an occasion for the greatest gratification and gratitude. They who look back to the scene will have only sunny memories of it.

The Fair closed with auction sales of the articles left on hand on Wednesday evening; and the total receipts will undoubtedly foot up over FOUR HUNDRED THOUSAND DOLLARS!

RALLY!

Rally, for our native land!
Heart to heart, and hand to hand,
  Freedom's rights maintaining;
Rally till from shore to shore
Treason's voice is heard no more,
  Not a foe remaining!

Rally, for our native land!
Giving back with willing hand
  All we have unto her;
Comfort, riches—what are they?
Life itself can never pay
  Half the service due her!

Rally, for our native land!
In this hour of peril stand
  Ever her defender!
True, as God in Heaven doth reign,
Truth and justice to maintain
  We Will Victory send her!   W. W. C.

THE SANITARY COMMISSION.

The Sanitary Commission is simply the National Sympathy for the Soldier and his Friends, organized into an INSTITUTION, to make it permanent, and systematized in its operations, to make these most extensive and most effective, while at the same time preventing them from interfering with the military or medical operations of the Government.

The Government must, of necessity, do its work for the disabled soldier, in a general, rapid, and uniform way; its first aim being to maintain and increase the efficiency of its armies, and its aid to those who are left in the hospitals, or who have fallen on the field, being administered on a certain average level, without the possibility of any careful and sympathetic discrimination of the cases of special hardship and need, which cases are still always occurring.

The Commission comes in, then, not to interfere at any point with the operations of the Government, but to supplement and complete these; supplying their deficiencies, and rendering the aid which they, in the nature of the case, cannot.

It commences its labors with the careful preliminary INSPECTION of Camps and Hospitals; and brings the best medical culture and skill which the country affords to bear upon the work of *preventing disease*, and removing or eradicating its causes.—In this way it has materially reduced the percentage of sickness throughout the army, and has conferred an unspeakable benefit on the National cause.

It follows the army next to the BATTLE-FIELD, and ministers to the soldiers wounded and sick after an engagement.—In the army the Medical department is dependent on the Quartermaster's department for the transportation of its supplies; and while an engagement is in progress everything must be subordinated to the rapid forwarding of those military supplies, guns, ammunition, etc., which are instantly needed on the ground, to prevent defeat, or turn defeat into victory. The Sanitary Commission, therefore, having but one branch to attend to, and having its independent means of transportation, gets its supplies upon the ground *sooner* than the Government can; while, in addition to this, it furnishes fresh clothing, fruits, jellies, wines, fresh meats, and other delicacies, which the Government, without the risk of incalculable waste, cannot undertake to afford.

From the Battle-field, it follows the soldier to the Hospital; and gives him there the care of nurses more tender, assiduous, accomplished, and attentive than the Government can furnish, with supplies of food more choice and tempting, and of clothing more carefully selected and adapted to his individual wants. It puts a cultivated and consecrated woman in the Hospital ward, to make it a cheerful and homelike place; to bring into it books, music, flowers, birds, prints, etc.; to write letters for those who cannot write for themselves; and to diffuse, through the otherwise gloomy apartment, an atmosphere of womanly sympathy and serenity.

If the mother or the sister of the suffering soldier comes to visit him at the Hospital, and personally to wait on him, the Government can of course do nothing for her. It would invite every species of imposition if it attempted it. But the Sanitary Commission provides a Home for her, where she can be comfortably lodged and fed, at a small expense, or—if she is very poor—at no expense at all, until she returns. At the same time it takes the utmost care that this assistance shall not be abused.

When the disabled soldier is discharged from the Hospital, the Government is released from further care of him the moment his papers are in his hands. The Commission then again takes him in hand; keeps him out of the clutch of the knaves and sharpers, who are always on the watch for him at just that point; supplies him with a comfortable home for the day or more of his tarrying in the city; furnishes him with tickets for his journey home at half-price—through an arrangement it makes with Railroad Companies; sends as agent with him, if he is too sick to travel alone; and afterwards collects for him ARREARS OF PAY, in sums varying from three dollars to three or four hundred—all without charge; though the last operation, the collection of pay, often involves a long, tedious, and widely extended correspondence.

If the man has died, in the camp or in the hospital, and his friends have lost trace of him, the Commission even undertakes the work of finding out where he died, and of learning and reporting all the particulars possible concerning his sickness, death, and burial; a work which absolutely *could not* be accomplished except through such a philanthropic, widely-ramified, National Institution.

It is perfectly palpable, then, from this rapid and cursory sketch of the office and work of the Sanitary Commission, that it needs large amounts of READY MONEY, over and above the supplies of articles which are constantly sent to it, to continue its beneficent operations. Aside from the aid which it furnishes to the wounded on the battle-field, it conducts Five other classes of operations for the benefit of soldiers and their friends; and for these it must employ many permanent agents, and pay each of them a moderate salary—though its principal officers, as we have said before, receive no compensation whatever for their services. It requires $40,000 a month, to enable it to do all its work. And never was money better expended than that which passes through its Treasury.

It has prevented disease. It has alleviated pain. It has saved multitudes of precious lives. It has comforted, without exaggeration, *Millions* of anxious hearts. It has given expression to the longing love and sympathy alike of the poorest and the richest from the midst of whom the army has gone forth. And it has constantly, nobly, and most powerfully reënforced the army itself—more than by thousands added to its ranks—through the exhibition which it has made of the love and enthusiastic admiration of the Nation toward the Army:—the Nation, whose right hand undoubtedly the Government is; but whose left hand, nearest its heart, strong to save if not, strike, and full of gifts, has been from the very beginning of the War to THE SANITARY COMMISSION.

SCRAP FROM A HOSPITAL JOURNAL.

—G. is doing well. Last Saturday the ball that he received in his lungs fifteen months ago was extracted. It was taken from the back, lodged just between two of the ribs. His Colonel chanced to come in just after the operation was performed. He had not seen him before since he was lying, left for dead, on the battle-field. G. is happy to be freed from the leaden weight, but asks, with a rueful voice, if I think the surgeon, who has done so much for him, "means to keep the ball?" He could not refuse it if it were asked, yet cannot bear the thought of parting with it after carrying it about with him for a year and a quarter.

BULLY FOR MEMMINGER.

O master-race, blest with superlative parts!
You are not only peerless in science and arts;
But you top the whole world in mechanical skill,
And of this the tip-top is your Memminger's mill.

Not a soul threw a sneer on Fourdrinier's brags,
When he'd got his machine, fed at one end with rags,
At the other to pour out, in wonderful style,
A paper-flood flowing on mile after mile.

But whereas the Gaul grinds his rags into cash,
The Memminger grandly converts *his* to trash
So perfect, a ton of it doesn't begin
To pay for a tithe of the rags he dumps in!

Yet, month after month, the blind Samson grinds on,
From day-peep to sunset, from sunset to dawn;
Sublimely unmoved, though all Dixie assert
Each hour yields but sequence of dirtier dirt.

O! boss of the grand rags-and-lampblack concern!
By far the best course you can hit on to learn
What's the matter the outcome's so monstrously mean,
Is—to run *yourself* bodily through the machine!

For, though you may fall the Rag-Imp to discover,
You'll gain the great blessing of being "ground over,"
Or ground to dead dust—which were luckier still
For the dupes of your infinite Shinplaster Mill!
BROOKLYN, 1864.   W. P. P.

TRUE enthusiasm is a mixture of admiration and love, directed to what is good and beautiful; it is an active, all-conquering sentiment. Narrow souls give themselves credit for enthusiasm, when they are merely astonished; and some ardent imaginations think they have enthusiasm, when they are merely affected by external brilliancy.

5.09 Emily Dickinson (1830–1886)
"Some keep the Sabbath going to church"
Here printed as "My Sabbath" in *The Round Table:*
A Weekly Record of the Notable, the Useful, and the Tasteful
New York, March 11, 1864
Amherst College Archives and Special Collections,
Emily Dickinson Collection

Shortly after "These are the days when birds come back" appeared in *The Drum Beat*, another poem, here titled "My Sabbath," was printed in this magazine, which strove to be a step up in quality from a daily newspaper. Edited by Charles Sweetser—another Amherst College alumnus—*The Round Table* was founded with noble aims and Sweetser refused, at first, to accept advertising to preserve the literary integrity of the magazine. This was the only published instance of "Some keep the Sabbath going to church" until the first posthumous edition of Dickinson's Poems appeared in 1890.

MY SABBATH.

Some keep the Sabbath going to church,
 I keep it staying at home,
With a bobolink for a chorister,
 And an orchard for a dome.

Some keep the Sabbath in surplice,
 I just wear my wings,
And instead of tolling the bell for church,
 Our little sexton sings.

God preaches—a noted clergyman,
 And the sermon is never long;
So instead of going to heaven at last,
 I'm going all along.

DIET IN THE WILDERNESS.—GOURMANDISE AT HOME.

WITH the aid of good rifles, travelers contrive to live tolerably in the wilderness. Of course cookery is a very simple process in the kitchenless regions beyond the frontiers of civilization; but the adventurous hunter who pursues and bags his dinner amid a thousand perils, provides himself during the exploit with a more pungent condiment than Carème or Savarin ever concocted—the sauce of appetite. Even lion-steak, if we are to believe Jules Girard, is not to be despised by the sportsman who has hunted a "lord with a big head" for twenty-four hours on an empty stomach in Algeria. But there are choicer meats than the musky flesh of leo to be had in Africa, and some of the recent explorers of its "antres vast and deserts wild" have favored us with descriptions of their banquets in Negroland that might tickle the exhausted palate of an over-fed alderman. Nothing spurs the jaded sense like novelty, and certainly there is no lack of this element in the African *carte.*

5.10 Photographer unknown
Charles Sweetser
Carte de visite photograph
Undated
Amherst College Archives and Special Collections,
Biographical Files

Charles Sweetser exemplifies the integrated network of
Dickinson's Amherst community and other friendships
through which her poems reached print. He was an Amherst
College alumnus and friend of Emily Fowler Ford's husband,
and was working at the *Brooklyn Daily Union* when that
newspaper lent its offices to *The Drum Beat*—the newspaper
that printed three of Dickinson's poems during its short run.
In 1863, Sweetser published Dickinson's "Some keep the
Sabbath going to church" in his magazine *The Round Table* (at
Cat. 5.10). The poem was printed anonymously, as were all ten
poems that appeared in her lifetime.

5.11 Emily Dickinson (1830–1886)
Letter to Thomas Niles,
about April 1883
Amherst College Archives
and Special Collections,
Emily Dickinson Collection,
AC 833

Only one of the ten poems that were printed
during Dickinson's lifetime appeared in a
book: *A Masque of Poets*, published in 1878
(Cat. 3.10, p. 53). The collection of anonymous verse was
edited by Thomas Niles, and he and Dickinson continued to
correspond after the book appeared. She regularly sent poems
for his consideration and comment; in this letter from April
1883, she asks him to "efface" the poems she had sent earlier
in favor of the ones enclosed. She also remarks on the *Life of
George Eliot* that he sent her the month before, dropping Eliot's
pseudonym to share her thoughts about "The Life of Marian
Evans."

Niles did not publish any of the poems Dickinson sent him.

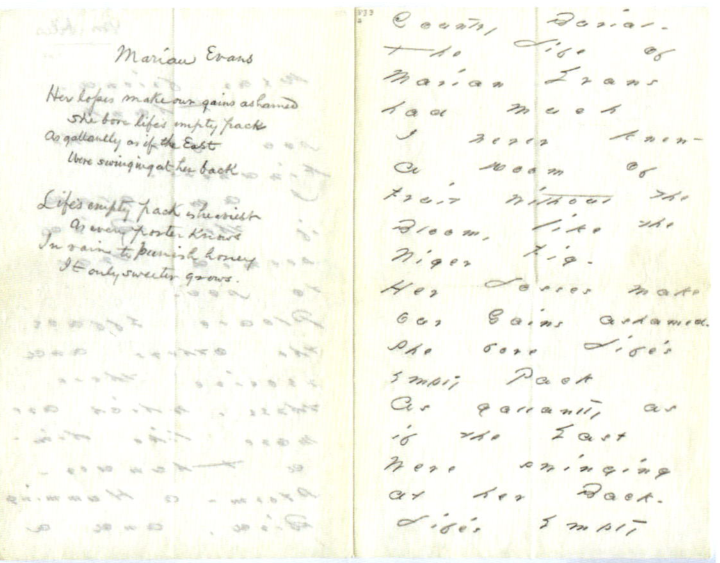

Posthumous Publications and Legacy

"It was not death for I stood up"

Emily Dickinson died at her home on May 15, 1886, possibly of a kidney disease. She left behind a trove of nearly 1,800 poems, only ten of which had been printed during her lifetime. Hundreds had been shared with her wide network of friends and correspondents, but Dickinson had kept her sets and fascicles—the hand-sewn manuscript booklets—entirely private, and these 1,100 poems were only discovered by her sister Lavinia after her death.

Lavinia quickly looked to Susan Dickinson, her sister-in-law and one of the poet's closest friends, to publish them. But work proceeded slowly, and Lavinia turned the manuscripts over to Mabel Loomis Todd, her brother Austin's mistress.

Todd dedicated much of the rest of her life to editing and publishing Dickinson's poetry. The first two books—in 1890 and 1891—were co-edited by Thomas Wentworth Higginson, the poet's old literary mentor. The editors faced many difficulties when interpreting Dickinson's challenging and unique manuscripts, and were further hindered by technology (Todd's typewriter did not have punctuation) and conventional practices. Nevertheless, more than 400 were brought out within ten years of Dickinson's death, and her indisputably strong literary reputation was quickly established.

Every editor of Dickinson's manuscripts has had to face the challenge of how to present a clearly unfinished manuscript, such as this one, as a printed poem. The single sheet from about 1879 is the sole source for the version of the poem published by Mabel Loomis Todd in 1896. Dickinson's crosses next to the words "imply" (in the left margin) and "function" (in the body of the last line), seen here, refer to alternate readings on back of the page. Additional lines, also on the back of the page, may be more alternate readings or may be an abandoned continuation of the poem. (See transcription at p. 181).

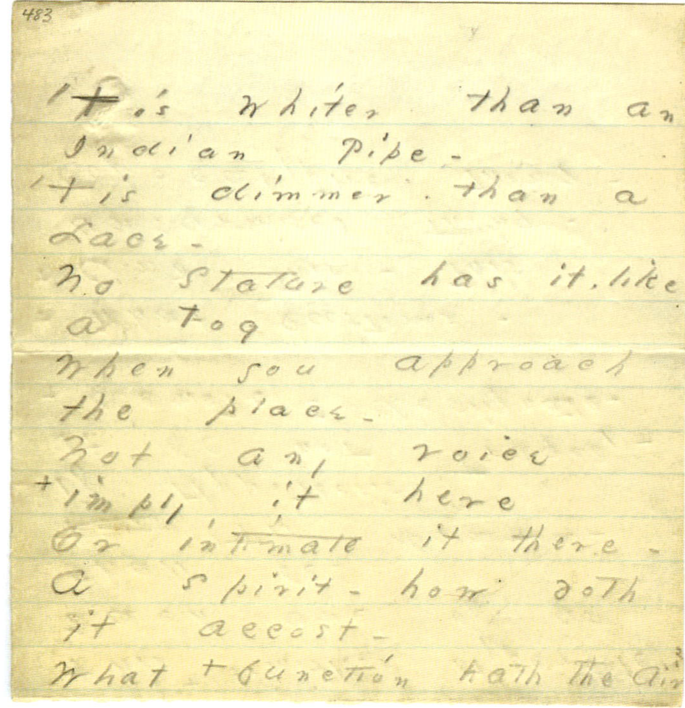

5.13 Mabel Loomis Todd (1856–1932)
Indian Pipes
Oil on card
1882
Amherst College Archives and Special Collections,
Emily Dickinson Collection, 1956.004

Mabel Loomis Todd sent this painting of Indian pipes to Emily
Dickinson in late summer 1882 while Todd was staying in
Washington, D.C. Her signature mark—overlapping letters
M, L, and T—can be seen in the lower left corner. A rendition
of this piece was used to decorate the covers of all of the
editions of Dickinson's poetry and letters edited by Todd and
published by Roberts Brothers between 1890 and 1896.

5.14 Emily Dickinson (1830–1886)
Letter to Mabel Loomis Todd, September 1882
Amherst College Archives and Special Collections,
Emily Dickinson Collection, AC 765

In this letter, Dickinson thanks Mabel Loomis Todd for the
gift of the Indian pipes painting: "That without suspecting
it you should send me the preferred flower of life, seems
almost supernatural, and the sweet glee that I felt at meeting
it, I could confide to none." Todd arrived in Amherst in 1881
and began a passionate love affair with Austin Dickinson the
following year. Although the entire Dickinson family would
experience the strain of the open secret of their affair in the
years ahead, this exchange of the painting and letter happened
before Austin and Mabel's relationship became intimate.

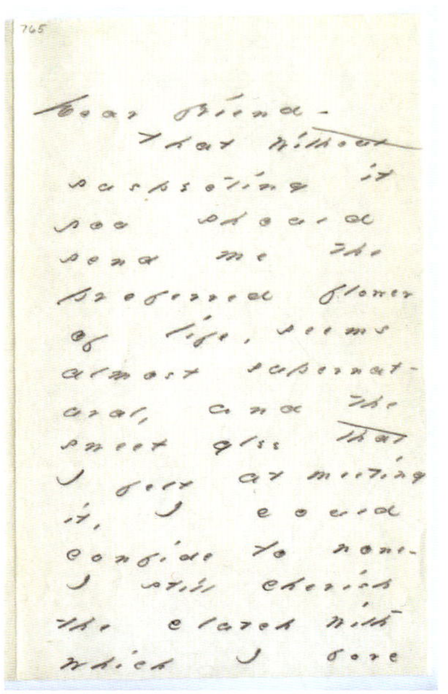
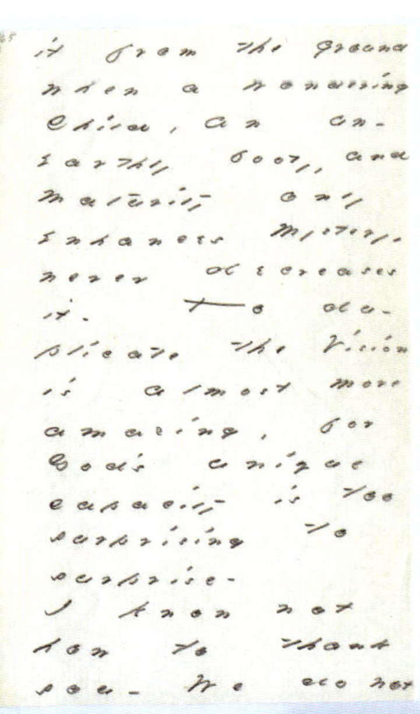
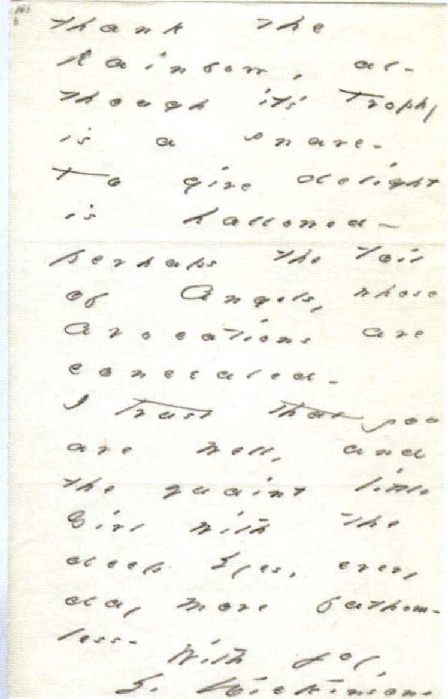

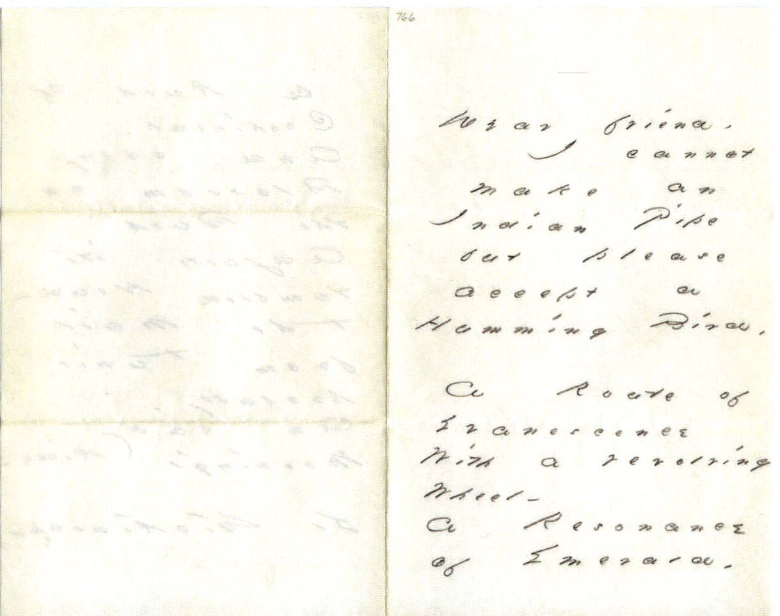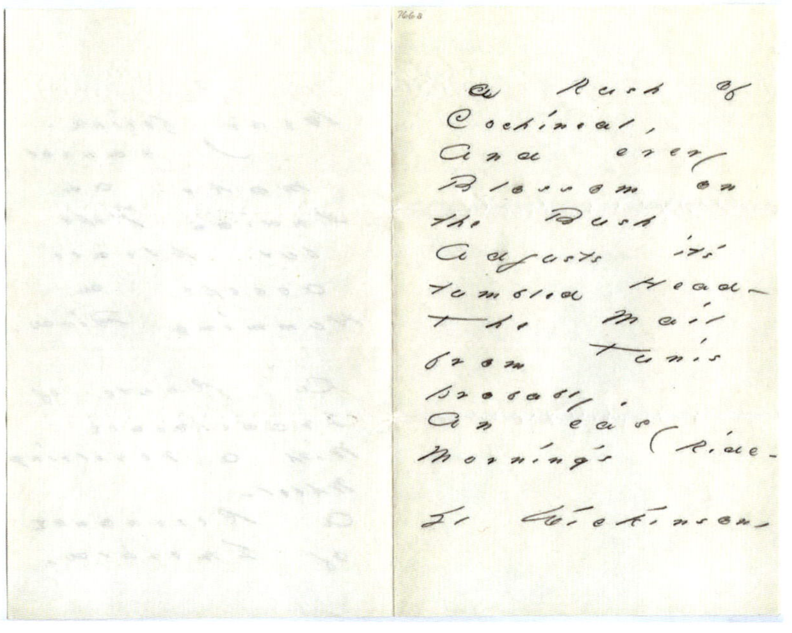

Dear friend,
      I   cannot
make   an
Indian   Pipe
but   please
accept   a
Humming   Bird —

    A   Route   of
Evanescence
With   a   revolving
Wheel —
  A   Resonance
  Of   Emerald —

    A   Rush   of
Cochineal —
And   every
Blossom   on
the Bush
  Adjusts its'
tumbled Head —
The   mail
from   Tunis
probably —
An   easy
Morning's   Ride —

E. Dickinson —

5.15   Emily Dickinson (1830–1886).
Letter including "A Route of / Evanescence"
to Mabel Loomis Todd, 1882
Amherst College Archives and Special Collections,
Emily Dickinson Collection, AC 766

Dickinson's genuine delight at Todd's painting of Indian
pipes is reinforced with this poem sent soon after. Except for
small variations in punctuation, this fair copy of "A route of
evanescence" is identical to the one Dickinson sent to Helen
Hunt Jackson three years before (Cat. 3.09, p. 52). Dickinson
also sent this poem to her cousins Louise and Fanny Norcross,
Sarah Tuckerman, and Thomas Wentworth Higginson. It was
also among those she enclosed with her letter to Thomas Niles
in April 1883 (Cat. 5.11, p. 74). In all the instances, Dickinson
directly associated this poem with the humming bird.

October 1882. Letter composed in pencil by Dickinson to Mabel Loomis Todd on two leaves
of a folded sheet of wove, cream stationery watermarked WESTON'S LINEN RECORD
1881 and folded horizontally into thirds for mailing. Unfolded the sheet measures 20.3 x
25.4 cm.; each leaf measures 20.3 x 12.7 cm. Dickinson addressed the envelope, also in
pencil, herself: "Mrs Todd — ." On the second leaf, the "A" in the line "A Rush of" has been
reformed. The poem inscribed in the body of the letter, "A Route of / Evanescence," is one
of the few poems Dickinson sent to a wide range of correspondents: Helen Hunt Jackson
(1879); Frances and Louise Norcross (1879, original MS lost); Sarah Tuckerman (1880),
T. W. Higginson (1880), Mabel Loomis Todd (MS above); and Thomas Niles (1883). In
addition to the six copies sent to others, Dickinson retained one variant copy. The copies
sent to Helen Hunt Jackson and Thomas Niles are included in this exhibition (see Cat. 3.09,
AC 816, and Cat. 5.11, AC 833).

5.16 Emily Dickinson (1830–1886)
"A route of evanescence"
Poem transcribed by Fanny Norcross, ca. 1889
Amherst College Archives and Special Collections,
Emily Dickinson Collection, Tr. 45

As part of her work editing Dickinson's manuscripts for publication in the 1890s, Mabel Loomis Todd contacted many of Dickinson's friends to ask for poems or letters they might be willing to share. Many correspondents sent their originals in Dickinson's hand, but others made transcriptions for her.

This manuscript includes "A route of evanescence" along with several other poems Dickinson sent to her cousins Fanny and Louise Norcross. Dickinson never titled her poems, but here "Humming bird" is placed above the text. Although Dickinson's original is not extant, she clearly made reference to the hummingbird somewhere in the copy sent to her cousins.

5.17 Mabel Loomis Todd (1856–1932)
Transcription of Emily Dickinson's alternate word choices for "A Route of Evanescence," undated
Amherst College Archives and Special Collections,
Emily Dickinson Collection, Tr. 3

This small slip of paper testifies to the extent of Todd's editorial work on Dickinson's poems and letters. In addition to the copy she received directly from the poet and the transcription she received from the Norcrosses (both at left), this note is evidence that Todd saw Dickinson's original draft (not on view) of "A Route of Evanescence" and noted the alternate wording for the adjective "revolving" in the second line:

> *dissolving wheel*
> *dissembling* ˝
> *renewing* ˝

Considering that all the copies she sent to friends use the phrase "revolving wheel," it is clear that Dickinson made a definite choice in this instance.

5.18   Emily Dickinson (1830–1886)
 “Honey grows everywhere”
 Fragment, undated
 Amherst College Archives and Special Collections,
 Emily Dickinson Collection, AC 214

5.19   Emily Dickinson (1830–1886)
 “Honey grows everywhere”
 Fragment transcribed by Mabel Loomis Todd, undated
 Amherst College Archives and Special Collections,
 Emily Dickinson Collection, AC 214a

The Amherst College archives holds nearly 900 transcriptions
of Dickinson's manuscripts made by Mabel Loomis Todd
and her assistants during the 1890s. No piece of Dickinson's
writing was too small, as illustrated by Todd's attempt to
turn this slim piece of paper with barely legible handwriting
(above) into something worthy of publication. Notes on Todd's
transcription (below) indicate she had selected this text for
inclusion in a proposed "Year Book" and that she classified
it as "Prose"—possibly for a section of Dickinson's writing
that fell outside the category of poetry and letters. Todd's
book never materialized, but the title was used in 1948 for an
unrelated project.

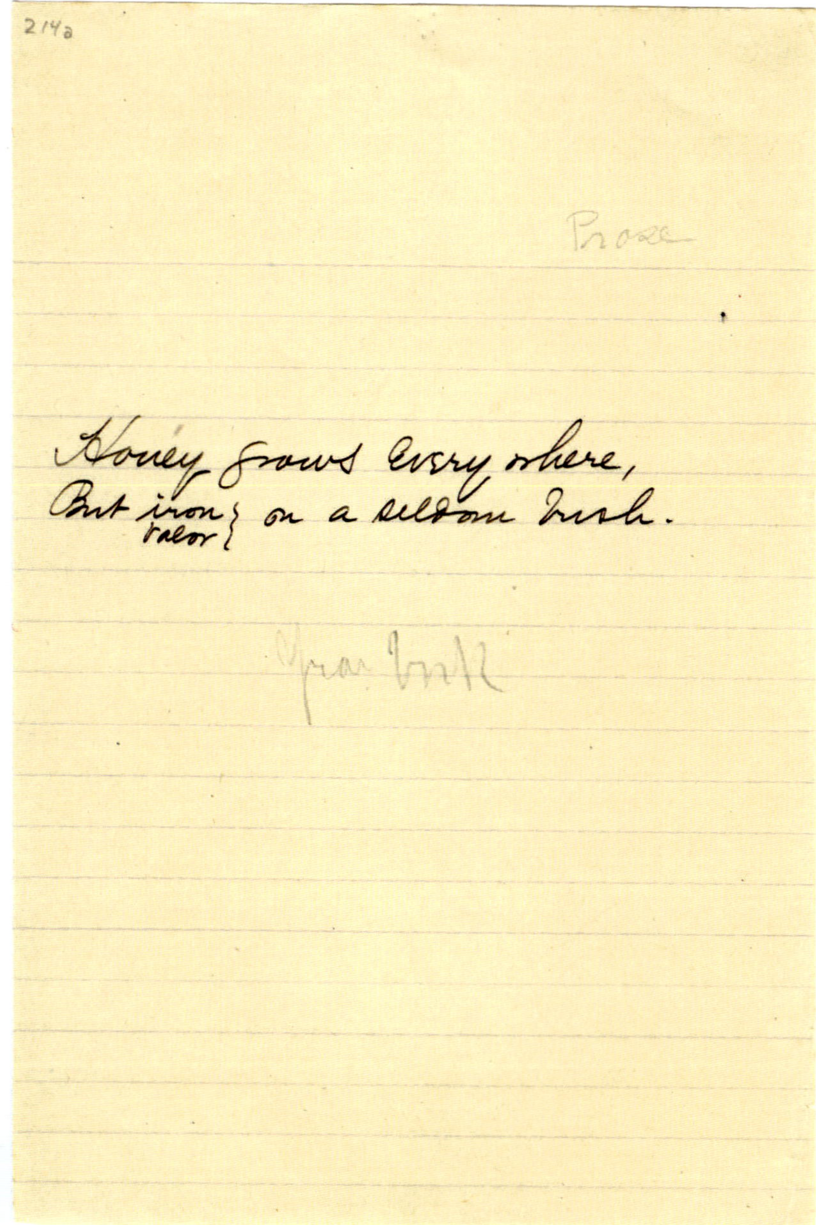

The first two books of Dickinson's poetry published after her death were edited collaboratively by Mabel Loomis Todd and Thomas Wentworth Higginson. The number of hands involved in shaping the first volume is clear from Higginson's mention in this letter of Mr. Baxter's criticisms, which had been communicated in a letter to the publisher Thomas Niles, who passed them along. Mr. Baxter had remarked: "There is hardly one of these poems which does not bear marks of unusual and remarkable talent; there is hardly one of them which is not marked by an extraordinary crudity of workmanship."

Here, Higginson asks Todd to revise some of the poems in light of that criticism.

It was not Death, for
I stood up,
And all the Dead, lie down -
It was not Night, for
all the Bells
Put out their tongues, for Noon.

It was not Frost, for on
my +Flesh   +Knees
I felt Siroccos - crawl -
Nor Fire - for just my +
Marble feet   +Two
Could keep a Chancel, cool -

And yet, it tasted, like
them all,
the Figures I have seen
Set orderly, for Burial,
Reminded me, of mine -

As if my life were shaven,
And fitted to a frame,
And could not breathe
without a key,
And 'twas like Midnight,
some -

When everything that ticked -
has stopped -
And Space stares all around,
Or Grisly frosts - first Au-
tumn morns,
Repeal the Beating Ground -

But, most, like Chaos -
Stopless - Cool -
Without a Chance, or Spar -
Or even a Report of Land -
to justify - Despair.

IT WAS NOT DEATH, FOR I STOOD UP,
AND ALL THE DEAD, LIE DOWN—
IT WAS NOT NIGHT, FOR ALL THE BELLS
PUT OUT THEIR TONGUES, FOR NOON.

IT WAS NOT FROST, FOR ON MY FLESH
I FELT SIROCCOS CRAWL—
NOR FIRE, BOR JUST MY MARBLE FEET
COULD KEEP A CHANCEL COOL.

AND YET, IT TASTED LIKE THEM ALL,
THE FGGUBSS I HAVE SEEN
SETORBERLY, FOR BURIAL,
REMIDDED ME OF MINE,

AS IF MY LIFE WERE SHAVEN,
AND FITTED TO A FRAME,
AND COULD NOT BREATHE WITHOUT A KEY,
ADD 'TWAS LIKE MIDNIGHT, SOME—

WHEN EVERYTHING THAT TICKED HAS STOPPED—
ADD SPACE STABBS, ALL ABOUBD,
BR GRISLY FROSTS— FISS AUTUMN MBRNS,
B PPEA

*Vol. II
fasc 85*

5.21 Emily Dickinson (1830–1886)
"It was not death, for / I stood up"
Poem, dated ca. summer 1862
Amherst College Archives and Special Collections,
Emily Dickinson Collection, AC 85

5.22 Emily Dickinson (1830–1886)
"It was not death, for I stood up"
Typed transcription, undated
Amherst College Archives and Special Collections,
Emily Dickinson Collection, TR 886

Mabel Loomis Todd began typewriting transcriptions of Dickinson's poems in the late 1880s. The Hammond typewriter was introduced in 1884; Todd used this machine to transcribe more than 200 of Dickinson's poems. Here, she selected Dickinson's original text over the variants—"knows" and "two"—added by Dickinson in pencil at a later time. The machine's lack of lower-case letters and punctuation made it impossible to capture many basic elements of Dickinson's originals.

The transcription also has the notation "Vol. II" indicating it was included in the 1891 collection *Poems: Second Series*, as well as a reference to "fasc 85"—the number Todd assigned to the fascicle, seen here at left.

5.23   Emily Dickinson (1830–1886)
"A pang is more / conspicuous in Spring"
Poem, dated ca. 1881
Amherst College Archives and Special Collections,
Emily Dickinson Collection, AC 109

Dickinson's earliest editors took their copy-text
primarily from her fascicles, with their relatively tidy and
straightforward presentation of the poet's work. The drama
in this late poem, with Dickinson's reflections on "Minute
Effulgencies and Winds," is heightened by the implied
movement in the shape of the paper. It remained unpublished
until 1945 when Mabel Loomis Todd's daughter, Millicent
Todd Bingham, published *Bolts of Melody: New Poems of Emily
Dickinson*. The poem appeared here with no mention of the
unusual shape of the manuscript, and omitted Dickinson's
variant included in the body of the poem.

Bingham's exhaustive research into the Dickinson
manuscripts she inherited filled three additional books;
in 1956, she donated her entire collection of Dickinson
manuscripts, her mother's editorial correspondence, and
many of her own working papers to Amherst College.

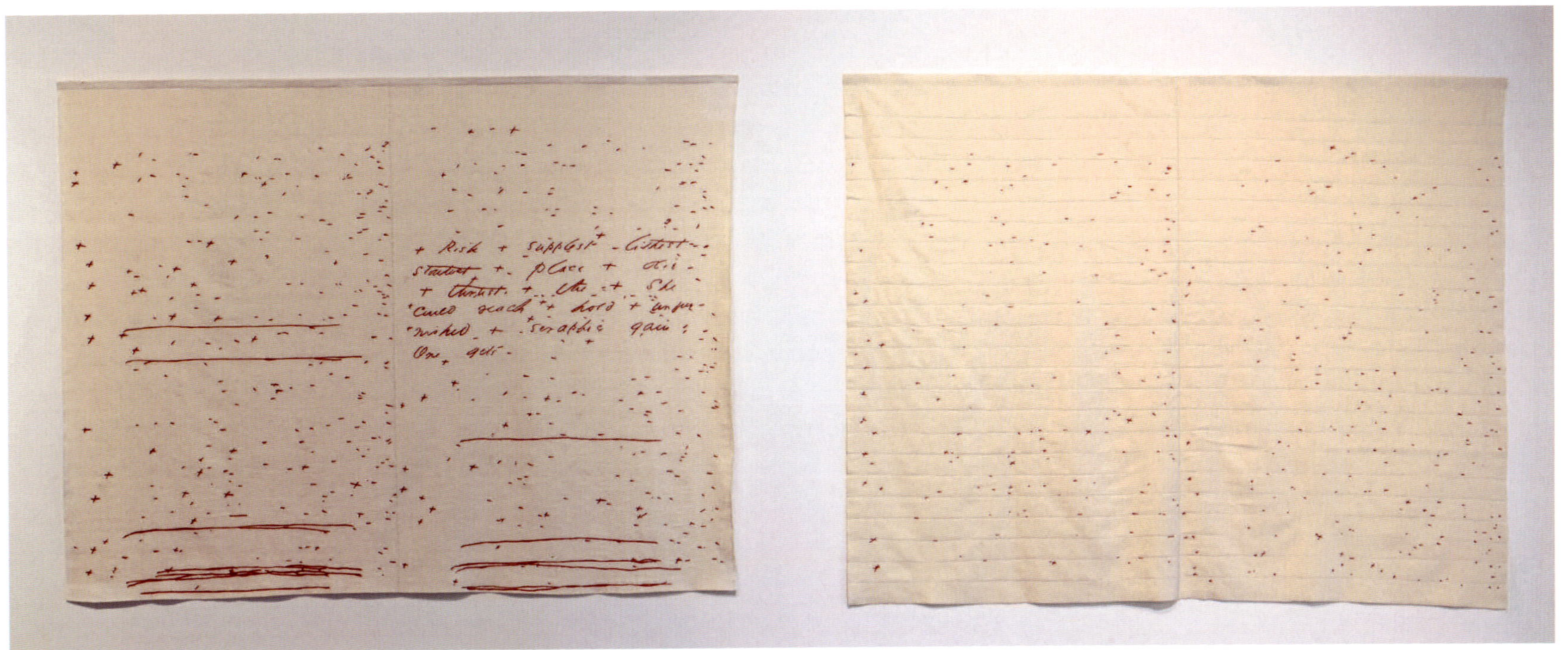

5.24 Jen Bervin (b. 1972)
The Composite Marks of Fascicle 28 and
The Composite Marks of Fascicle 38
Installation View, The Power Plant (Toronto, Canada)
Photograph by Toni Hafkenscheid

Jen Bervin (b. 1972)
The Dickinson Composites
New York: Granary Books, 2010
Amherst College Archives and Special Collections,
xxN7433 .B47 D53 2010

This interpretation of Dickinson's notation system stands
in contrast to the many editions of Dickinson's poetry that
routinely omitted these marks and often failed to mention
other unusual features of Dickinson's manuscripts. Jen
Bervin, a contemporary visual artist and writer, selected six
of Dickinson's handsewn fascicles, and then overlaid digital
images of all the non-textual marks to generate images that
guided her embroidery of quilts measuring six feet by eight
feet (above). Each copy of the limited edition published by
Granary Books (left) includes two machine sewn and hand-
embroidered samples—excerpts from Composites 28 and 38,
in the same materials as the original quilts. Bervin has written
that she "wanted to visually reassert the vital presence of the
omitted marks, to raise questions about them."

5.25 Emily Dickinson (1830–1886)
Poems
Boston: Roberts Brothers, 1890
Amherst College Archives and Special Collections,
Emily Dickinson Collection, PS1541.A1 1890 Ser.1

This volume of 125 poems, edited by Mabel Loomis Todd and
Thomas Wentworth Higginson, was published in October of
1890. Appearing four years after Dickinson's death, it was the
first collected edition of her work. Five hundred copies were
sold the day it was published, and it was reissued eleven times
within the year; this copy was given by Todd to her parents
shortly after it appeared. The Indian pipes on the cover are
based on the painting she had sent Dickinson years earlier
(Cat. 5.13, p. 77).

In the preface, Higginson emphasizes Dickinson's peculiarity
and reclusiveness, as did Todd in her many public lectures
about the poet. Already the subject of gossip and speculation
during her lifetime, fascination with Dickinson's personal life
grew with her literary reputation.

Frontispiece Shown at Figure 1, p. 6:

5.26 Emily Dickinson (1830–1886)
Poems, Second Series
Boston: Roberts Brothers, 1891
Morgan Library & Museum,
Gift of William H. McCarthy, Jr.
PML 47569

With hundreds of manuscripts to choose from, Todd and
Higginson published a second book of poems in October
1891. This edition includes a four-page "Fac-simile of
'Renunciation,' by Emily Dickinson," the first published
reproduction of a Dickinson manuscript. The preface
describes the discovery of the true extent of Dickinson's
literary output when her sister Lavinia found the fascicles and
friends began sharing their Dickinson manuscripts with the
editors.

"I'm Nobody! Who are you?" is the first poem in the section
of the book titled "Life." Dickinson's editors made many
alterations to the poet's punctuation. Here, they changed her
distinctive dash to a more standard comma in the line: "How
public, like a frog — "

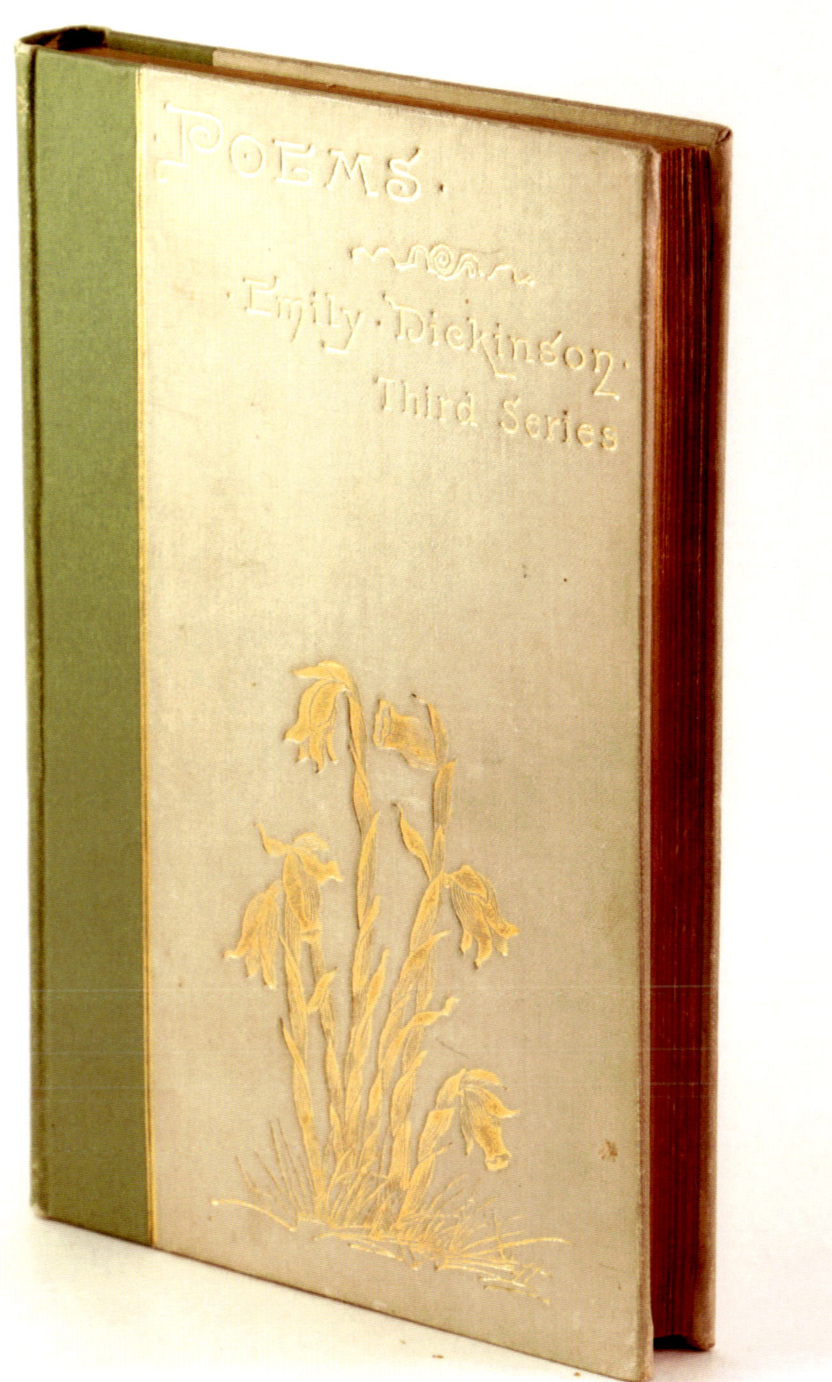

5.27 Emily Dickinson (1830–1886)
Poems: Third Series
Boston: Roberts Bros., 1896
Amherst College Archives and Special Collections,
Emily Dickinson Collection, PS1541.A1 1896 Ser.3

An edition of Dickinson's letters appeared in 1894, followed by this third collection of previously unpublished poems in 1896. Higginson withdrew from the project after *Poems: Second Series* in 1891, leaving Todd to carry on without him.

Austin Dickinson died in 1895. The animosity between his widow, Susan, and his mistress, Mabel Loomis Todd, erupted in a lawsuit over real estate in 1898. Todd lost the case, but maintained possession of hundreds of Dickinson's manuscripts; these she kept locked away until 1931 when she collaborated with her daughter, Millicent Todd Bingham, on a revised edition of Dickinson's letters. Roberts Brothers used Todd's Indian pipes the cover of all three series of *Poems* and the *Letters*.

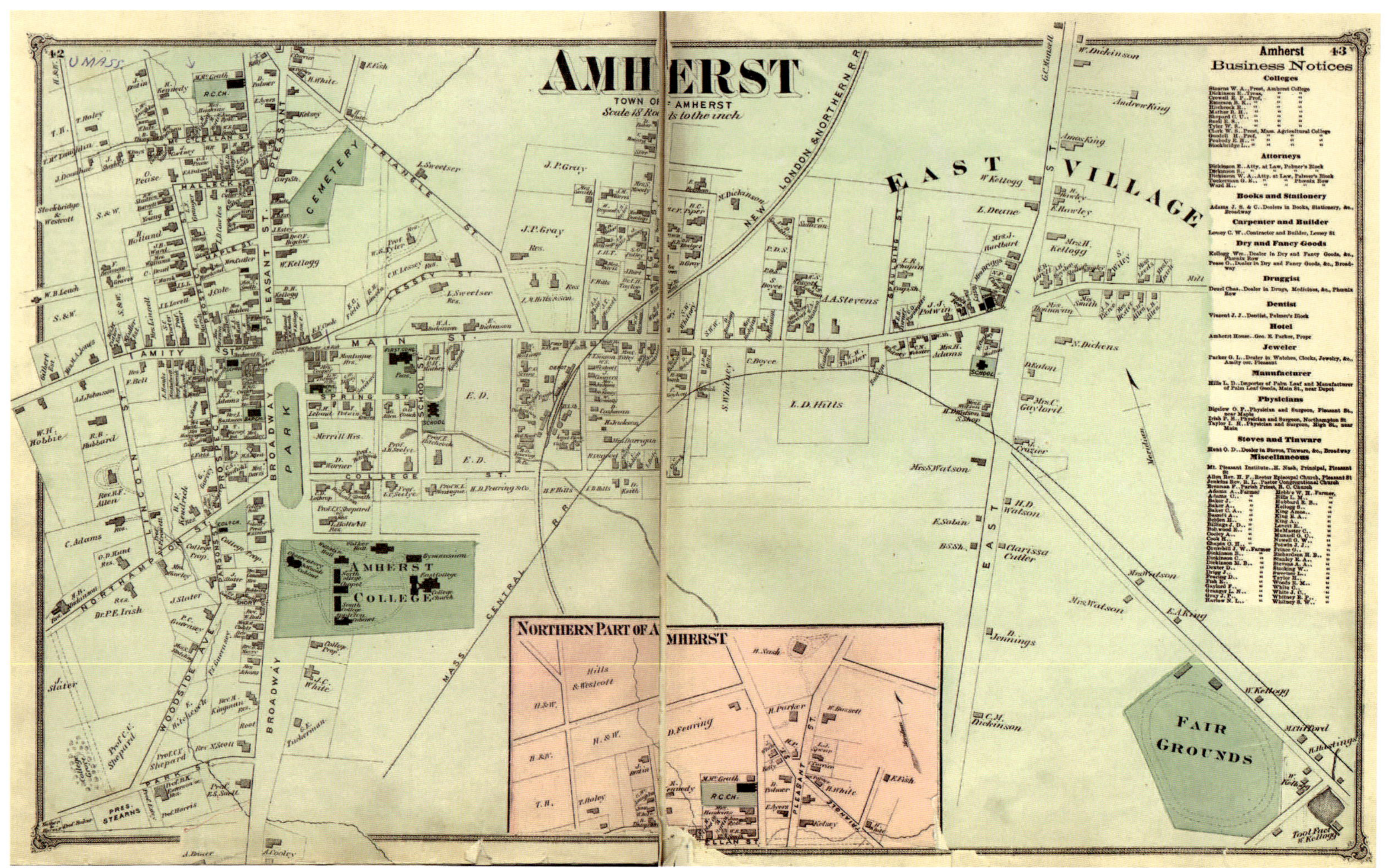

A map of Amherst, from *County Atlas of Hampshire, Massachusetts, from actual surveys by and under the direction of F[rederick] W. Beers* (New York: F. W. Beers, 1873). The Dickinson family homes are on the north side of Main Street on the left page of the map: "W. A Dickinson" and "E. Dickinson." Amherst College Archives and Special Collections.

Emily Dickinson:
Manuscripts, Maps, and a Poetics of Cartography

Marta Werner

And this, essentially is what maps give us, *reality,* a reality that exceeds our vision, our reach, the span of our days, a reality we achieve no other way. We are always mapping the invisible or the unattainable or the erasable, the future or the past, the whatever-is-not-here-present-to-our-senses-now and, through the gift that the map gives us, transmuting it into everything it is not ... *into the real.*

—Denis Wood[1]

The Gulf behind – was not –
The Continents – were new –
Eternity – it was – before
Eternity was due –

—Emily Dickinson
from "It was a quiet Way – " [H 86][2]

Manuscripts

The word "map" comes from the Latin *mappa,* for "napkin, cloth, sheet," and refers to the material on which the early maps were drawn by hand. Like the map, the manuscript exists first as a material body. In its diverse strata and trajectories the manuscript is more than a metaphoric map. If we look carefully, we see contours,

---

1. Denis Wood, with John Fels, *The Power of Maps* (New York: The Guilford Press, 1992), 4-5.

2. The citations to Dickinson's writings will always be to the manuscript and the archive in which that manuscript is housed. These are as follows: AC: Amherst College Archives and Special Collections; BPL: Boston Public Library; H: Houghton Library, Harvard University; MA: The Morgan Library & Museum; NYPL: New York Public Library. For printed versions of Dickinson's writings see Ralph W. Franklin's *The Poems of Emily Dickinson,* Variorum edition (3 vols.) (Cambridge, Mass.: The Belknap Press of Harvard University Press, 1998), here designated "Fr.," and Thomas H. Johnson's and Theodora Ward's *The Letters of Emily Dickinson* (3 vols.) (Cambridge, Mass.: The Belknap Press of Harvard University Press, 1958), here designated "JL." For Dickinson's letters to Susan Gilbert Dickinson, see Martha Nell Smith and Ellen Louise Hart, eds. *Open Me Carefully: Emily Dickinson's Intimate Letters to Susan Huntington Dickinson* (Ashfield, Mass.: Paris Press, 1998).

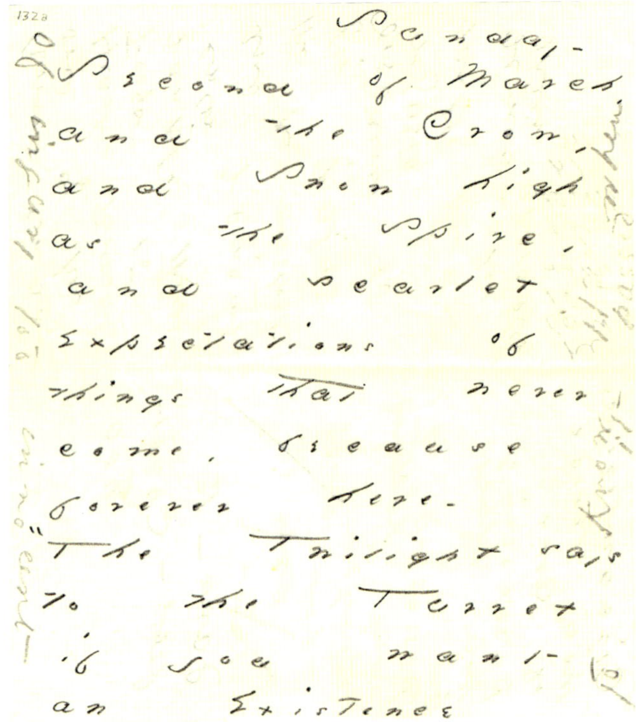
Sunday –
Second of March,
and the Crow,
and Snow high
as the Spire,
and scarlet
Expectations of
things that never
come, because
forever here.
"The Twilight rays
to the Turret

Figure 1: "Sunday – / Second of March,"= March 2, 1884, Amherst College Archives and Special Collections, Emily Dickinson Collection, AC 132a.

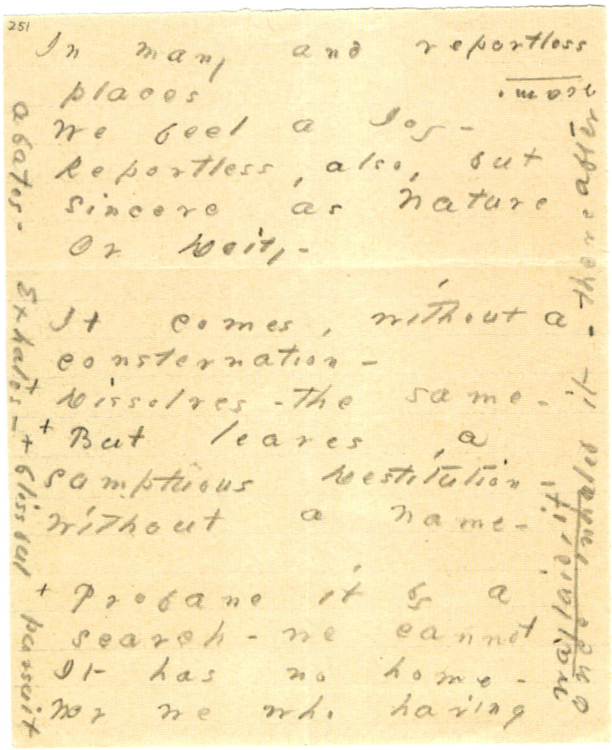
In many and reportless
places
We feel a Joy –
Reportless, also, but
Sincere as Nature
Or Deity –
It comes, without a
consternation –
Dissolves – the same –
But leaves a
sumptuous Destitution –
Without a Name –
Profane it by a
search – we cannot
It has no home –
Nor we who having

Figure 2: "In many and reportless / places", ca. 1876, Amherst College Archives and Special Collections, Emily Dickinson Collection, AC 251.

boundaries, the grooves where pencil has pressed, the lines where the iron gall has cut its acidic furrows. And like the maps we unfolded and marveled at as children, some of the first things we notice about a manuscript are its shape, borders, and colors. Indeed, the manuscript possesses many of the attributes of what today's cartographers call the "deep map": it is multi-layered and three-dimensional, as much process as product; it entails the inscription of a subjectivity while also registering the many forces—historical, cultural, geographical, environmental—that shape that subjectivity and circulate beyond it. Visible but not fully decipherable, mutable and suspended between presence and absence, every manuscript, like every map, is irreducibly unique.

After working for many years with Dickinson's manuscripts, I sometimes imagine them as pages from a vast, overflowing book of maps. They are aids to our navigation of the world; they give meaning to the ideas of near and far; they have the power to console us when we are lost for a moment or forever. The topography alluded to in Dickinson's poems is varied and sweeping. In them she traverses plains and mountains, forests and rivers, whole seas. Terrain changes quickly, and in a single step it is possible to cross from one hemisphere to another, or from one world to the next: "Of River or of Ridge < + Of Fathom or of League > / + Defies Topography – <+ Forbid that any know –>" (AC 86-13/14). If the fascicles—those forty lightly bound volumes Dickinson probably made between 1858 and 1864—form a kind of poetic atlas, her many unbound poems on single sheets or partial sheets seem like close-ups or bright fragments torn from an infinite but now vanished map.[3] Consider, for a moment, two "insets" from this late, lost map. The first (Figure 1) composed on laid, Irish linen paper and imagined by some to be the draft of a letter and by others a poem, maps the zone between dusk and dark; the second (Figure 2), composed on a rectangle of cream, blue-ruled paper, charts the coordinates of joy.

Although no place names appear to identify the site, there are still landmarks to orient us. The first letter-poem maps a Sabbath day in late winter, somewhere in the northern hemisphere where the latitude may be measured by the height of snow, the season's birds, and the church's spire. It is a map of the future's manifestation in the present—the "forever here –" of our "scarlet / Expectations," and of the epiphany of twilight itself, the dialogue between the tilted, rotating earth and the sun in the moment of its fall below the horizon. For the human observer in this scene, twilight is a period or region of obscurity and ambiguity. But even as the poem-as-lyric invites us to mark the relation between human existence and the more-than-human rays of the atmosphere, so the poem-as-map reminds us that agency—the power

3. The dating of Dickinson's manuscripts is a challenging project, and while much material evidence (especially handwriting evidence) supports the dating schema presented by Ralph W. Franklin, dating Dickinson's work remains more art than science. I have used Johnson and Franklin's estimates for the numbers of Dickinson's poems and letters belonging to specific years and ranges of years. Although there is still—and is likely to always be—debate concerning the exact number of poems and letters composed, copied, or circulated within a year or range of years, I believe Johnson and Franklin's estimates are strong enough to support a reading of trends in both the poems and the correspondence. This said, the dating of the manuscripts must be considered an ongoing project.

of annunciation—belongs to the world's phenomena far more than to ourselves. The Twilight breaks into the letter-poem, interrupting the mapping of the human realm, whose central landmark is the spire, and unsettling our sense of scale by pointing to the further, unmapped realm of the Cosmos.

In the second late lyric poem, "In many and reportless / places," Dickinson alludes to the limitations of conventional maps as guides in our pursuit of rapture. Instead of providing a route to the nameless site of "Joy –" opened by the nearly simultaneous advent and withdrawal of rapture and experienced by the speaker as immersion in "sumptuous Destitution – ," the poem points the way beyond longitude and latitude. Here, Dickinson implies, the curvature of the earth makes scale meaningless for calculating the distance in time or space between two positions. Rather, by roaming aimlessly over an inestimable expanse, the poet becomes a new kind of cartographer. The map she traces is not the map of well-traveled ways, but the map whose North, South, East and West, like midnight and morning, change places—and on which distances are measured in prosodic pauses or the inhalations and exhalations of the wanderers and of Joy itself.

Marking both limit and threshold, the border of the manuscript is also the dividing line between two territories, two hemispheres we call "text" and "world." As scholars have long maintained, Dickinson's manuscripts raise questions about borders—their uncertainty, and especially their capacity to change.

While Sharon Cameron's work on the fascicles shows how the rows of variants following Dickinson's poems transform ends into apparently moving edges (see Figure 4), Susan Howe's work questions where the border can be drawn between poems and letters, manuscripts and drawings. "Sometimes," Howe writes, "letters are poems with a salutation and signature. Sometimes poems are letters with a salutation and a signature. If limits disappear where will we find bearings?"[4]

❧

Before we cross over the manuscript's outer border into its interior, we must first shed what are often the even unconscious matrices of the printed page, the organization of our visual expectations imposed by the unyielding edges of the typographer's chase. It is not easy to reshape how we think and speak of "the manuscript page" without the lurking comparison of the clean, printed page, separated into text block, invisible but tangible lines created by sorts of type and margins against which we

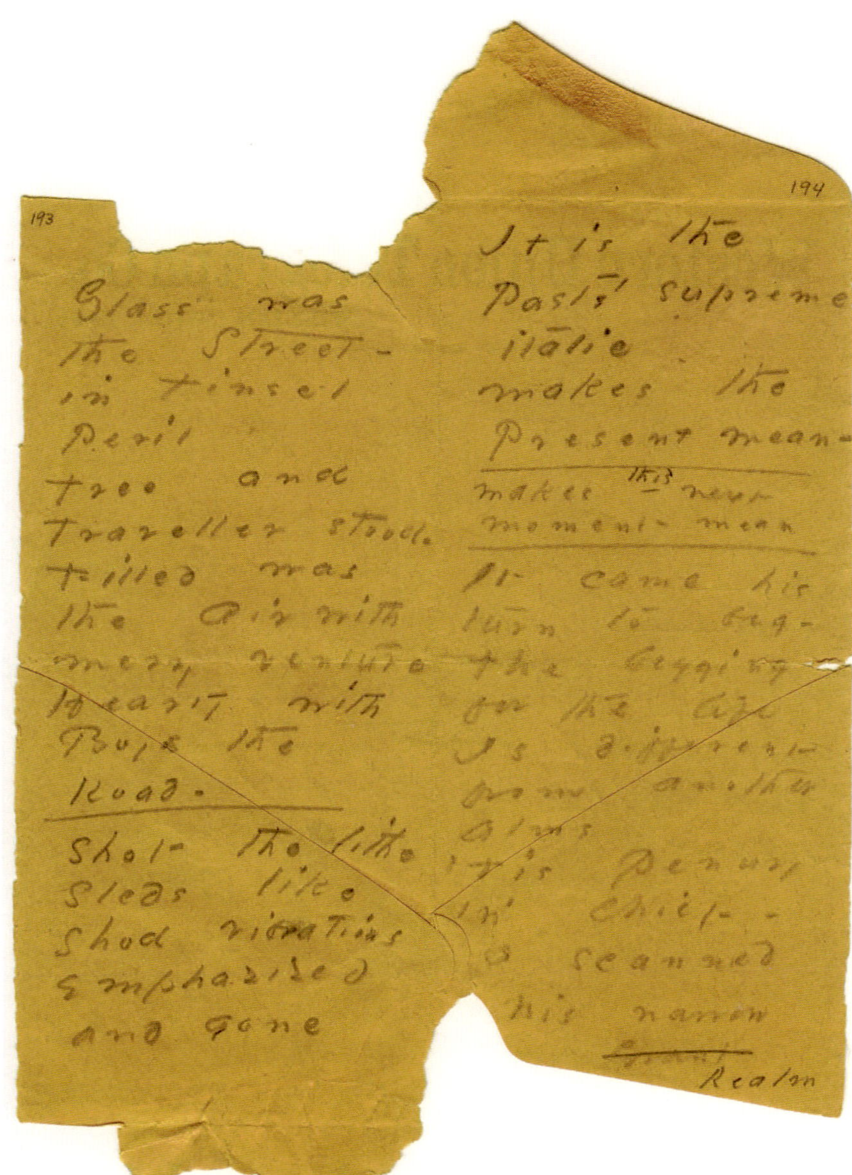

Figure 3: "Glass was / the Street – "; "It came his / turn to beg – ," ca. 1880, Amherst College Archives and Special Collections, Emily Dickinson Collection, AC 193/194. See also AC 450 Cat. 4.13, p. 65; and Figure 1, p. 139).

Figure 4: Variants "moving" the edges of "The Birds begun at / Four o'Clock," ca. 1864, Amherst College Archives and Special Collections, Emily Dickinson Collection, AC 81-8 (detail).

---

4. See Sharon Cameron's *Choosing Not Choosing: Dickinson's Fascicles* (Chicago: University of Chicago Press, 1993). See also Susan Howe, "These Flames and Generosities of the Heart: Emily Dickinson and the Illogic of Sumptuary Values," in *Sulfur* 28 (Spring 1991), 145.

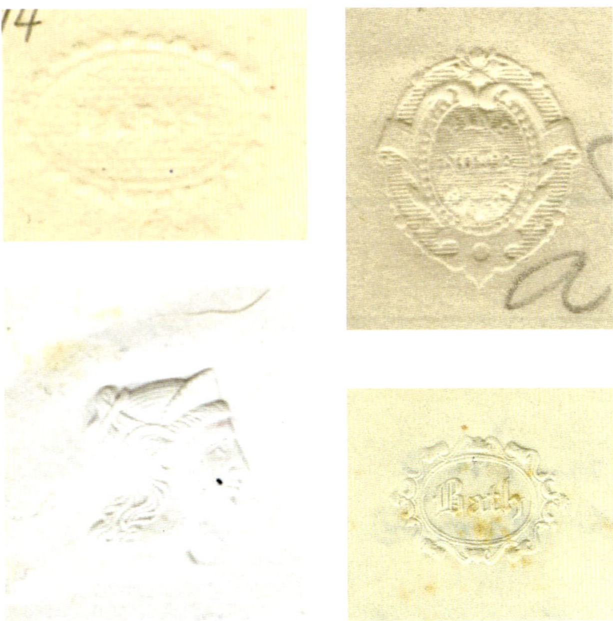

Figure 5: Examples of embossing found on Dickinson's stationery. Top row, left to right: Paris, Fine Note Paper. Bottom row, left to right: female figurehead (Athena?), Bath. Amherst College Archives and Special Collections, Emily Dickinson Collection, AC 274, AC 654, AC 129, AC 240.

might be tempted to measure Dickinson's unique pagescapes. But Dickinson constructs her pages, pressing their edges, boundaries, and material definitions even beyond "page" to under the flaps of the envelopes that might have once been intended to serve as carrier for her prose and poetic missives. Dickinson's "pages" bend, crowd, disorient and reorder the space of textuality. Once we cross over the manuscript's outer edges and into its multiple surfaces of text and experimentation, unruled spaces, and potentially boundless chronologies fathomable perhaps only by the author, there are many topographical features to ponder: the density or translucence of the paper, its chain lines or the fibers of its weave, the watermarks and the tactile patterns of its embossing, the thickness and color of its rulings. In Dickinson's case the topography of the leaf—the "pagescape"— extends the inner world of the poet, her memory and imagination. In her drafts we often see Dickinson gravitating towards different zones of a manuscript to experiment with lexical choices and make a trial of variants, while in her carefully wrought copies we might see her scripts as continuing the visual cadences of the filaments in the paper's weave.

For many viewers, the most arresting feature of the pagescape of Dickinson's works is her handwriting: unlike the martial lines of print, whose uniformity is guaranteed by the chase, we find channels of ink or pencil running across the manuscript and sideways along its edges, sometimes seeming to create a frame or decorative border for the text. From her cursive of the 1840s, described by Dickinson's childhood friend Emily Fowler Ford as "very beautiful—small, clear, and finished,"[5] and the writing of her middle years, which Thomas Wentworth Higginson famously described as the "fossil bird tracks of that town,"[6] to the ghostlier demarcations characteristic of the late pencil drafts of the 1880s, the evolution of Dickinson's handwriting over several decades is linked to her compositional process and to the aesthetics that inform them. And while a quick comparison of a manuscript from the 1840s to another of Dickinson's from the later years would seem to reveal two entirely dissimilar productions, a longer study illuminates subtle but striking continuities in her hand. Dickinson's tendency, for example, toward forming long, tapered descenders in her minuscule "y's," and the detached and right-crossing strokes of her majuscule "T's" that will become pronounced in her later hand are already present to some degree in her hand of the 1840s. So, too, the angled slant of her early writing continues in her later work.[7] (Compare, for example, Cat. 2.09, p. 32, with Cat. 5.07, p. 71.)

The art of writing by hand is an intricate cognitive process that requires the writer to sense both pen and paper, position and move the writing instrument, and direct

5. Emily Fowler Ford, "Growing Up with Emily Dickinson: A Remembrance" in *Emily Dickinson: Early Feminist Essays (1886-1915)*, http://www.earlywomenmasters.net/essays/authors/fowler/ fowler.html.

6. Thomas Wentworth Higginson, "Emily Dickinson's Letters," *The Atlantic,* October, 1891: http://www.theatlantic.com/magazine/archive/1891/10/emily-dickinsons-letters/306524/.

7. For an interesting new study on handwriting, see Anne Trubek's *The History and Uncertain Future of Handwriting* (New York and London: Bloomsbury Publishing, 2016).

The Networked Recluse

this drive by thought. Not mental automaticity, but, rather, the listening through the body, the harmonized movement of mind and body, brings writing into being. Between the 1850s and the 1880s, Dickinson's letterforms grew in expressiveness as they more fully transcended the need to render a conventionalized set of alphabetic symbols. In many works in fair copy from the 1870s and 1880s Dickinson's hand-wrought kerning and tracking of letters and words together with her practice of stretching writing to the very perimeter of the paper imparts a net- or mesh-like quality to the leaves. Noting her own experience of this change in her friend's hand, Fowler-Ford wrote, "Later, though her writing retained its elegance, it became difficult to read."[8] The degree to which we share Fowler Ford's experience of estrangement when encountering Dickinson's later manuscripts may be attributed in part to the changes of scale—magnification—of her alphabetic forms, the reduction in conjoined and flowing letters, and to the expansive apertures separating words. Absorbing our entire range of vision even as they recede into a deep remoteness, these manuscripts seem to occupy a space both very close and immeasurably far away. Following her letterforms across the years, it is possible to dream of becoming a connoisseur of her singular calligraphy.

In recent years visual artists have responded to what Susan Howe first called the "mysterious sensuous expression"[9] of Dickinson's scripts in a myriad of ways: Kiki Smith answered with *Sampler*; Jen Bervin with the exquisite series *The Dickinson Composites*, in which the individual pieces resemble star charts (Figure 7, next page); and Howe's long-time partner, the artist David von Schlegell, used string and graphite to produce a series of spare works on paper that resemble both Dickinson's scripts and the strings she used to tie the fascicles together (Figure 8, next page). They were the last drawings he ever made.[10]

Dickinson's manuscript witnesses reveal a wide array of states: there are worksheet drafts, crowded and still alive with variants, addenda, and cancellations; intermediate drafts copied from earlier drafts but still forever suspended somewhere between the opposing reflexes of composition and completion; immaculate fair copies of poems, some bound into fascicles, some on single sheets; and fair copies of poems that left Dickinson's desk to circulate in the realm of readers. Each is a thing of meaning and of beauty, though for different reasons and in different ways. To begin with, though, the very terms "rough draft," "intermediate copy," and "fair copy" that I have used above—and that are such common tender in the world of publication—do not fully reflect the varied textual conditions of Dickinson's manuscripts. Although some determinations of state are straightforward—a poem composed in a rough-copy broken cursive, with multiple cancellations, additions, and variants

---

8. Emily Fowler Ford, "Growing Up with Emily Dickinson: A Remembrance."

9. Howe, "These Flames and Generosities of the Heart," 43.

10. von Schlegell composed these last drawings while he was living in Buffalo, New York; they were first exhibited at the Nina Freudenheim Gallery in 1992.

Figure 6: Random letterforms A-Z (sans "X"), with representative marks of punctuation, ca. 1858-1885, The Morgan Library & Museum and Amherst College Archives and Special Collections, Emily Dickinson Collection, AC 450; AC 450; AC 766; AC 88-13; AC 766; AC 84-2; AC 106; AC 217; AC 827; AC 816; AC 106; AC 450; AC 851; MA 1357; AC 80-8; AC 813; AC 814; AC 251; AC 88-13; AC 88-13; MA 1556; AC 84-4; AC 106; AC 83-5; AC 84-2; AC 84-2; AC 80-8; AC 83-4; AC 855; AC 851; AC 132; AC 813; AC 217; AC 106.

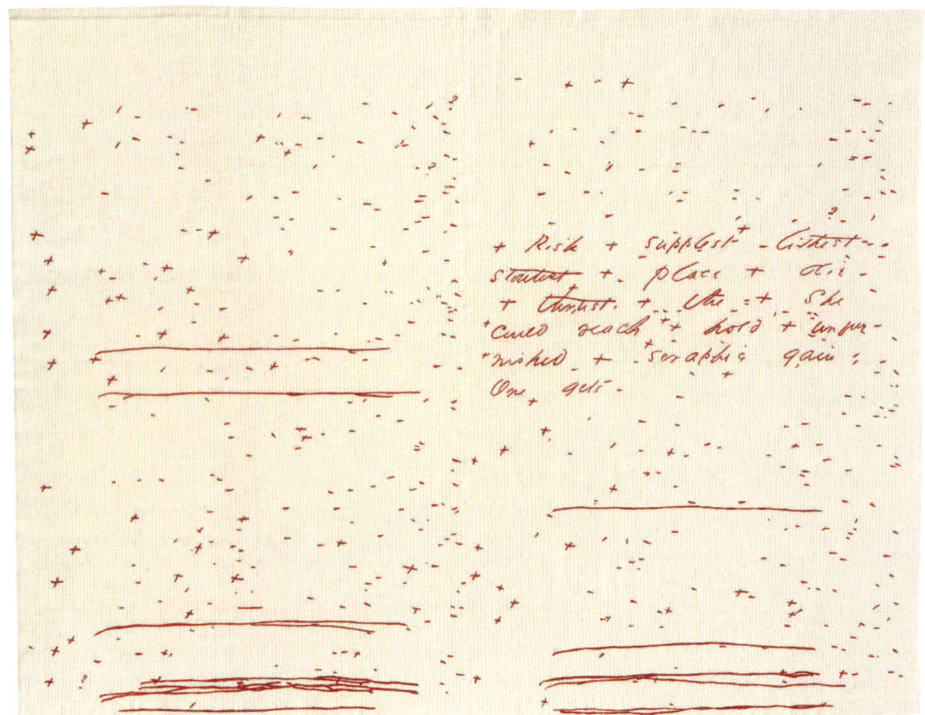

Figure 7: Jen Bervin, *The Composite Marks of Fascicle 28,* 2008. Cotton and silk thread on cotton batting backed with muslin, 6 x 8 ft. Photograph courtesy of the artist.

Figure 8: David von Schlegell, *Untitled*, late drawing with graphite and string. Private Collection.

on a torn scrap of wrapping paper likely falls into the category of "rough draft"; while a poem containing no cancellations, additions, or variants copied onto embossed stationery in a flowing hand and preserved among Dickinson's own papers likely falls into the category of "fair copy"—others fall somewhere between these poles. In many cases, Dickinson's manuscripts exhibit a discordant mixture of features, e.g., a poem composed in Dickinson's rough-copy cursive but inscribed on a leaf of fine stationery; a poem composed throughout in a fair-copy hand but speckled with authorial variants and emendations, and so on. At the moment, the best classification for manuscripts falling somewhere along this continuum may be "service copies"; that is, copies meant for the author's continued consideration and experimentation, or even copies once destined to be "final" that then, in moments of *pentimento*, underwent additional revision, inevitably changing their status from "fair" and "final" to potential antegraphs from which the poet-scribe would have penned new, unblemished copies. Even the term "service copy," though, conceals the vast range of very different intermediate documents found between Dickinson's rough drafts and final copies; for while the associations among early drafts and later versions of a poem may help us to reconstruct Dickinson's compositional practices and strategies, these associations may also be elusive since there is always a potential break between each state of the text in the course of its unfolding.

One example of the varied and multiple states between process and completion of her manuscripts are the fair copies of poems Dickinson prepared as gifts for specific recipients. In many ways—especially in their careful preparation and their iconic richness—they seem identical with Dickinson's final copies. Yet if we equate these "gift copies" with "final copies" we sacrifice essential differences between two subtle states of completion, and misconstrue Dickinson's relationship to both. The limited circulation of these gift-poems cannot be understood as a form of "publication" as we think of it today, nor as it was thought of in her day. First, Dickinson never sent the same poem to more than six recipients, and in the overwhelming majority of the cases poems were sent to one person alone. In many of these cases, she contextualized the gift poem in ways that underscored the private, uniquely aimed nature of the communication between sender and addressee, and, in at least a few cases, she altered the gift-poem in ways we may regard as the embodied witness of the contact between two interiorities. Second, while the poems disseminated in this manner are free of variants and emendations, the state of the gift copy often marks a moment in the trajectory of a poem toward a later, emended and potentially final form. Evidence for this claim may be found in Dickinson's practice of retain-

The Networked Recluse

ing not a copy of the gift-poem, but, rather, an alternative (and unresolved) service copy with one or more variants.[11]

Fair-copy and final manuscripts, executed with care and art, can seem almost purged of time. To some scholars, these manuscripts may be valued as mirrors of an author's "final intentions," while the collector is drawn to them as to shining keepsakes or relics. By contrast, the service manuscripts and, most especially, the worksheet manuscripts, are profoundly time-bound. With the intermediate manuscript acting as a way-station between compositional states, the initial worksheet draft, often rapidly executed and initially bewildering to the eye, is prized as a map of the itinerary traced by the writer in the very hour of composition—what Clarice Lispector called "the hour of the star," when knowing and not knowing meet.[12] In describing this quality of the draft, Daniel Farrar calls attention not only to its ephemerality, but also to the instability of the writer-reader held ransom by the compositional process:

> The draft has no reader. No other reader, that is, than the writer himself: the signs on the page, iconic or otherwise, have no addressee other than their own writer. They are meant for his eyes only, but this does not mean that there is a perfect identity between the writing and reading agencies. The draft page is the locus of a dialogue between the writer and his later self or selves....[13]

Often in Dickinson's rough-copy drafts, the recto seems more serene and orderly than the verso, as if she struck out with a clear sense of direction, but soon entered a crisis in which she was summoned by the east and west, the north and south of a poem's contradictory desires. And sometimes, Dickinson revisited a poem apparently finished many years earlier, returning not simply to change a word or two or refine a passage but to un-write it in order to reenter the compositional process.

The draft keeps watch over unforeseeable conditions; it seeks to preserve possibility. Such is the case with one exquisite manuscript of the poem "Two Butterflies went / out at Noon − ." First composed in the summer of 1863 when Dickinson sent it to her Norcross cousins, a second copy was bound into Fascicle 25 around the same time; the poem was then laid away for almost fifteen years. But in 1878, Dickinson returned to the poem—generating a worksheet draft (Figure 9, next page) described by Thomas H. Johnson as a "fascinating document of poetic creativeness in travail."[14] After copying the first two lines of the bound copy almost verbatim, she was suddenly drawn by new currents of thought. To follow Dickinson's changes of

---

11. For several examples of this phenomenon, see manuscripts AC 693, H 336, H 368, AC 413, AC 344, and AC 491.

12. See Clarice Lispector, *The Hour of the Star* (New York: New Directions Books, 1992).

13. Daniel Ferrer, "The open space of the draft page: James Joyce and Modern Manuscripts," *Item*, http://www.item.ens.fr/index.php?id=23616.

14. See Thomas H. Johnson's JP533n in *The Poems of Emily Dickinson* (3 vols.), Thomas H. Johnson, ed. (Cambridge, Mass.: The Belknap Press of Harvard University Press, 1955), 410: "It is a penciled worksheet draft set down on both sides of a half sheet of stationery. It is rare among the surviving worksheets in the degree of its complication. The redaction evidently never resulted in a finished poem, but it is a fascinating document of poetic creativeness in travail."

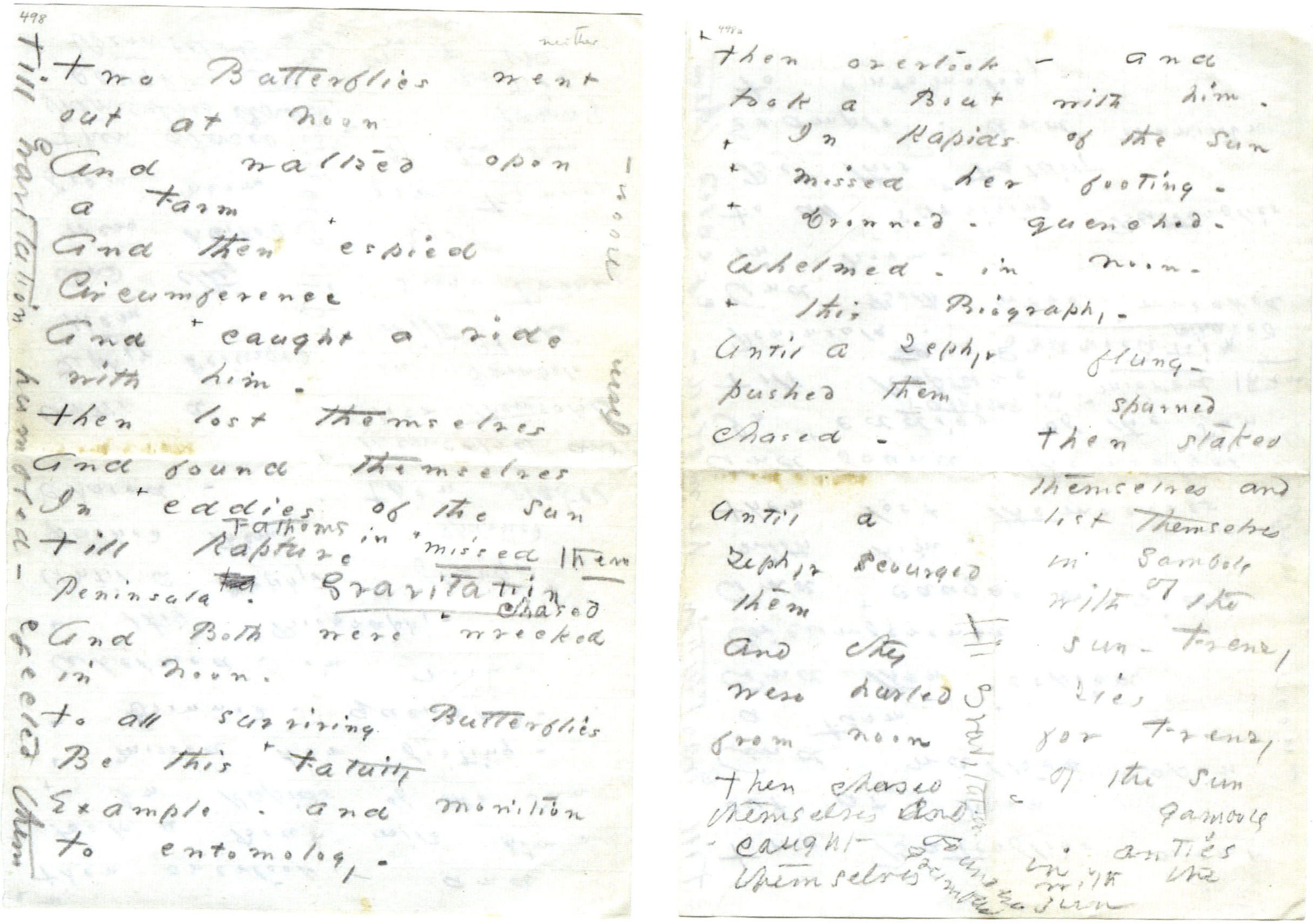

Figure 9: "Two Butterflies went / out at Noon" (ca. 1878), Amherst College Archives and Special Collections, Emily Dickinson Collection, AC 498.

direction, to go with her into the melée of blind ends and unexpected clearings, is to find—with Paul Valéry—that "there is nothing more beautiful than a beautiful rough draft."[15]

On the face of "Two Butterflies" it is possible to see a poetic correlate of the continental glide through geologic time proposed in the world maps of the early nineteenth century. Like James Hutton's theory that the geologic processes contributing to the earth's formation have "no vestige of a beginning, [no] prospect of an end," so Dickinson's worksheets make manifest the potentially limitless process of a poem's unfolding.[16] On this manuscript no word is cancelled, but whirlwinds of authorial possibilities swirl into vortexes before dissolving into a free drift defying the determining force that attracts all bodies toward the center of the earth: "…+ eddies of… Fathoms in…the Sun…+Rapids of the Sun… Till Rapture _missed_

15. Paul Valery, *Cahiers* XV, 421; quoted in Serge Bourjea, "Rhombos Eye, Dance, Trace: The Writing Process in Valery's Rough Drafts," *Yale French Studies* (84) (1994), 145.

16. The paper Hutton read to the Royal Society of Edinburgh in 1785 is entitled "Theory of the Earth, or an Investigation of the Laws Observable in the Composition, Dissolution and Restoration of Land Upon the Globe."

Peninsula… Gravitation chased… missed her footing… + Drowned… +quenched − …
them… Till Gravitation humbled − … ejected… them… in Noon …from Noon… whelmed −
in Noon… Until a zephyr scourged them and they were hurled from noon… Till Gravitation
fumbled… grumbled… Then chased themselves and caught themselves… Then staked
themselves and lost themselves in Gambols with the sun… Frenzies for… for Frenzy of the
sun… gambols… antics in the sun…."[17]

Figure 10: Fascicle string, Fascicle 39, Amherst College Archives and
Special Collections, AC 81.

Like maps opened to the elements, the manuscripts Dickinson abandoned more
than a century ago have suffered exposure to light and air that have darkened their
pages while simultaneously bleaching the ink and lead marks etched into them.
The color of the inks we see in Dickinson's fair copies before 1870, now often a
sepia brown, may once have been brownish-black or a rich purple-black, derived
as they likely were from iron gall; while the crispness of the pencil writing typical
of her later years has softened, sometimes smudged into near-illegibility. The extra-
textual elements, too, show signs of wear. The strings—some white, others twisted
blue and white or red and white—that bound individual fascicles together are worn
and frayed, while the straight pins Dickinson used to join, sometimes only briefly,
different documents show signs of rusting. On one particularly beautiful holograph
of the poem "Baffled for just a Day or two − " (see Cat. 2.26, p. 44), the wasted
remains of a rosebud plucked by Dickinson in 1859 from her garden, and soon after
fastened with green ribbon (later reinforced with tape in the century following her
death) to a poem-letter sent to Elizabeth Holland, are signal reminders of the frag-
ile, contingent nature of all human works subject to the forces of time and nature.

Maps

How can one both move and carry along with one the fermenting depths which are also,
at every point, influenced by the pressure of events around them? And how can one
possibly do this so that the result is readable?

—Hugh Trevor-Roper[18]

That's when I knew we could write poems in maps. That's when I began thinking serious-
ly about a poetics of cartography.

—Denis Wood[19]

In 1998, forty-three years after Johnson's critical edition of Dickinson's poetry,
Franklin's variorum edition of her poems was published. Several years after the
turn of the new millennium, three major archives of Dickinson's manuscripts—the
Amherst College Library, the Houghton Library, and the Boston Public Library—
began the long-awaited process of making digital surrogates of those manuscripts

---

17. My representation of variants here is intended to be suggestive. For an attempt to find order in
the midst of chaos, see Ralph W. Franklin's extensive notes for Fr. 571.

18. The passage by Hugh Trevor-Roper was quoted in Keith Thomas, "A Highly Paradoxical
Historian," *New York Review of Books* (April 12, 2007), 53-57.

19. Denis Wood, "Everything Sings: Maps for a Narrative Atlas," https://placesjournal.org/article/
everything-sings-maps-for-a-narrative-atlas/

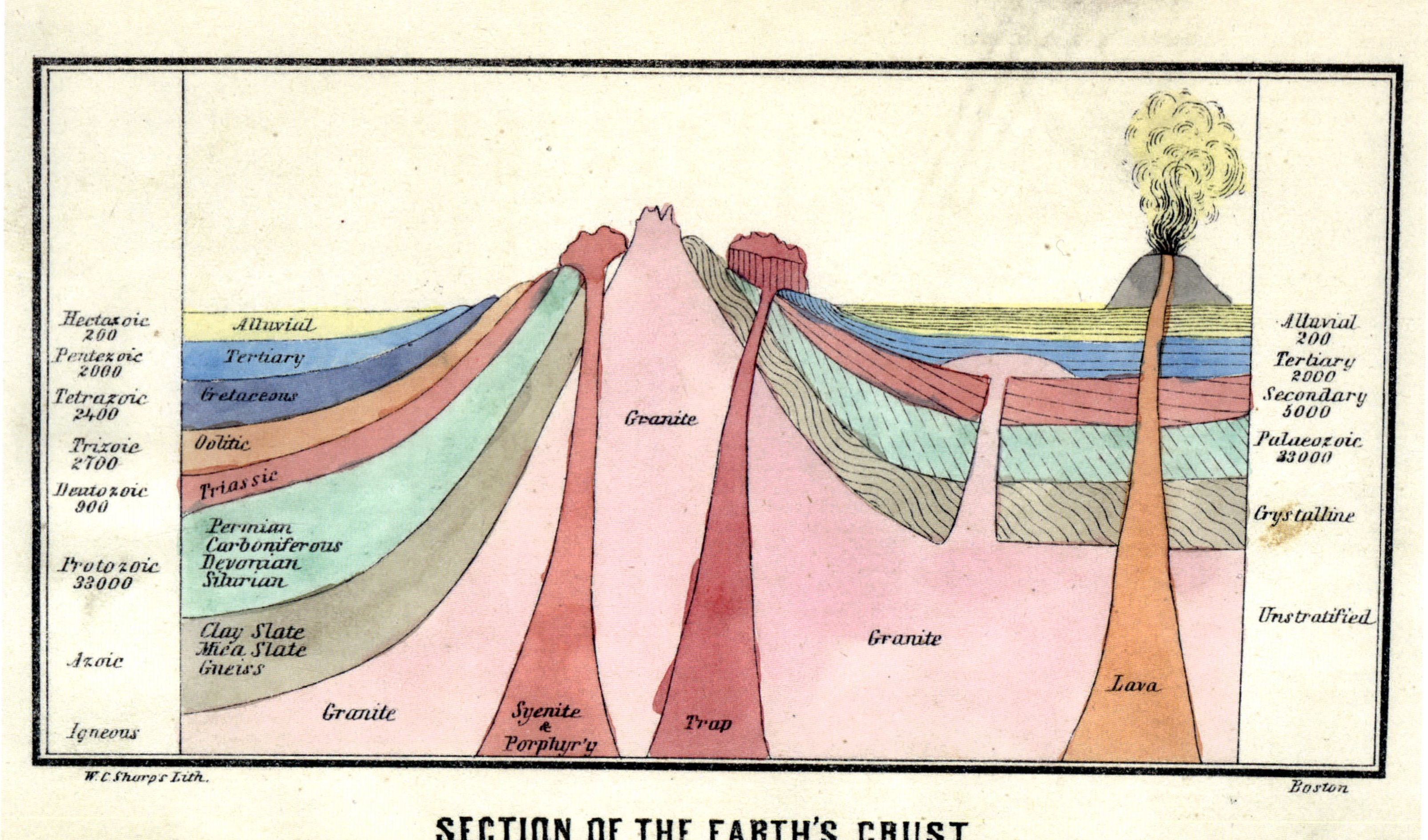

Figure 11: Frontispiece for Edward Hitchcock's *The Religion of Geology* (1851). Hand-colored lithograph showing a "Section of the Earth's Crust." Amherst College Archives and Special Collections, QE22.H67 R25.

available online.[20] The same might well be true in the near future for Dickinson's letters, originally published in a scholarly edition produced in 1958 by Johnson and his assistant Theodora Ward, even though many of her letters have yet to be digitized. Certainly, the day will soon dawn when we will have printed and digital access to every extant manuscript Dickinson left behind. These two sets of tools provide valuable insights into the interpretative expanse of her production (editions) and their singular material constructions (digital facsimiles).

Yet the constraints of the edition, driven by its scholarly goal of finding system in language, poetics, and rhetorical structures, are echoed in the solitary presence of each individual document that concretizes even the ethereal poetic moments in pen and paper that were bound—and earthbound—to the writer's biographical context: a late morning in the sun of her room with its south and west facing windows on a

---

20. Access to digital surrogates of Dickinson's manuscripts has expanded and improved exponentially in the past years. The Amherst College Archives and Special Collections led the way, digitizing its entire collection of Dickinson manuscripts (including poems and letters) in the fall of 2012, granting viewers permission to use the images free of charge: see https://acdc.amherst.edu/browse/collection/ed. This opening of the archives was followed by similar gestures by the Boston Public Library (http://archon.bpl.org/index.php?p=core%2Fsearch&q=Higginson+to+Dickinson&content=1) and the Houghton Library, Harvard University (The Emily Dickinson Archive; http://www.edickinson.org).

Sabbath day in early Spring 1861 when, the "Violets" by her side, she composed a message to the addressee known only as "Master," or an endless night in October 1883 when her young nephew "traveled from the Full," but left her "moving on in the Dark" where "Awe is the first Hand that is held to us — " and "Course" is replaced by "Boundlessness — " (H B91).

Historically, maps have never been static. They have represented the essence of movement and travel and of relative distances: relationships of space, potentially ever-changing geologic, civic, and political units, boundaries to be traversed. Originally prepared as charts for sea and land routes, real and imagined, they often included reminders of propulsion and transport: winds and rivers. To map was to convey movement and trajectory, but also position and bearings. We know, as some of the correspondence suggests, that "Dickinson" cannot be a solipsistic set of meanings, but rather—as we suspect—a dazzlingly complex array of contexts, human and natural, and experiences that inform many different worlds of meaning in Dickinson's writings. To gain access to the kind of orientation to her work that traces the movement of Dickinson's texts, to plumb the "depth, texture, tension, and resonance" in the moment of its execution and meanings, we can now resort to an additional, third tool, one that helps us map those contexts and experiences.[21] These would be "deep maps" of her writings on which to trace the potentially undis-covered itineraries of and influences on her creative experience, maps, perhaps, of regions previously unmappable.

In the nineteenth century, the advent of an early form of infographics encouraged the creation of new kinds of maps capable of fusing thousands of pieces of data into one picture—showing, as naturalist and mapmaker Alexander von Humboldt wrote, "the simultaneous action and connecting links of the forces which pervade the universe."[22] Among the maps in an atlas of Dickinson's work and world we might find maps representing the deep geological past of that corner of the world in which she lived as the leading geologists and old-earth creationists of her time would have understood it, overlaid with newer accounts of that billion-year history of continen-tal collisions and drift, volcanic arcs, and multiple ice-ages. So, too, we might find maps charting the topographic features of the planet's surface, the region's fauna and flora, its weather events and soundscape.[23] The distant links between this lost earth and Dickinson's work are evoked in Higginson's description of Dickinson's handwriting as resembling the fossil tracks of prehistoric birds—a remark doubt-

Figure 12: Orra White Hitchcock, Drawing of five lines of fossil footprints, 1828–1840. Pen and ink on linen, 90 x 189 cm. Amherst College Archives and Special Collections.

---

21. David J. Bodenhamer, "Narrating Space and Place," in *Deep Maps and Spatial Narratives*, David J. Bodenhamer, John Corrigan, and Trevor M. Harris, eds. (Bloomington: Indiana University Press, 2015), 22.

22. See "The Exquisite 19th-Century Infographics That Explained The History Of The Natural World," http://itsinfographics.com/the-exquisite-19th-century-infographics-that-explained-the-history-of-the-natural-world/

23. For example, Dickinson's contemporary, Sabra Snell, collaborated with her father, Ebenezer Snell, Amherst College Professor of Mathematics, on a weather journal that spanned the years 1835-1902. For more information on this work, see my "The Weather (of) Documents," *ESQ* (62) (3), 2016, 318-369.

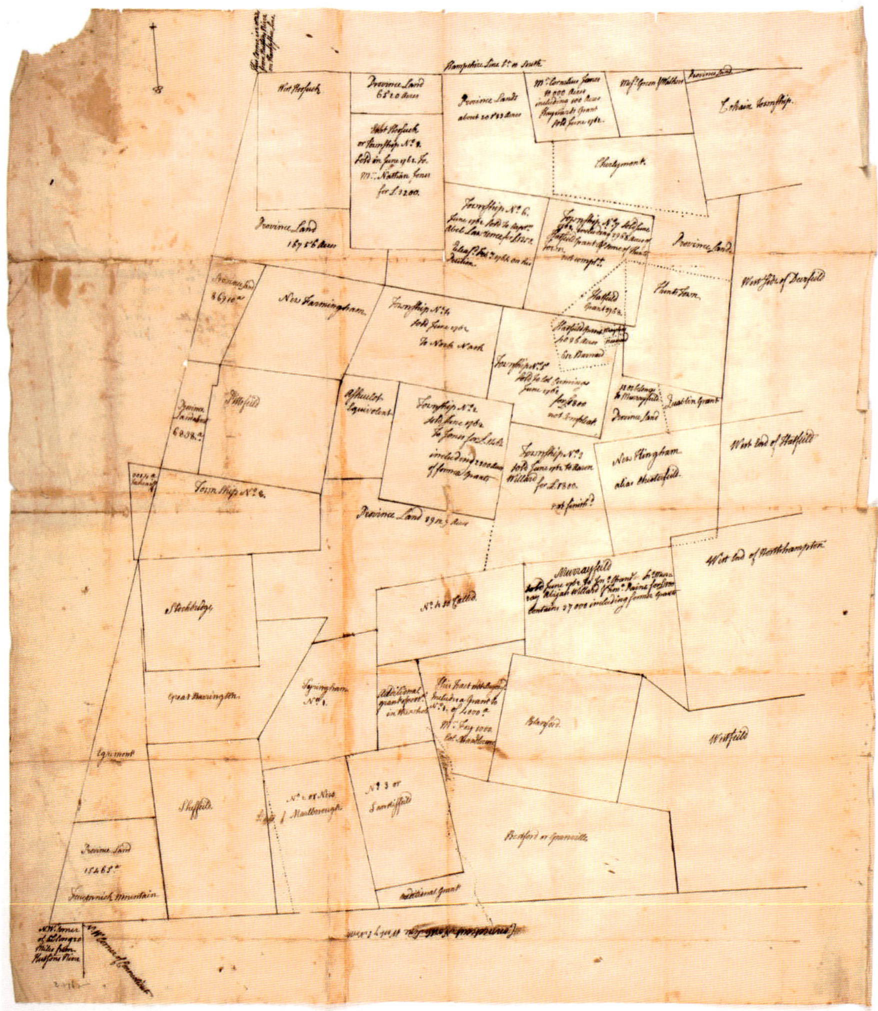

Figure 13: Maps of the towns of Western Massachusetts, 1783. Berkshire County (Mass.), Franklin County (Mass.), Hampden County (Mass.)., Hampshire County (Mass.) American Antiquarian Society Collection.

less alluding to the specimens found by Amherst Professor Edward Hitchcock in the bedrock and preserved by the glacial ice. And they are captured in Dickinson's herbarium, overflowing with nineteenth-century plant specimens—the delicate and brief issue of millennia of ecological changes (See Cat. 2.06 and 2.07, pp. 28-29).[24]

Other maps of different orientations replete with many overlays might chart patterns of human settlement and conflicts in the Connecticut River Valley across the centuries. In these maps of cultural emplacement, the generations of Dickinsons who inhabited Amherst are visible only in the very uppermost layers, where inlays

24. Dickinson's passion for botany, expressed materially in her herbarium—her "first 'book,'" as Judith Farr writes—was fostered by her early education at Amherst Academy. Founded by Samuel Fowler Dickinson and Noah Webster, it was, as Richard Sewall writes, "no ordinary school." By the time Dickinson was admitted to the Academy, the science curriculum reflected the marked influence of Edward Hitchcock, a geologist, astronomer, botanist, religious divine, and professor at (and later president of) Amherst College. Dickinson noted Hitchcock's sway over her thinking in an 1877 letter to Thomas W. Higginson: "When Flowers annually died and I was a child, I used to read Dr. Hitchcock's Book on The Flowers of North America. This comforted their Absence—assuring me they lived" (JL 488). In 2006, a facsimile edition of Dickinson's herbarium was published by The Belknap Press of Harvard University Press, making a surrogate of this beautiful artifact widely available. Judith Farr's "Preface" and Richard B. Sewall's essay "Science and the Poet: Emily Dickinson's Herbarium and 'The Clue Divine'," along with Ray Angelo's "Catalog of Plant Specimens," frame this volume.

might show the more intimate patterns of their habitation: their dwelling places, the institutions with which they were involved, the sites of their graves. With some magnification we might begin to trace the pathways of their settling, leaving, re-settling, and perishing in that vale. Some maps might even show us who escapes and who remains. They may allow us to see enacted the tighter and tighter coiling of the family unit as Edward Dickinson enclosed his wife and children inside the Homestead and The Evergreens. In the inventory of artifacts accompanying each detailed inlay, we would find family daguerreotypes, volumes from the Homestead's or Evergreen's libraries, writing instruments, locks of hair, fragments of stationery, linen and crockery, fallow seeds from Dickinson's conservatory—all the pearls and detritus that might be unearthed in the course of an archaeological excavation.

The new deep maps represent both the vastness of the world's macro-phenomena and its most minute and intimate details. They unfold in different shapes and sizes; they will challenge notions of scale—collapsing or expanding distances arbitrarily—and also of time, whose flow they may immeasurably accelerate or momentarily freeze to reveal the "chaos or simultaneity of lived existence."[25] In the atlas, however, the maps of Dickinson's exterior world are still few in comparison to the maps of the interior world—or worlds—of Dickinson's writings. Worlds *mise en abime*.

Essential to any map is its orientation, its north star or fixed point from which all other orientations and movement are figured and generated. In the case of "Dickinson's maps" this would be her eighteen-inch square cherry and pine desk, now replicated in the house at 280 Main Street in Amherst, the original ironically estranged from Dickinson's contexts in Harvard's Houghton Library. In the thousands of images of the desk and its dopplegangers we find strewn across the Internet, it is often bathed in sunlight or lamplight, with a single fascicle laid on an otherwise pristine and vacated surface.

This image of Dickinson's desk is so familiar to her readers, so imprinted on our imaginations, that we think of it not as an image at all, but rather as a memory interiorized, justly our own. But the memory is also troubling: How could this delicate table have withstood the weight of Dickinson's books or the force of her hand in the "white heat" of writing every day across the days of more than thirty years? Just beyond the familiar image, another, more uncanny image of the desk is forming. In this image the desk is piled high with volumes, some closed but others standing open at pages Dickinson may have been re-reading; the desk is heavy with the correspondence she has received and is replying to, and with the poems she is composing or copying. The topography of the desk is perpetually changing, altered both by Dickinson, who shuffles the layers of papers, exposing some and burying others, and by forces less visible or accountable: winds blowing from the west-facing windows, time itself.[26]

Figure 14: A reproduction of Dickinson's desk at the Dickinson Homestead. Photograph courtesy of The Emily Dickinson Museum.

---

25. David J. Bodenhamer, "Narrating Space and Place," 17.

26. For other reflections on Dickinson's desk, for example, see my installation "Imagining Emily Dickinson's Desks, 1870-1885" (http://www.emilydickinson.org/node/211), and Linda Russo's

A map of the surface of Dickinson's desk charts our imagination of her material-immaterial space of creation that emanates from 42 37.6129, -72 51.4388. For although we cannot witness her in the moment of writing—this moment remains forever closed to us who are always too late—we may carefully begin to reconstruct it by making a series of enquiries, then mapping possible answers to them; or, if no answers are forthcoming, by mapping the questions themselves: Does Dickinson turn into the free space of writing at particular hours or open spaces of her days? Does she write quickly or slowly? Does she compose poems as single lyrics, or sometimes as series? In constructing a fascicle, does she search among poems accumulated over years or choose only from her most recent works? Does she copy the poems destined for a single fascicle all at once, arranging and binding them together immediately? Or are the patterns of her selecting, copying, arranging, and binding less hurried and more varied? Does Dickinson re-read poems before binding them? Is the event of binding one full of violence, or does it call for the lightest of touches? What prompts her returns to particular fascicles and her revisions—sometimes many years later—of poems that appeared at an earlier time to have reached a finished state?

And perhaps of equal importance for a poet uninterested in the cultural mechanisms of publication, how does she care for her archives? When Dickinson ceases her practice of binding poems into fascicles, how does she keep order among the hundreds of documents accumulating around her? Do fascicles and poems on loose sheets lie together? Does she separate poems, letter-drafts, and fragments? How might her understanding of order itself have changed over time? In our accounting of Dickinson's countless hours, no question feels final. What lay open on the cherry table on that day in April of 1862 when she first wrote to Thomas Wentworth Higginson to ask him if her poems "breathed"? What rested on her desk on May 15, 1886—the day when her breath stopped forever? What was there the day after her death? And how and when was the desk at last cleared of its unruly contents, turned back into an empty signifier, an empty point of reference?

Decades of new research and new ways of evaluating the solid information we already have might be devoted to mapping the changing topography of Dickinson's desk at different moments over the course of her writing life. Each new map, however detailed, would reveal the need for yet another, still more exact inset to chart a smaller region. So, too, each would simultaneously illuminate the need for a wider map on which to trace the enigmatic routes of two groups of writings: those Dickinson sent out to span the miles, with the hope that they would reach their singular addressees in the world she shared with them; and those she held back—perhaps with the equally strong hope that they would span the centuries to be received at last by strangers.

We will never know exactly how many letters Emily Dickinson wrote or how many correspondents she engaged. The custom, still followed in her day, of burning

lyrical and intimate *To Think of Her Writing Awash in Light* (Boulder, Co.: Subito Press, 2016).

private letters in the wake of a person's death not only led to the wholesale destruction of the letters Dickinson received—among them, no doubt, letters from Susan Gilbert Dickinson, Thomas Wentworth Higginson, and Otis Lord—but almost certainly rendered irrecoverable letters she may have written to others, including Benjamin Newton, Charles Wadsworth, and even, if such a one existed, to the figure known only as "Master." Other letters no longer extant may have been claimed by the chaos of the Civil War. And still others might have fallen victim to the upheavals in her correspondents' lives or the estranging nature of time in which the things of the world vanish.

Yet despite both the known and unknown lacunæ that puncture this record, over one thousand of Dickinson's letters to over eighty recipients have survived. Thus although Dickinson rarely traveled very far beyond the boundaries of Amherst—or even, in the later years, past the grounds of the family home—she moved freely through time and across space through her writings. Moreover, even though Dickinson's correspondence survives in the end as a one-way message, each of the missives that issues from her desk contains multiple contexts that connect it to her "travel" beyond her room, in which her "wanderings" in that smaller space mirror something of the eventual movement of her writing beyond the confines of the Homestead.[27]

To better map the overarching scope and range of Dickinson's correspondence, especially its relation to her poetry, we might divide Dickinson's writing into six provisional phases.[28]

- The initial phase, beginning in 1842, the year assigned to Dickinson's earliest extant letter, and ending in 1852, features only letters:[29] At least ninety-seven letters to nine correspondents can be assigned to these years.

---

27. Among Dickinson's most cherished correspondents, many of whom are represented in the Morgan's exhibition, we find Susan Huntington Gilbert Dickinson, the poet's beloved sister-in-law; Thomas Wentworth Higginson, author, abolitionist, and champion of women's rights; Samuel Bowles, editor of *The Republican*; Fanny and Louise Norcross, Dickinson's cousins from Cambridgeport, Mass.; and Elizabeth Holland, the wife of Josiah Holland and one of Dickinson's closest confidants.

28. In his three volume edition of Dickinson's letters published in 1958, Thomas H. Johnson divides the letters into twelve phases: (1) 1842-1846 (1-14); (2) 1847-1848, (15-26); (3) 1849-1850 (27-39); (4) 1851-1854 (40-176); (5) 1855-1857 (177-186); (6) 1858-1861 (187-245); (7) 1862-1865 (246-313); (8) 1866-1869 (314-37); (9) 1870-1874 (338-431); (10) 1875-1879 (432-626); (11) 1880-1883 (627-878); (12) 1884-1886 (879-1045). For Johnson's rationale concerning the divisions in the letters, see his section notes in *The Letters of Emily Dickinson*. Johnson and Ralph W. Franklin are more conservative in their division of Dickinson's poems. In *The Poems of Emily Dickinson*, *Including variant readings critically compared with all known manuscripts* (3 vols.) (Cambridge, Mass.: The Belknap Press of Harvard University Press, 1955), Johnson suggests only three implicit phases: (1) 1850-1862 (1-494); (2) 1862-1870 (495-1176); and (3) 1870-1886 (1177-1775), each phase occupying a single volume. In *The Poems of Emily Dickinson*, Variorum Edition, Ralph W. Franklin follows Johnson's earlier schema, though with some variations: volume 1 contains poems assigned to the years 1850-1863 (1-526); volume 2 contains poems assigned to the years 1863-1873 (527-1287); and volume 3 contains poems assigned to the years 1873-1886 (1288-1789). In *Open Me Carefully*, Martha Nell Smith and Ellen Louise Hart offer yet another schema for thinking about the divisions of Dickinson's letters to her sister-in-law.

29. Two early valentines composed by Dickinson also belong to these years; these works are clearly juvenilia, and I have considered them as separate from Dickinson's larger poetic project. Since,

- The second phase would cover the brief, five-year period between 1853 and 1857. Although only two poems from these years survive—"On this wondrous sea" (1853) and "I have a Bird in spring" (1854)—both of which were first sent to Susan Gilbert (Dickinson), it must have been a period of considerable poetic experimentation. Among the eighty-eight extant letters falling within these years, several to Henry Emmons allude explicitly to their frequent exchange of poems, and while the overall number of correspondents remains relatively stable, the intensification of the correspondence with Susan and the opening of a correspondence with Elizabeth and Josiah Holland signal an important outward shift in her writing.

- The third phase coincides with the years of fascicle binding, 1858 to 1864, and the most devastating years of the Civil War. During this period, Dickinson's production of poems reached its greatest intensity—in these years, she composed or copied at least 886 poems. While during this phase of her writing life Dickinson clearly privileged the production of poems over letters, the simple ratio of number of poems (886) to number of letters (113) during these years occludes significant changes in the direction and style of Dickinson's letters and the degree to which Dickinson's practice of sending poems to particular correspondents, most fully established during this phase, may help to drive her larger artistic project. At this juncture, we see the falling away of many of Dickinson's early correspondences with school friends, and the initiation of further ranging epistolary relationships. Dickinson's correspondence with Thomas Wentworth Higginson opens during these years, as do her correspondences with Samuel Bowles and Fanny and Louisa Norcross. The "Master" writings, too, belong to this period—though they do not continue beyond it, as do the others.

- The fourth phase spans only the years 1865 to 1869, but nonetheless constitutes a fairly distinct period. In these years both Dickinson's poetic production and (especially) her correspondence are radically curtailed: only one hundred and seventy two poems and thirty-six letters fall within these years. Although the reasons for her withdrawal from correspondence at this time may never be fully uncovered, it seems likely that in the wake of the fascicle project and the closing of her private bindery, Dickinson entered a term of withdrawal. Her circle of correspondents contracts, but in so doing magnifies our understanding of those with whom Dickinson felt the most intimate of bonds.

- Throughout the 1870s and the first few years of the 1880s, Dickinson channels new, if elegiac, energies into writing. These years, constituting the fifth phase, are a rich mine for poems, letters, and those writings that vibrate between prose and verse. Between 1870 and 1883, letters (540) only slightly outnumber poems (463), even as the line dividing one genre from another

moreover, they were sent to specific addressees, they may count among her letters.

is progressively blurred. The range of correspondents swells again, too, far exceeding the number of correspondents in any other period.

- Finally, in the last two years of Dickinson's life, 1884 to 1886, and the concluding phase of her writing, we see registered in her work the toll of so many personal losses. It may be that, as Thomas Johnson believed, Dickinson underwent a breakdown of some form in the summer of 1884;[30] by 1885 she was certainly suffering from the illness that would take her life the following year. Still, she continued to write, now reversing the pattern of her previous fallow period, producing more than fifty poems and 165 letters.

This final phase offers us unique but helpful materials for mapping, for example, the last year of Dickinson's life. Mapping outwardly from her desk, we can begin to trace the perhaps multiple and surprising trajectories of old and new connections both among longstanding friends and among the tools of genre with which she communicated. In that last year it would seem that poem and letter are often indistinguishable, both missives that are often simultaneous in their roles as personal and existential connection. Among the nineteen extant messages that are assignable to the last year of her life, we find brief notes to neighbors, often thanking them for small kindnesses to her during her illness, as well as two longer letters to Charles Clarke, both focused on her memory of Charles Wadsworth, who had visited Dickinson in Amherst in 1880 after a lacuna of more than twenty years: "The last time he came in Life, I was with my Lilies and Heliotropes…. 'Where did you come from,' I said, for he spoke like an Apparition – " (AC 743). If Dickinson corresponded with Wadsworth during those twenty years, the correspondence has not survived—evidence equally of the precarious existence of "live" or "sent" letters and their (and our) almost infinite trust in their addressees.

For the most part, though, in the months preceding Dickinson's death, her missives found their way to her most enduring and beloved interlocutors: Susan Dickinson (1830–1913), Frances and Louisa Norcross (Fanny and Loo, respectively 1847–1919 and 1842–1896), and the Unitarian abolitionist Thomas Wentworth Higginson (1823–1911). But what trajectories in time and space did these messages take on? As Dickinson seems ever more compromised in her physical health, the question requires ever greater care in tracing the complex paths of her works from her desk to their addresses and beyond.

The notes to Susan are especially brief, though a new quality of trust and fullness attaches to them. It is not, or so it seems, that illness kept Dickinson from writing more, but rather that language had no place anymore as the vehicle through which they sought to conjure the presence of each other.

   I was

   just writing

   these very

---

30. Johnson forwards this suggestion in his introduction to the letters Dickinson wrote between 1884 and 1886. Johnson, *The Letters of Emily Dickinson*, 808.

words to you,
"Susan fronts
on the Gulf
Stream," when
Vinnie entered
with the Sea —
Dare I touch
the Coincidence?
Do you remem-
ber what whis-
pered to
"Horatio"?
            Emily —
[H B65, early 1866]

How lovely
every Solace!
This long,
short, penance
"Even I regain
my freedom
with a Sigh"
            Emily —
[H B128, early 1886]

At last the correspondence that had spanned thirty-six years and included the sharing of at least 250 poems ended with a seven-word note: "Thank you, dear Sue — for every solace —" (H B101).[31] And yet how resonant the last messages are: Susan, fronting on the Gulf Stream, turns into the Sea and Solace at once. She is the survivor—"what whispered"—left to tell Dickinson's tale. The final dateable poem from Dickinson to Susan Dickinson was sent across the space between their two adjacent houses on Main Street two years earlier in October of 1884 and marked the anniversary of eight-year-old Gilbert Dickinson's death from typhoid fever: "Some Arrows slay but whom they strike — / But this slew all <u>but </u>him — / Who so appareled his Escape — / Too trackless for a Tomb —" (H B145). Among her own papers, Dickinson kept a partial draft of the letter, including the opening line of the poem. To this draft she pinned a second, narrow strip of paper repeating the words, "Most Arrows." The liberating "Sigh" and "solace" of her final missives lay in quiet contrast—a coda—to the slaying arrow of her last poem to Susan. Each is a consolation defined in part by the intimacy of closest family not two hundred yards apart, consigned to paper and *carried* that distance and yet retained in partial—and personal—draft form with the potential variant of "Most." "Most" was not designed to

---

31. In a note accompanying this message, Thomas H. Johnson writes, "Another manuscript (HCL L24), unfolded and apparently never sent, was probably a trial start for this letter: 'Dear Sue, Thank y.'" See *The Letters of Emily Dickinson*, L1030.

travel those few yards. But in time, after Dickinson's death, its survival gives birth to an additional trajectory the traveled "Some" now takes.

In 1884, Dickinson also sent poems to her Norcross cousins for the last time. The poems, "We send the / Wave to find / the Wave −" (AC 641) and "The going from a world we know" (MS destroyed; see Fr. 1662A), appear to have traveled to the Norcrosses, who that very year moved from Cambridge to Concord, only a short time after their composition. The miles from her desk to Concord seem less urgent than the time required to cover the ground. If a version of the first poem survives among Dickinson's papers only in draft form, the second—and last—poem did not linger in Dickinson's hands even in draft, but seems instead to have been pulled with "We send the Wave," finding its sole geography in flight from the known world "Forgetting to return."

Even more fleetingly, the two letters from the year of Dickinson's death to her Norcross cousins exist only in transcripts made by Fanny and Loo, now intimate copyists of Dickinson's erased hand, perhaps during Mabel Loomis Todd's prepa-ration of Dickinson's letters for publication. In the letter of March 1886 to her cousins, Dickinson alludes to the serious illness that had confined her to bed for more than five months. It proves to be a distance from her desk greater than that of the journey to Concord, a departure that in those five months in grave health must have seemed perilous: "I scarcely know where to begin," she writes, "but love is always a safe place" (MS destroyed; see JL 1034). She asks if their winter has been "a tender shelter"; she wishes to know what they have been reading. When she writes again, it is May 1886, just days before her death. To the cousins with whom she had corresponded for twenty-seven years, Dickinson sent her last, most telegraphic message. Elliptical in the extreme, again we must read the message in the transcription ultimately provided by Louise, who—following the tradition of her day—destroyed all original manuscripts she and her sister had received from Dickinson after Frances's own death: "Little Cousins, Called back. Emily" (MS destroyed; see JL 1046). At once complete, even authoritative, and yet broken off, Dickinson's last written words are a private allusion to a book she and her cousins shared, an unadorned statement of fact, and an invitation to wonder.[32] The faint shadow of the missive's intimacy, now solely in Louise's hand, and the shared title grow even fainter with the proximity of Dickinson's impending death. The message that seems so simple in Louise's now distant hand—in time and miles—is instantly weighty and existential, the opposite of Calvino's "lightness," as it came from Dickinson's pen. It hints at the ineluctable privacy of our condition even as it registers our equally inescapable desire to send out a signal, a flare that might counter this "infinite remoteness" from each other at the moment we step off the edge of the world.

---

32. The book alluded to in the letter was Hugh Conway's *Called Back* (Bristol: J. W. Arrowsmith; London : Simpkin, Marshall, 1884).

Dickinson bade farewell to Higginson in a three-letter sequence. In the early spring of 1886, she rallied long enough to write a long message in response to his winter letter inquiring if she had heard of the death of Helen Hunt Jackson. The opening of Dickinson's letter conveys her gratitude for Higginson's sonnet honoring the memory of Jackson and tenders a stanza of her own composed in 1884 but revised at this moment to fit the occasion. In the first and final circulation of the poem, the pronoun "Herself," that renames Jackson, replaces "the Dawn" of the earlier copy of record:

> Not knowing
> when the Dawn
> will come,
> I open every
> Door,
> Or has it
> Feathers, like
> a Bird,
> Or Billows,
> like a Shore –
> [AC 303]

In the second part of her letter, Dickinson informs Higginson of her own grave sickness and of the fragile hope that she may be emerging from it: "I have been very ill, Dear friend, since November, bereft of Book and Thought, by the Doctor's reproof, but begin to roam in my Room now –" (BPL Higg 101). Here, the desk materializes for her again—but the distances within her own room, where she "roams," are greater due to the illness—and, for a moment, perhaps, she leafs through the materials that have collected on it in the past months, or sifts through the poems and other writings she composed over the last quarter century and that she will soon be leaving forever. The time of the letter—the very act of penning it—suggests an alternative space, a dual condition of calling upon her distant friend from her desk. Suddenly realizing through the touch of physical suffering that she was in the clasp of divine power, Dickinson's last lines summon the energies of an earlier time as they avow poetry as a response on the order of prayer to human and cosmic mystery. Maintaining her hold on the Angel, she demands of him, as her ransom, a blessing: "Audacity of Bliss, said Jacob to the Angel 'I will not let thee go except I bless thee' – Pugilist and Poet, Jacob was correct – Your Scholar – " (BPL Higg 101).

In April, Dickinson wrote again to Higginson, seemingly before enough time had passed for him to send a response to her previous message. Into this letter, Dickinson copies the last two poems she would ever write and the only poems assigned to the year 1886. A draft of the first poem, "The Immortality / she gave" (AC 810), was found among Dickinson's papers; no copy of the second poem, however, appears to have survived:

> Of Glory not a
> Beam is left
> But her Eternal
> House –
> The Asterisk is
> for the Dead,
> The Living, for
> the Stars –
> [BPL Higg 114]

Was it too late for Dickinson to have made a copy for her records? Did she know there was no reason to retain a final "author's copy" of these last poems? Even as Dickinson is writing the lines, moving her hand across the paper, she is departing the world. The poem falls from her hands into ours, enjoining us to mark the place the dead once occupied, and to guarantee that the stars will not go out above us. For once, Dickinson's words are fixed and invariant: there will be no further versions of this poem. Yet such invariance is possible only at the very moment when the material has become immaterial, when the "Eternal House" (of art) stands perfected; all the while, no beam survives whole. While the dead turn into stars, the works they leave behind remain embodied, fallen things, still subject to the laws of the corporeal realm, to chance and time. Each fallen, vulnerable, and lovely artifact is part of the life of the past, a clue to the meaning of that past receding ever more quickly from us who live in the age of speed. How do we map what stands at the edge of, and defines, the Timeless? Is it enough to chart the trajectory of a letter and its component poems as arriving at their destination?

In her first letter to Higginson, datable to April of 1862, Dickinson had asked him if her poetry "breathed –" (BPL, Higg 50). Now in her final message to him, written just days before her death, her question about poetry becomes a question about immortality. Containing neither salutation nor signature, are her questions a letter? a poem?

> Deity – does
> He live
> now?
> My friend –
> does he
> breathe?

Rarely given to comment on the visual aspects of Dickinson's writing, about this composition Thomas H. Johnson noted the spatial orientation of Dickinson's script, a ductus that had at this point changed: "The handwriting shows an extreme slant and wide spacing of letters" (JL 1045n). In the open spaces between the words, bird and wave, the "Billows of / Circumference" (AC 111) figure the undulant motions of the world between firmaments that connect the eternal, her dear friend the Unitarian minister, and the sign of the living body: breath. The directionality of our

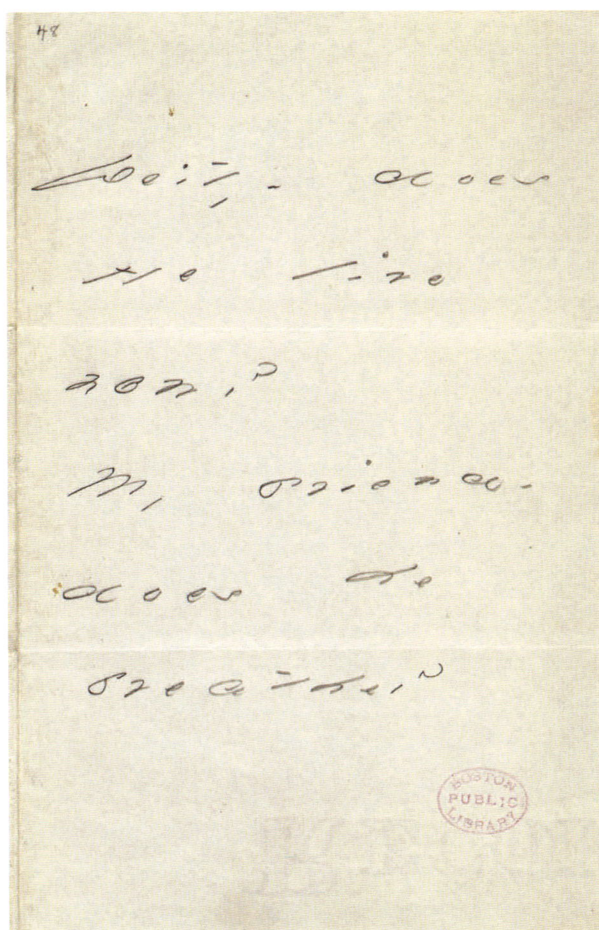

Figure 15: Dickinson's last communication with Thomas W. Higginson, May 1866. Boston Public Library, Emily Dickinson Collection, BPL Higg 48.

map here fails, even in terms of the missive's genre. All that guides us in plotting trajectories is her farewell in the closure of two questions.

The importance of Dickinson's manuscripts—and of all primary sources—inheres not simply in the information that we can extract from them, but, rather in the uniqueness of their physical forms—like maps that help us to decipher—through patient study, something of the dynamics and hidden forces of the culture that brought them into being, and that deliver them to the hands of her family, friends and readers, and finally into our hands.

As people, letters, and poems move along temporal and spatial trajectories, they trace narratives that may come to light through the process of mapping. By following these different bodies as they cross boundaries at once literal and figurative, tangible and intangible, we may begin to understand something of the fears and the desires, the imaginings and limitations of the writer, her readers, and the documents themselves. Following closely, we find ourselves in exterior and interior regions whose coordinates we are taking for the first time. In their essay "Inscribing the Past: Depth as Narrative in Historical Spacetime," Philip J. Ethington and Nobuko Toyosawa observe, "Maps of any form, be they pictorial or textual, only spottily represent the total landscape in any era. If the lived world were really like the maps we make of it, we would fall into huge gaps of nothingness between small islands of reality."[33] Readers of Dickinson recognize this experience. We come to a poem or a letter, a "small island of reality," and to another and another, and just when we are getting our bearings, we step off the edge into nothingness. Parts of the map are missing. To traverse this negative space, the reader must become cartographer, de-territorializing—perhaps even exiling—herself in order to draw new routes and byways. In the new atlas of Dickinson's writings that I imagine, the legend is missing, and in its place we find a series of questions: Why do some letters and poems travel with godspeed, while others go astray or lie unsent? What makes a letter weighty or light as air? What is the "destination" of the unsent letter, and who is the addressee of such a document? Why does a correspondence begin and later break off—terminate—in a particular moment and place? And what makes it commence again after the lapse of many years? What poems journey as companions to letters or to each other, and which ones always travel alone?

To follow a particular correspondence, that is, the letters and the poems accompanying them, is to discover the furthest distance a letter or a poem traveled across space or time; but it is also to question the ways in which distance and closeness are conceptualized and measured by the writer and her correspondents. For when ideas of scale are fundamentally altered, so too meanings of "near" and "far" may shift: the distant may become near and the near remote. It is not only the curvature of the Earth's surface that complicates the ratio of distance on the map to the corresponding distance on the ground, but rather the changing horizon of the spatial

---

33. Philip J. Ethington and Nobuko Toyosawa, "Inscribing the Past: Depth as Narrative in Historical Spacetime", in Bodenhamer, Corrigan, and Harris, eds., *Deep Maps and Spatial Narratives*, 88.

 The Networked Recluse

imaginary. To track poems and letters to their different destinations, and to trace the multiple contexts and trajectories in which they are created and formed, may be to unfold a map of a writer's imagination of her interlocutors, while also revealing the addresses of these readers and the scenes of their reading. Who were these correspondents who saved Dickinson's poems and letters — sometimes even the briefest of messages — all their lives? Who were they to Dickinson, and who was she to them? How many of them knew each other and knew that they were secret sharers in a common circle? What narratives of desire or ambition, of grief, consolation, or delight, of salutation and farewell, does the mapping of each correspondence disclose? Finally, to map Dickinson's correspondences and the circulation of her poems in the world is also to call for an account of the far greater number of poems and other writings that remained unshared in her time. To shadow the writings never sent to anyone, yet carefully preserved among Dickinson's papers, may reveal the coordinates of a writer not less but more hermetic than we once imagined.

Deep Maps unfold slowly. They move, as Cliff McLucas notes, "at a speed of landform or weather."[34] The mapping of Dickinson's years and hours, her works and world, is a project as deep as the past—and as unfathomable as the future. We imagine that the maps we make will call upon us to recalculate the distances—textual and geographical, cultural and emotional—between poems, letters, writers, and readers. What fierce and tender cartographies will emerge from our attempts to map the flow of events of the past, however, cannot be wholly known prior to their making. The endeavor will no doubt be corrective of our speculations and conjectures, compelling the re-interpretation of the data we trusted as telling us only one truth rather than the multiple contextual truths of Dickinson's desk and writing.

Still further, over the course of mapping Dickinson's passage through spacetime, her poems and letters may at last appear not only as the work of a singular, *sui generis* human mind of nineteenth-century North America but also of the forces of indifferent nature across many centuries. In the imaginary atlas of Dickinson's writings and world may also be a "ghost map" on which the invisible traces of past actions on the landscape will be made visible, and fragile biofacts, geofacts, and artifacts will be scattered together in a vast ecosystem where the fossil prints of prehistoric dinosaurs once believed to be primeval birds and the poems in a handwriting resembling them lie open for interpretation without end.

The Morgan's admirable project of curating and ordering for us such unique witnesses and artifacts connected to Dickinson's world reminds us of the rich and unique contexts that punctuate the narrative that elucidates Dickinson herself. These materials draw us still today, not just as precious objects to examine, but for where they lead us when, after that first glance, they draw us onto the path and trajectory that sends us traveling through to a different time, a different culture, a

34. This passage from Cliff McLucas appears at http://metamedia.standford.edu/~mshanks/ projects/deep-mapping.html, accessed August 2016.

different place. Powerful maps, they move us further than we could normally go—
into the soul of a twenty-three-year-old writing of a "wondrous sea" from her room
in a house looking onto Amherst's West Cemetery.

Acknowledgments

I thank Carolyn Vega, Assistant Curator, Literary and Historical Manuscripts,
The Morgan Library & Museum, and Mike Kelly, Head, Archives and Special
Collections, Amherst College, for their collaboration on the current exhibition of
Dickinson manuscripts and artifacts at The Morgan Library. It offers viewers new
access to Dickinson's works and world. I would also like to thank Margaret Dakin,
Archivist, Amherst College, and Leslie Morris, Curator of Manuscripts, Houghton
Library, for sharing with me their intimate knowledge of Dickinson's manuscripts.
My greatest debt is to the editors, early and late, of Dickinson's writings, whose
work has fostered a deeper understanding of Dickinson's manuscripts and textual
practice.

Sumptuous Destitution

Richard Wilbur

At some point Emily Dickinson sent her whole Calvinist vocabulary into exile, telling it not to come back until it would subserve her own sense of things.

Of course, that is not a true story, but it is a way of saying what I find most remarkable in Emily Dickinson. She inherited a great and overbearing vocabulary which, had she used it submissively, would have forced her to express an established theology and psychology. But she would not let that vocabulary write her poems for her. There lies the real difference between a poet like Emily Dickinson and a fine versifier like Isaac Watts. To be sure, Emily Dickinson also wrote in the metres of hymnody, and paraphrased the Bible, and made her poems turn on great words like Immortality and Salvation and Election. But in her poems those great words are not merely being themselves; they have been adopted, for expressive purposes; they have been taken personally, and therefore redefined.

The poems of Emily Dickinson are a continual appeal to experience, motivated by an arrogant passion for the truth. "Truth is so rare a thing," she once said, "it is delightful to tell it." And, sending some poems to Colonel Higginson, she wrote, "Excuse them, if they are untrue." And again, to the same correspondent, she observed, "Candor is the only wile"— meaning that the writer's bag of tricks need contain one trick only, the trick of being honest. That her taste for truth involved a regard for objective fact need not be argued: we have her poem on the snake, and that on the hummingbird, and they are small masterpieces of exact description. She liked accuracy; she liked solid and homely detail; and even in her most exalted poems we are surprised and reassured by buckets, shawls, or buzzing flies.

Editor's Note: This essay originally appeared as a contribution to *Emily Dickinson; Three Views*, a volume published by the Amherst College Press in 1960 containing, in addition to this essay, contributions from Archibald MacLeish and Louise Bogan. It is republished here by kind permission of the author. The numbers appearing after Wilbur's quotations of Dickinson's poems correspond to the index numbers assigned to the poems by Thomas H. Johnson.

But her chief truthfulness lay in her insistence on discovering the facts of her inner experience. She was a Linnaeus to the phenomena of her own consciousness, describing and distinguishing the states and motions of her soul. The results of this "psychic reconnaissance," as Professor Whicher called it, were several. For one thing, it made her articulate about inward matters which poetry had never so sharply defined; specifically, it made her capable of writing two such lines as these:

> A perfect, paralyzing bliss
> Contented as despair.

We often assent to the shock of a paradox before we understand it, but those lines are so just and so concentrated as to explode their meaning instantly in the mind. They did not come so easily, I think, to Emily Dickinson. Unless I guess wrongly as to chronology, such lines were the fruit of long poetic research; the poet had worked toward them through much study of the way certain emotions can usurp consciousness entirely, annulling our sense of past and future, canceling near and far, converting all time and space to a joyous or grievous here and now. It is in their ways of annihilating time and space that bliss and despair are comparable.

Which leads me to a second consequence of Emily Dickinson's self-analysis. It is one thing to assert as pious doctrine that the soul has power, with God's grace, to master circumstance. It is another thing to find out personally, as Emily Dickinson did in writing her psychological poems, that the aspect of the world is in no way constant, that the power of external things depends on our state of mind, that the soul selects its own society and may, if granted strength to do so, select a superior order and scope of consciousness which will render it finally invulnerable. She learned these things by witnessing her own courageous spirit.

Another result of Emily Dickinson's introspection was that she discovered some grounds, in the nature of her soul and its affections, for a personal conception of such ideas as Heaven and Immortality, and so managed a precarious convergence between her inner experience and her religious inheritance. What I want to attempt now is a rough sketch of the imaginative logic by which she did this. I had better say before I start that I shall often seem demonstrably wrong, because Emily Dickinson, like many poets, was consistent in her concerns but inconsistent in her attitudes. The following, therefore, is merely an opinion as to her main drift.

Emily Dickinson never lets us forget for very long that in some respects life gave her short measure; and indeed it is possible to see the greater part of her poetry as an effort to cope with her sense of privation. I think that for her there were three major privations: she was deprived of an orthodox and steady religious faith; she was deprived of love; she was deprived of literary recognition.

At the age of 17, after a series of revival meetings at Mount Holyoke Seminary, Emily Dickinson found that she must refuse to become a professing Christian. To some modern minds this may seem to have been a sensible and necessary step; and surely it was a step toward becoming such a poet as she became. But for her, no pleasure in her own integrity could then eradicate the feeling that she had betrayed a deficiency, a want of grace. In her letters to Abiah Root she tells of the enhancing effect of conversion on her fellow-students, and says of herself in a famous passage:

> *I* am one of the lingering bad ones, and so do I slink away, and pause and ponder, and ponder and pause, and do work without knowing why, not surely, for this brief world, and more sure it is not for heaven, and I ask what this message *means* that they ask for so very eagerly: *you* know of this depth and fulness, will you try to tell me about it?

There is humor in that, and stubbornness, and a bit of characteristic lurking pride: but there is also an anguished sense of having separated herself, through some dry incapacity, from spiritual community, from purpose, and from magnitude of life. As a child of evangelical Amherst, she inevitably thought of purposive, heroic life as requiring a vigorous faith. Out of such a thought she later wrote:

> The abdication of Belief
> Makes the Behavior small—
> Better an ignis fatuus
> Than no illume at all— (1551)

That hers *was* a species of religious personality goes without saying; but by her refusal of such ideas as original sin, redemption, hell, and election, she made it impossible for herself—as Professor Whicher observed—"to share the religious life of her generation." She became an unsteady congregation of one.

Her second privation, the privation of love, is one with which her poems and her biographies have made us exceedingly familiar, though some biographical facts remain conjectural. She had the good fortune, at least once, to bestow her heart on another; but she seems to have found her life, in great part, a history of loneliness, separation, and bereavement.

As for literary fame, some will deny that Emily Dickinson ever greatly desired it, and certainly there is evidence mostly from her latter years, to support such a view. She *did* write that "Publication is the auction/Of the mind of man." And she *did* say to Helen Hunt Jackson, "How can you print a piece of your soul?" But earlier, in 1861, she had frankly expressed to Sue Dickinson the hope that "sometime" she might make her kinfolk proud of her. The truth is, I think, that Emily Dickinson knew she was good, and began her career with a normal appetite for recognition. I think that she later came, with some reason, to despair of being understood or properly valued, and so directed against her hopes of fame what was by then a well-developed disposition to renounce. That she wrote a good number of poems about fame supports my view: the subjects to which a poet returns are those which vex him.

What did Emily Dickinson do, as a poet, with her sense of privation? One thing she quite often did was to pose as the laureate and attorney of the empty-handed, and question God about the economy of His creation. Why, she asked, is a fatherly God so sparing of His presence? Why is there never a sign that prayers are heard?

Why does Nature tell us no comforting news of its Maker? Why do some receive a whole loaf, while others must starve on a crumb? Where is the benevolence in shipwreck and earthquake? By asking such questions as these, she turned complaint into critique, and used her own sufferings as experiential evidence about the nature of the deity. The God who emerges from these poems is a God who does not answer, an unrevealed God whom one cannot confidently approach through Nature or through doctrine.

But there was another way in which Emily Dickinson dealt with her sentiment of lack—another emotional strategy which was both more frequent and more fruitful. I refer to her repeated assertion of the paradox that privation is more plentiful than plenty; that to renounce is to possess the more; that "The Banquit of abstemiousness/Defaces that of wine." We all know how the poet illustrated this ascetic paradox in her behavior—how in her latter years she chose to live in relative retirement, keeping the world, even in its dearest aspects, at a physical remove. She would write her friends, telling them how she missed them, then flee upstairs when they came to see her; afterward, she might send a note of apology, offering the odd explanation that "We shun because we prize." Any reader of Dickinson biographies can furnish other examples, dramatic or homely, of this prizing and shunning, this yearning and renouncing: in my own mind's eye is a picture of Emily Dickinson watching a gay circus caravan from the distance of her chamber window.

In her inner life, as well, she came to keep the world's images, even the images of things passionately desired, at the remove which renunciation makes; and her poetry at its most mature continually proclaims that to lose or forego what we desire is somehow to gain. We may say, if we like, with some of the poet's commentators, that this central paradox of her thought is a rationalization of her neurotic plight; but we had better add that it is also a discovery of something about the soul. Let me read you a little poem of psychological observation which, whatever its date of composition may logically be considered as an approach to that discovery.

> Undue Significance a starving man attaches
> To Food —
> Far off — He sighs — and therefore — Hopeless —
> And therefore — Good—
>
> Partaken — it relieves — indeed —
> But proves us
> That Spices fly
> In the Receipt — It was the Distance —
> Was Savory — (439)

This poem describes an educational experience, in which a starving man is brought to distinguish between appetite and desire. So long as he despairs of sustenance, the man conceives it with the eye of desire as infinitely delicious. But when, after all, he secures it and appeases his hunger, he finds that its imagined spices have flown.

The moral is plain: once an object has been magnified by desire, it cannot be wholly possessed by appetite.

The poet is not concerned, in this poem, with passing any judgment. She is simply describing the way things go in the human soul, telling us that the frustration of appetite awakens or abets desire, and that the effect of intense desiring is to render any finite satisfaction disappointing. Now I want to read you another well-known poem, in which Emily Dickinson was again considering privation and possession, and the modes of enjoyment possible to each. In this case, I think, a judgment is strongly implied.

> Success is counted sweetest
> By those who ne'er succeed.
> To comprehend a nectar
> Requires sorest need.
>
> Not one of all the purple Host
> Who took the Flag today
> Can tell the definition
> So clear of Victory
>
> As he defeated — dying —
> On whose forbidden ear
> The distant strains of triumph
> Burst agonized and clear! (67)

Certainly Emily Dickinson's critics are right in calling this poem an expression of the idea of compensation—of the idea that every evil confers some balancing good, that through bitterness we learn to appreciate the sweet, that "Water is taught by thirst." The defeated and dying soldier of this poem is compensated by a greater awareness of the meaning of victory than the victors themselves can have: he can comprehend the joy of success through its polar contrast to his own despair.

The poem surely does say that; yet it seems to me that there is something further implied. On a first reading, we are much impressed with the wretchedness of the dying soldier's lot, and an improved understanding of the nature of victory may seem small compensation for defeat and death; but the more one ponders this poem the likelier it grows that Emily Dickinson is arguing the *superiority* of defeat to victory, of frustration to satisfaction, and of anguished comprehension to mere possession. What do the victors have but victory, a victory which they cannot fully savor or clearly define? They have paid for their triumph by a sacrifice of awareness; a material gain has cost them a spiritual loss. For the dying soldier, the case is reversed: defeat and death are attended by an increase of awareness, and material loss has led to spiritual gain. Emily Dickinson would think that the better bargain.

In the first of these two poems I have read, it was possible to imagine the poet as saying that a starving man's visions of food are but wish fulfillments, and hence illusory; but the second poem assures us of the contrary—assures us that food, or victory, or any other good thing is best comprehended by the eye of desire from the vantage of privation. We must now ask in what way desire can define things, what comprehension of nectars it can have beyond a sense of inaccessible sweetness.

Since Emily Dickinson was not a philosopher, and never set forth her thought in any orderly way, I shall answer that quotation from the seventeenth-century divine Thomas Traherne. Conveniently for us, Traherne is thinking, in this brief meditation, about food—specifically, about acorns—as perceived by appetite and by desire.

> The service of things and their excellencies are spiritual: being objects not of the eye, but of the mind: and you more spiritual by how much more you esteem them. Pigs eat acorns, but neither consider the sun that gave them life, nor the influences of the heavens by which they were nourished, nor the very root of the tree from whence they came. This being the work of Angels, who in a wide and clear light see even the sea that gave them moisture: And feed upon that acorn spiritually while they know the ends for which it was created, and feast upon all these as upon a World of Joys within it: while to ignorant swine that eat the shell, it is an empty husk of no taste nor delightful savor.[1]

Emily Dickinson could not have written that, for various reasons, a major reason being that she could not see in Nature any revelations of divine purpose. But like Traherne she discovered that the soul has an infinite hunger, a hunger to possess all things. (That discovery, I suspect, was the major fruit of her introspection.) And like Traherne she distinguished two ways of possessing things, the way of appetite and the way of desire. What Traherne said of the pig she said of her favorite insect:

> Auto da Fe and Judgment —
> Are nothing to the Bee —
> His separation from His Rose —
> To Him — sums Misery — (620)

The creature of appetite (whether insect or human) pursues satisfaction, and strives to possess the object in itself; it cannot imagine the vaster economy of desire, in which the pain of abstinence is justified by moments of infinite joy, and the object is spiritually possessed, not merely for itself, but more truly as an index of the All. That is how one comprehends a nectar. Miss Dickinson's bee does not comprehend the rose which it plunders, because the truer sweetness of the rose lies beyond the rose, in its relationship to the whole of being; but she would say that Gerard Manley Hopkins comprehends a bluebell when, having noticed its intrinsic beauties, he adds, "I know the beauty of Our Lord by it." And here is an eight-line poem of her own, in which she comprehends the full sweetness of water.

> We thirst at first — 'tis Nature's Act —
> And later — when we die —
> A little Water supplicate —
> Of fingers going by —
>
> It intimates the finer want —
> Whose adequate supply

---

1. Wilbur here quotes from Thomas Traherne, *Centuries of Meditation*. See *The Works of Thomas Traherne* (5 vol.), ed. Jan Ross (Cambridge, U.K.: Boydell and Brewer, D.S. Brewer, 2013), vol. 5, 15, §26.

> Is that Great Water in the West —
> Termed Immortality — (726)

Emily Dickinson elected the economy of desire, and called her privation good, rendering it positive by renunciation. And so she came to live in a huge world of delectable distances. Far-off words like "Brazil" or "Ciracassian" appear continually in her poems as symbols or things distanced by loss or renunciation, yet infinitely prized and yearned-for. So identified in her mind are distance and delight that, when ravished by the sight of a hummingbird in her garden, she calls it "the mail from Tunis." And not only are the objects of her desire distant; they are also very often moving away, their sweetness increasing in proportion to their remoteness. "To disappear enhances," one of the poems begins, and another closes with these lines:

> The Mountain — at a given distance —
> In Amber — lies —
> Approached — the Amber flits — a little —
> And That's — the Skies — (572)

To the eye of desire, all things are seen in a profound perspective, either moving or gesturing toward the vanishing-point. Or to use a figure which may be closer to Miss Dickinson's thought, to the eye of desire the world is a centrifuge, in which all things are straining or flying toward the occult circumference. In some such way, Emily Dickinson conceived her world, and it was in a spatial metaphor that she gave her personal definition of Heaven. "Heaven," she said, "is what I cannot reach."

At times it seems that there is nothing in her world but her own soul, with its attendant abstraction, and, at a vast remove, the inscrutable Heaven. On most of what might intervene she has closed the valves of her attention, and what mortal objects she does acknowledge are riddled by desire to the point of transparency. Here is a sentence from her correspondence: "Enough is of so vast a sweetness, I suppose it never occurs, only pathetic counterfeits." The writer of that sentence could not invest her longings in any finite object. Again she wrote, "Emblem is immeasurable—that is why it is better than fulfillment, which can be drained." For such a sensibility, it was natural and necessary that things be touched with infinity. Therefore her nature poetry, when most serious, does not play descriptively with birds or flowers but presents us repeatedly with dawn, noon, and sunset, those grand ceremonial moments of the day which argue the splendor of Paradise. Or it shows us the ordinary landscape transformed by the electric brilliance of a storm; or it shows us the fields succumbing to the annual mystery of death. In her love-poems, Emily Dickinson was at first covetous of the beloved himself; indeed, she could be idolatrous, going so far as to say that his face, should she see it again in Heaven, would eclipse the face of Jesus. But in what I take to be her later work the beloved's lineaments, which were never very distinct, vanish entirely; he becomes pure emblem, a symbol of remote spiritual joy, and so is all but absorbed into the idea of Heaven. The lost beloved is, as one poem declares, "infinite when gone," and in such lines as the following we are aware of him mainly as an instrument in the poet's commerce with the beyond.

> Of all the Souls that stand create —
> I have elected — One —
> When Sense from Spirit — files away —
> And Subterfuge — is done —
> When that which is — and that which was —
> Apart — intrinsic — stand —
> And this brief Tragedy of Flesh —
> Is shifted — like a Sand —
> When Figures show their royal Front —
> And Mists — are carved away,
> Behold the Atom — I preferred —
> To all the lists of Clay! (664)

In this extraordinary poem, the corporeal beloved is seen as if from another and immaterial existence, and in such perspective his earthly person is but an atom of clay. His risen spirit, we presume, is more imposing, but it is certainly not in focus. What the rapt and thudding lines of this poem portray is the poet's own magnificence of soul -her fidelity to desire, her confidence of Heaven, her contempt of the world. Like Cleopatra's final speeches, this poem is an irresistible demonstration of spiritual status, in which the super natural is so royally demanded that skepticism is disarmed. A part of its effect derives, by the way, from the fact that the life to come is described in an ambiguous present tense, so that we half-suppose the speaker to be already in Heaven.

There were times when Emily Dickinson supposed this of herself, and I want to close by making a partial guess at the logic of her claims to beatitude. It seems to me that she generally saw Heaven as a kind of infinitely remote bank, in which, she hoped, her untouched felicities were drawing interest. Parting, she said, was all she knew of it. Hence it is surprising to find her saying, in some poems, that Heaven has drawn near to her, and that in her soul's "superior instants" Eternity has disclosed to her "the colossal substance/Of immortality." Yet the contradiction can be understood, if we recall what sort of evidence was persuasive to Emily Dickinson.

"Too much of proof," she wrote, "affronts belief"; and she was little convinced either by doctrine or by theological reasoning. Her residual Calvinism was criticized and fortified by her study of her own soul in action, and from the phenomena of her soul she was capable of making the boldest inferences. That the sense of time is subject to the moods of the soul seemed to her a proof of the soul's eternity. Her intensity of grief for the dead, and her feeling of their continued presence, seemed to her arguments for the reunion of souls in Heaven. And when she found in herself infinite desires, "immortal longings," it seemed to her possible that such desires might somewhere be infinitely answered.

One psychic experience which she interpreted as beatitude was "glee," or as some would call it, euphoria. Now, a notable thing about glee or euphoria is its gratuitousness. It seems to come from nowhere, and it was this apparent sourcelessness of the emotion from which Emily Dickinson made her inference. "The 'happiness' without a cause," she said, "is the best happiness, for glee intuitive and lasting is the gift of God." Having foregone all earthly causes of happiness, she could only explain her glee, when it came, as a divine gift — a compensation in joy for what she had renounced in satisfaction, and a foretaste of the mood of Heaven. The experience of glee, as she records it, is boundless: all distances collapse, and the soul expands to the very circumference of things. Here is how she put it in one of her letters: "Abroad is close tonight and I have but to lift my hands to touch the 'Hights of Abraham.'" And one of her gleeful poems begins,

> 'Tis little — I could care for Pearls —
> Who own the ample sea —

How often she felt that way we cannot know, and it hardly matters. As Robert Frost has pointed out, happiness can make up in height for what it lacks in length; and the important thing for us, as for her, is that she construed the experience as a divine gift. So also she thought of the power to write poetry, a power which, as we know, came to her often; and poetry must have been the chief source of her sense of blessedness. The poetic impulses which visited her seemed "bulletins from Immortality," and by their means she converted all her losses into gains, and all the pains of her life to that clarity and repose which were to her the qualities of Heaven. So superior did she feel, as a poet, to earthly circumstance, and so strong was her faith in words, that she more than once presumed to view this life from the vantage of the grave.

In a manner of speaking, she *was* dead. And yet her poetry, with its articulate faithfulness to inner and outer truth, its insistence on maximum consciousness, is not an avoidance of life but an eccentric mastery of it. Let me close by reading you a last poem, in which she conveys both the extent of her repudiation and the extent of her happiness.

> The Missing All, prevented Me
> From missing minor Things.
> If nothing larger than a World's
> Departure from a Hinge
> Or Sun's extinction, be observed
> 'Twas not so large that I
> Could lift my Forehead from my work
> For Curiosity. (985)

A manuscript in Dickinson's hand as a map of her navigating the
processes of writing. Pages from Fascicle 84 (AC 84), ca. 1863.
Amherst College Archives and Special Collections.

Transcription and Transgression

Editor's Note: Susan Howe is a scholar, poet, and critic, whose 1985 *My Emily Dickinson* explored from a poetic perspective the cultural and literary influences that shaped Dickinson's world view. She is a Fellow of the American Academy of Arts and Sciences, and the recipient of the 2011 Bollingen Prize in American Poetry. Marta Werner, whose essay on "Emily Dickinson: Manuscrips, Maps, and a Poetics of Cartography" appears elsewhere in this volulme, is also the co-author of *The Gorgeous Nothings: Emily Dickinson's Envelope Poems* (New York: New Directions Books, 2013).

The conversation transcribed in this section took place at Howe's home in Guilford, Connecticut, on October 28, 2016.

Marta Werner: I once asked you how you had first encountered Emily Dickinson's poetry, and whether you had inherited Dickinson from your mother, but you said no, and then followed another line of descent through your father's family. Can you tell us a little more about this line of inheritance?

Susan Howe: I wrote *My Emily Dickinson* many years ago. Now, looking back, I realize she was there through my paternal grandfather or perhaps, in a more uncanny way, through my grandmother—even if she died four years before I was born. They were married in 1899. Her mother, Helen Huntington Quincy, grew up in Hadley and knew the Dickinsons. Both were devotees of the first Todd–Higginson editions of the 1890s. Aunt Helen said she could recite whole poems by heart. Grandpa, the author of many now out-of-print biographies and poems, was an assistant editor of the *Atlantic Monthly*, the magazine where Thomas Wentworth Higginson published "Letter to a Young Contributor"—the article that catalyzed Dickinson's twenty-five-year correspondence with him. Grandpa's book *Who Lived Here? A Baker's Dozen of Historic New England Homes and Their Occupants* has a chapter on the Dickinson house in Amherst, where he pays some attention to the history of her manuscripts.[1]

My childhood coincided with the war years and while our father away in Europe my mother, my sister and I took the subway from Cambridge to Boston for Sunday

---

1. M. A. DeWolfe Howe, *Who Lived Here? A Baker's Dozen of Historic New England Houses and Their Occupants* (Boston: Little, Brown, 1952).

lunches at his apartment. During those years Aunt Helen earned her living by doing monologues á la Ruth Draper and Cornelia Otis Skinner—her most witheringly affectionate satires were of genteel Bostonian matrons. As children we used to love watching her step into such characters. After the war she married and moved to New York but Sunday lunches at the apartment on Louisburg Square were a family ritual; we always spent Christmas there.

When Richard Sewall's biography of Dickinson was published I was living in New York, and Aunt Helen, who shared my love for her work, naturally got a copy. She was in the last weeks of the sudden illness that killed her. Because she didn't have the physical energy to read herself. I began to read it to her. She asked me to make marginal markings beside passages she planned to go back to when she was better. We both knew she would never get better. I never felt closer to her. It was as if we could only touch each other through reading aloud. This practice of self-discipline was above all a dread of any display of affection. Here is a passage from chapter two I checked for her, where Sewall quotes from a letter from Samuel G. Ward to Thomas W. Higginson:

> She [Dickinson] is the quintessence of that element we all have who are of the Puritan descent.... We came to this country to think our own thoughts with nobody to hinder.... We conversed with our own souls till we lost the art of communicating with other people. The typical family grew up strangers to each other, as in this case. It was *awfully* high, but awfully lonesome. Such prodigies of shyness do not exist elsewhere. [2]

I made the little pencil mark while the wide, un-thing that we couldn't say was there. This was in 1974.

MW: In retrospect, your early years in Cambridge seem to have determined the course of your life.

SH: Maybe—though I had no idea it would in play out in the way it has. During the 1940s and 50s my parents were close friends with a circle of ground-breaking Americanists at Harvard. Some of them were building American Studies as a radical new discipline. Some were involved in various ways with textual. Perry Miller, F. O. Matthiessen, Kenneth Murdoch, Jack Sweeney, Archibald MacLeish. Even Lillian Hellman was around a lot as well. In the 1940s, these now-canonical scholars were still on the fringe in a way. I mainly heard them going on at numerous cocktail parties and was very scornful. Being a faculty brat is complicated. Particularly if you were a girl during the 1940s and 50s.

MW: Your parents—at least in the stories you tell about them—were very different. But both of them loved words. Was writing your birthright?

SH: Everyone in the family seemed to have written books and this still goes on. A doctor or business man would have been nice; but no. On my father's side, there was great regard for the papers of writers. My father, who loved Cotton Mather,

---

2. Samuel G. Ward, letter to Thomas W. Higginson, ca. 1890; quoted in Richard Sewall, *The Life of Emily Dickinson* (2 vols.) (New York: Farrar, Straus and Giroux, 1974), 26.

was the biographer of the long-lived and wordy Justice Oliver Wendell Holmes' papers. We all blamed Holmes for driving him to an early grave. And here I am as an old woman still lured on by manuscripts of certain writers. My mother loved to recite Browning's "My Last Duchess" and passages from Milton's "Comus" as well as poems and passages from plays of Yeats. After he came back from the war, my father read *Nicholas Nickelby* and *The Pickwick Papers* to us before bed. The sense-memory of listening to the works of writers read aloud, loved and laughed over—has given me a particular ear for words read aloud.

MW: Long ago, before I ever read *My Emily Dickinson*, I heard you give a reading of your own work. And after that, I thought I might at last have some idea of how Dickinson's poems sounded. Your voice was fierce and spare. It almost cut the pages you read from.

SH: My Anglo-Irish mother insisted that Americans couldn't speak English correctly. Particularly Bostoninans. She could be merciless about very infinitesimal issues of pronunciation, like either/*eye-ther*, or dew/*dyew*. At the same time, I'm the daughter of an American father who was deeply involved with nineteenth-century American law and literature. What is thrilling about American writers of that century is how they place themselves within the registers of English literature as American writers. To me, to understand Dickinson truly you have to go back to the beginning, to the early crossing of the Atlantic Ocean from England to the New World. You have to trace the way the pulse of the English language slips into something different, into an American cadence. Noah Webster's 1844 *American Dictionary of the English Language* is in part a record of this change. But you can see it in earlier documents too. In the sermons of Jonathan Edwards, in the brokenness of the conversion narratives composed by the members of Thomas Shepard's congregation, in the captivity narratives by Mary Rowlandson and the other Puritans who lived on the edges and margins of the settlement most subject to Amerindian attacks. Richard Slotkin's *Regeneration Through Violence* tells this counter-story. And so does Patricia Caldwell's *The Puritan Conversion Narrative*.

At the same time, there are the voices of her own century. There is Emerson—the Emerson who springs from the same source as Edwards, from Calvinism. His essays are built up sentence by sentence. They tear the veil away from the face of the new world while also conveying a radical acceptance of the conditions of "this new yet unapproachable America."

MW: How did *My Emily Dickinson* begin?

SH: With my belief that she loved Charles Dickens. In the early letters exchanged between Dickinson and her brother, Austin—when he was away from home and falling in love with Susan—they had almost a code where "Dickens" stood in for things they couldn't say. I was really manic about this connection. I'm not saying I was right, but I was obsessed. Particularly with connections to David Copperfield.

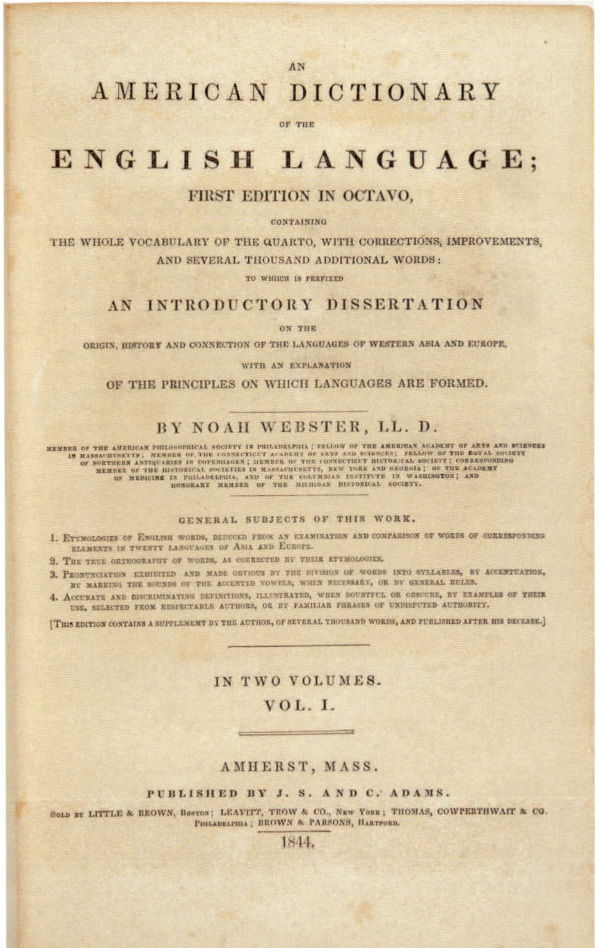

Figure 1: Title page to Noah Webster's *An American Dictionary of the English Language* (Amherst, Mass.: J. S. and C. Adams, 1844). Amherst College Archives and Special Collections.

And then to the similarity of their surnames, which wouldn't have been lost on her. This led, by tychic reasoning, to:

> My Life had stood – a
> Loaded Gun –

MW: Your reading of this poem is violent and beautiful. It's unlike any other reading, even the remarkable early reading given to us by Adrienne Rich.

SH: Adrienne Rich wrote about this poem in the 1970s, in the context of first-wave feminism. Certainly the poem speaks to women; it spoke to me. It's a poem about power. Much later, when I was teaching at Stanford, a speaker came who was researching guns in the Connecticut River Valley during the nineteenth century. This was the place that most of the guns in America were manufactured.

But my interest in the poem was elsewhere, in Dickinson's reading, in her sources. "My Life had stood – a / Loaded Gun –" sounds in a dark American key [Robert] Browning's "Childe Roland to the Dark Tower Came." I'm sure there is an acoustic connection to the Browning poem. It also resembles a Browning monologue. *My Emily Dickinson* began as a search for the soundings of her sources in her writing. I was tracing Dickinson's reading, her use of quotation and slant quotation. I wasn't thinking about the visual nature of the page—that came later—I was just listening. I was working from the Thomas Johnson editions. And when all is said and done, I think my prose essays are influenced by Johnson's edition of Emily Dickinson's letters.

MW: Why did you title your first scholarly work in such an apparently personal way—*My Emily Dickinson*?

SH: Because of her lines about George Eliot after Eliot's death:

> The look of the words as they lay in the print I shall never forget. Not their face in the casket could have had the eternity to me. Now, *my* George Eliot. The gift of belief which her greatness denied her, I trust she receives in the childhood of the kingdom of heaven. As childhood is earth's confiding time, perhaps having no childhood, she lost her way to the early trust, and no later came. Amazing human heart, a syllable can make to quake like jostled tree, what infinite for thee?[3]

The idea that a syllable can change everything is beautiful. And true. With Dickinson, it's about connectives, lack of connectives, syllables and that sense that one syllable is a life or death matter. And of course the lines gesture again to something both excruciatingly fundamental and profoundly unexplainable: Eternity.

MW: It's a haunting letter—the way she first registers Eliot's death by seeing the "words as they lay in the print." You can't rub them out. They are still and permanent.

SH: Yes. And they convey something of what I've been trying to express about sight and sound—that what you see is what you hear, what echoes very deep inside of you. But I also titled it that way because I was trying to say this is my interpretation. It

---

3. *The Letters of Emily Dickinson*, ed. Thomas H. Johnson and Theodora Ward (Cambridge, Mass.: The Belkap Press of Harvard University Press, 1986) at no. 710.

may not be a right one; it's just mine. I wasn't in academia when I wrote it. It was conceived and composed far outside of that space. And so it's an innocent book in a way that *The Birth-mark* essays can never be. By that time, I had my job at Buffalo. And there was no going back. I had changed.

MW: Can you say more about that change?

SH: Well, I felt completely insecure in academia. It was the age of French theory, and at the same time we had so many fine scholars in English, too—Ken Dauber, Neil Schmitz, Bob Daly. They had written scholarly books on writers that I cared about. They modeled a kind of discipline for me as well as an encouragement to my enthusiastic eccentricity. I didn't want to disappoint. And it was crucial to me that I not make mistakes, that I be correct. You've got to ground yourself somewhere in fact, in history. Looking back, I remember the terror I felt. But it was a good terror.

MW: It's not possible, even if you wished to, to return to that state of innocence. But is it possible, in the work you're engaged in now, to reach a new space of reconciliation and restoration?

SH: I don't know. Thinking about it all these years later, I'm drawn to other lines in the same letter on George Eliot's death; rereading the lines "As childhood is earth's confiding time." Earth was not confiding if you were a child during the 1940s, even if you were an American child. In those dark times, Sunday dinners at my grandfather's seemed sheltering. Now that we seem to be involved in endless war, I think of him often. Of his study crammed with books. He was the sweetest person. He was otherworldly, as if he had stepped out of the nineteenth century.

MW: Much of the force of *My Emily Dickinson* comes from its concentration. It's such an intense book. But so is your later work, *The Birth-mark*. Each chapter unfolds on its own terms; and each chapter might fall out of the book to live an autonomous life. But together they also propose unforeseen connections, complex intertextualities.

SH: Well, that's the way I always work; I don't know any other way. I haven't looked at Dickinson for quite a while; I opened the books again because you were coming. But once you do, you wonder why you closed them. She's just—she's incomparable. There are certain poets who defy comparison with anyone. You can't compare Shakespeare. You can't compare Keats. And you can't compare Dickinson.

MW: So there's something *sui generis* about Dickinson?

SH: Yes. She is *sui generis*. And so powerful. Now, every time any woman writes a poem the critics say, oh, so-and-so like Emily Dickinson. She's not! There is no other. I love Sharon Cameron's reading of Dickinson's poetry as a "poetry of variance." There's a kind of—

MW: A kind of excess?

SH: Yes, excess. And that's what her two authorized male editors have failed to account for or represent. Dickinson is a poet of excess, a boundary-crosser. Often the scholarly apparatus of these editions functions like a net to trap her in. But of course she who refused title and number ultimately escapes all nets.

I think she came to believe that writing is essentially between you and God, or between you and space, between you and nothingness. But what do I know? "'No' is the—"

MW: "...wildest word we consign to Language."[4]

SH: Yes. There's something so supremely daring about such negation.

MW: It's perhaps the affirmation of a negative theology: "Faith is Doubt."[5]

SH: Yes. John of the Cross, or even Jonathan Edwards, where nothing is everything.

❧

MW: It might be said that you found Emily Dickinson twice. First as a lyric poet, and then again as a visual artist. At what moment did you first lay eyes on her manuscript pages?

SH: For me, the visual field of Dickinson's manuscripts brings us to the central mystery, the absolute mystery of the relationship between sound and sight, to the idea that every mark is an acoustic mark that you make on paper. And so there is some kind of unity between what we see—what we put down on that piece of paper—and what we hear in the mind's ear. It is ultimately inexplicable, but that's what it is, a unity.

MW: *My Emily Dickinson* was published in 1985, four years after Franklin's edition of Dickinson's *Manuscript Books*,[6] but almost no one seemed to know about it.

SH: It's true. When I wrote *My Emily Dickinson* I hadn't seen her manuscripts—well, I had seen a few facsimiles, but only in isolated contexts. Franklin's edition was revelatory. Before I ever saw an original, I saw his work. I couldn't believe my eyes. I saw just a whole other Emily Dickinson. The line breaks, the enjambments amazed me. And I was overwhelmed by the revolutions in Dickinson's poetic forms in the space of a few years. The early work was neatly handwritten, conventionally lineated. It almost felt repressed. Later, stanzas break open and lines, even words, break open. Variants are more frequent. By the time you reach the final fascicle, you are left wondering, What am I reading? There's no answer. It is a radical ambiguity—which tends to be lost in print editions presenting poems.

MW: A few years after the publication of *The Manuscript Books*, Franklin's edition of *The Master Letters of Emily Dickinson* was published. Had your sense of astonishment

---

4. Ibid.

5. Johnson and Ward, eds., *The Letters of Emily Dickinson* at no. 912.

6. *The Manuscript Books of Emily Dickinson* (2 vols.), ed. Ralph W. Franklin (Cambridge, Mass.: The Belknap Press of Harvard University Press, 1981).

over Dickinson's holographs diminished by this time, or did this edition take you newly by surprise?

SH: I was shocked. I thought Johnson's edition of Dickinson was an heroic thing because he had preserved her dashes and capitals. This goes for the letters as well. For me, the Master Letters register a crisis of conversion over Dickinson's assumption of her power, which was terrifying. The struggle documented in these letters, if they even are letters, is paralleled in the early fascicles. And both the poems in the fascicles from this period and the letters are littered with quotations from her reading, too. Charlotte and Emily Bronte are all over the place. Ruskin and Emerson are embedded too, and so many others. One might say they are passionate pastiches. At the same time, they carry an erotic force. The documents themselves may look fragile, but they are volcanic.

MW: I was captivated by Franklin's edition of the Master Letters long ago, and I still love it.

SH: Oh, I love it too. And I hate it. My copy is littered with savage notes. He tried to contain the power of the manuscripts he had typographically set free by placing them into an envelope that comes with the edition. Ironically, I was talking about this just the other day at an event about your *The Gorgeous Nothings*, the fragments Dickinson wrote on envelopes.

MW: Yes, because the envelope marks a boundary. You put the letters in the envelope, you address them "The Master Letters," and suddenly that's what they are—that's all they are: letters a to man she called "Master."

SH: Right. That's it. But what are they?

MW: And why she did save them when she did not routinely save drafts of letters? Two of them, and one of them especially, is a very rough draft, but she kept them all for more than a quarter of a century—kept them until her death in 1886. Franklin was right to imagine that they stand at the heart of her mystery. But which mystery? I don't believe you can think about these documents without thinking about the boundaries around them, and how they might be re-drawn; about which other documents potentially belong in this constellation of "Master" letters (or poems).

The dating of these letters—which we owe to Johnson and Franklin—is interesting. She writes the first letter in 1858, the same year we think she begins binding poems into fascicles, and the last letter belongs to the year 1861. And after she writes that first beautiful but rather stiff fair-copy "letter" in 1858, you see Dickinson moving further and further into the explosively experimental space of the later two letters. The change can't be explained simply by reference to the "state" of the documents, that is, of going from fair to rough copies. No, there's something parallel going on in these so-called letters and Dickinson's poems. When you read these three letters you see, in radically condensed form, the future of the fascicles. There's a change of direction between 1858 and 1861. Maybe it's a change in her thinking about authorial intention; maybe it's a change in her notion of audience; maybe it's both or something else entirely. But you can't read these works and not feel it. Whoever—whatever—the Master was, and we may never know, the address—which is not a name after all, but both the promise and the screen of a name—is also the summons to experimentation.

You recently read one of the "Master Letters" in New York City. What was the response from the audience?

SH: Yes, I read the third and possibly the final letter in the sequence that begins,

> If you saw a bullet
> hit a Bird – and he told you
> he was'nt shot...

It was in small artist bookstore, a young audience. And they were—well, they had no words. After the reading people came up to me and said they couldn't believe these letters came out of the nineteenth century. The letters were a revelation to them—just as they had been to me when I first read them in Franklin's edition. And to give him credit in his transcriptions, he followed her line breaks, and this was a huge step in the editorial history. There you hear, because it's a crucial acoustic difference, the brokenness of the language.

MW: The territory of the transcription, especially in Dickinson scholarship, can feel like a textual scholar's no-man's land. How do you think we should transcribe Dickinson's writings?

SH: I don't know. Sometimes I think it just can't be done. On the one hand, the physical line breaks need to be preserved. But when you break the handwritten lines the way they're broken on the page in a typed transcription, you lose her sense of the page as a field of words spreading from edge to edge. You end up with a narrow little ribbon of print. But even the meticulous representation of her spacing does not preserve the air of the original leaves. There is no solution. But the best editions—or the most daring ones— still take the problem on, even when their editors know the transcriptions will be failures.

MW: The trouble is, where do you stop when you're doing a diplomatic transcription? For even after you reproduce the size, the letter forms exactly, and measure the spaces between letters and words, and after you trace the punctuation, the lengths and angles of the dashes, and even after you have recorded every stray mark, you realize you're leaving something else out—or failing to capture something essential. And so there's always something blind about the transcript.

SH: Yes. That's what I've realized after all these years.

MW: You can't do it.

SH: You can't do it. But I do admire the attempt. One fault of the Franklin edition of Dickinson's Manuscript Books is there is no attempt at transcription, and so no encounter with many of the fundamental questions of how to represent Dickinson's writing process. On the other hand, the Cornell editions of Yeats and the Garland Shelley are exemplary. They propose a model of what should have been done for Dickinson. And in both these cases it wasn't one male editor constructing the final version of a poet, but groups of editors collaborating, perhaps even differing in their ideas of what should be represented and how

MW: But the transcription is fallen. It is always fallen.

SH: It is fallen. In the transcription you're trying to go back to the beginning and make things right again. You're trying to go back before the fall into print. You can't. But then just recognize that. So this is fallen. So just allow it to fall.

MW: Are we in the age of the transcription?

SH: I think we are. For so long I have been fascinated by the original manuscript page, but now my fascination is with the transcription. And now I even see that all my work is really influenced by transcriptions, by the solutions transcribers imagine for textual problems. What are you going to do with text positioned upside down, or with crossed writing? How are symbols and authorial marks represented?

MW: That's interesting. Is it possible for a transcription, limited as it is, to carry something of the original across—perhaps even something that would otherwise be lost?

SH: There is something, I think. In the case of Dickinson, the printed transcription conveys a percussive element that we're not immediately aware of when we look at the handwritten documents. The "*silver* scruple." The "Bobolink − / and *his* − a *silver* scruple." It's that sharp thing in Dickinson that is so, to me, American.

> I've got a cough as
> big as a thimble − but
> I dont care for that −
> I've got a Tomahawk
> in my side but that
> dont hurt me much,
> Her Master
> stabs her more −

Wordsworth wouldn't say that, but she does.

MW: And here we are, witnessing the miracle of sight and sound again.

❧

MW: The Master Letters lead us into the larger region of Dickinson's letters—the many, many letters she sent away without any hope that she would see them again, or that one day they would be re-gathered. Indeed, we'll never know how many escaped the multiple attempts at gathering in the late nineteenth and early twentieth centuries. What does this say about Dickinson, this willingness to send lines and passages away forever?

SH: That's what is so unimaginable—the way she could just throw beautiful lines into letters and send them away.

MW: Dickinson's late letters are among the most beautiful documents I know. You've mentioned that you feel drawn to them now, at this moment in your life.

SH: They're unbelievable—there may be nothing more beautiful. You turn a page and the lines are suddenly there. What does she write to Susan? "I was just writing these very words to you, 'Susan fronts on the Gulf Stream,' when Vinnie entered with the Sea. Dare I touch the Coincidence? Do you remember what whispered to "Horatio"?[7] Maybe Vinnie had entered with her volume of Keats, who once wrote Keats once wrote that Shakespeare was the sea. But maybe not.

MW: There is a change in the letters after the death of Gilbert, Dickinson's young nephew. Dickinson is very ill during this time—Johnson thinks she suffers some form of breakdown—but the letters of this period are exquisite witnesses of her powers as elegist.

SH: Yes. And you see that after Gilbert's death the only possible response is acknowledgment of the mystery you can never hope to solve.

MW: "Awe is the first Hand that is held to us," she wrote to Susan in that October of 1883.

SH: The death of a child is beyond words, yet Dickinson found them. "Moving on in the Dark like Loaded Boats at Night, though there is no Course, there is Boundlessness – ."[8] It's strange, but just now as I'm remembering my grandmother through her love of Dickinson's poems, I remember that her mother had a sister, Abigail, who died at the age of ten. Her mother never got over it and it affected all the siblings. They lived in Hadley, and were friends with the Dickinsons. The deaths of Gilbert and Abigail would have forged a connection between the Dickinsons and the Quincys. I have often seen Abigail's tiny gravestone in our family plot.

MW: In the landscape of the late letters, in the soundscape of loss, it is still possible to be astonished by the beauty of the world.

SH: Yes. And we're in the Edenic landscape of the Connecticut River Valley, the landscape of Jonathan Edwards. For me, Edwards is the very expression of the cusp of the fall from grace. Dickinson is aware of the fall, in a way, too. We hear it in her letters. A few nights ago, I copied out this passage from a letter Dickinson wrote two years after Gilbert's death. It's a letter I adore:

"Open the Door," was his last Cry – "The Boys are waiting for me!" Quite used to his Commandment, his little Aunt obeyed, and still two years and many Days, and he does not return. Where makes my Lark his Nest? But Corinthians' bugle obliterates the birds. So covering your loved heart, to keep it from another shot.[9]

---

7. Johnson and Ward, eds., *The Letters of Emily Dickinson* at no. 1028.

8. Ibid. at no. 871.

9. Ibid. at no. 1020.

And there is the shot again. The one we hear ring out in "My Life had stood – a /
Loaded Gun – " Jesus. It's devastating, with regard to belief. At the same time, it's
written totally in the language of the Bible.

MW: If she is aware of the fall, does she think there's the possibility of salvation?

SH: When Dickinson goes to Mount Holyoke, she meets up with Mary Lyon and
for exactly a year she lives under the intense, laser-like focus of Lyon on the state
of her soul.

MW: And she will not confess in there. She holds out. And then, abruptly, she leaves.

SH: I think it's one of the ways in which she's most deeply an enigma. I don't think
you do know the state of her soul. I think one day she's one thing, and another day,
she's another. I don't think she was a believer in Lyon's understanding of the term,
but you see what she is a believer is in the Word. And that's the thing about the
Bible, the King James Version of the Bible. I believe in words. I would like to have
"The Lord is my shepherd" read over me when I am dying, its music would comfort
me in the way certain hymns do. I don't go to church; but I believe in, "The Lord is
my shepherd. I shall not want." And I don't want it made politically correct. I don't
want it corrected. It's got to be that version, that Word, the Word of God—or the
Word of King James.

MW:

> Let down the Bars,
> Oh Death
> The tired Flocks
> come in
> Whose bleating ceases
> to repeat
> Whose wandering
> is done –
> Thine is the stillest
> night
> Thine the securest <Paternal>
> Fold
> Too near Thou art
> for seeking Thee
> Too tender, <willing>
> to be told – <called>[10]

SH: But then the fragment, "God cannot discontinue <anul> himself. This appall-
ing trust is at times all that remains – ."[11]

---

10. *The Poems of Emily Dickinson*, Variorum Edition (3 vols.), ed. Ralph W. Franklin (Cambridge,
Mass.: The Belknap Press of Harvard University Press, 1998), at no. 1117.

11. Johnson, ed., *The Letters of Emily Dickinson*, at Prose Fragment 34.

MW: For me, Dickinson is the poet who hazards all. Who knows all is hazarded in the Word: "What a Hazard an accent is!"[12] The peril is made palpable in the way the word "Hazard" stretches across an entire line. I wonder: Is your Emily Dickinson a hermetic poet, or was she just waiting for a reader—a stranger—willing to cross that vast nothingness and meet her?

SH: I think she started as a writer hoping for future publication. But the deeper she went into writing, the more she moved away from the idea of audience. The same thing happens with Melville after *Moby Dick*. Even that was a flop. But in *Pierre*, there's a more intense, if only partly conscious, moving away. I think Dickinson, like Melville, reached the conclusion that it simply doesn't matter who reads what you have written. What matters is what you got at that moment.

⁂

MW: For almost as long as I have known you, I have dreamed of following you through the archives and into the feeling you describe so beautifully in the final paragraph of *Spontaneous Particulars: The Telepathy of Archives*:

> …From somewhere in the twilight realm of sound a spirit of belief flares up at the point where meaning stops and the unreality of what seems most real floods over us. The inward ardor I feel while working in research libraries is intuitive. Its a sense of self-identification and trust, or the granting of grace in an ordinary room, in a secular time.[13]

How did this life affair with the archives begin, and how has it changed over time?

SH: Initially I saw the archives as sites of power and privilege. My first relation to them was that of an intruder. I was blocked from seeing what I wanted to see, what I had come to see—Dickinson's manuscripts at the Houghton Library! But the libraries are also homes to me. I love books. Some people think Dickinson suffered from agoraphobia. I am quite agoraphobic, too, I prefer stacks to streets. Now the ones at Sterling Library at Yale are overcrowded. Speaking of guns, all the books not many people read have been sent to off-site storage, in a building complex that was formerly the Winchester rifle factory. This means that odd unread books one used to discover by chance when you went looking for something else are lost. It's a sort of form of grace when you find it, something to do with chance connections.

MW: What you're saying reminds me of Wallace Stevens' lines in "The House was Quiet and the World was Calm":

> The words were spoken as if there was no book,
> Except that the reader leaned above the page,
>
> Wanted to lean, wanted much most to be
> The scholar to whom his book is true, to whom
>
> The summer night is like a perfection of thought.

---

12. Ibid. at no. 1011n.

13. Susan Howe, *Spontaneous Particulars: The Telepathy of Archives* (New York: Christine Burgin / New Directions Books, 2014), 63.

You have worked in many archives—magisterial places like Sterling, the Houghton, and others. But you also like to visit small, out-of-the-way archives.

SH: Yes, I also enjoy small local libraries. Usually they have local historical collections where you will find things that historicists have neglected, or you find an old book with the odd spelling from seventeenth century. I don't know. It's the peace found in the landscape of place.

MW: And now there is another kind of archive to get lost in as well—the digital archive. Do you find yourself wandering in those spaces as well?

SH: Well, it is thrilling that these archives exist. They show us a whole different way of reading someone like Dickinson, particularly. But the experience of searching the digital archive is entirely different. What is missing is the feeling that you're literally wandering in books made of paper along shelves in mysterious dark places that are slightly hard to get to. In the digital archives, there is a magnification of the visual aspects of the manuscript but at the same time a loss of its materiality. When I saw—and touched—the Master Letters in the archive at Amherst I could feel the fragility of the paper. And when I looked at Edwards' manuscripts in the Beinecke Library, I could touch the fibers of the rag paper and feel that it was made out of bits of material. The handwriting just bites into the paper. There's a sense in Dickinson literally that the word is skin, that it's almost the parchment. It comes down to a sense of touch, even a sense of smell.

You can't have everything, of course, and now so many people can see things in digital form that they would otherwise have been blind too. But there's also the worry that because things are digitized, the originals will be still more fiercely guarded.

❧

MW: Two years ago, The Drawing Center curated an exhibition of Dickinson's manuscripts. For the first time, they were presented to the public in beautiful glass vitrines as works of visual art. This exhibition seemed to fulfill one of your hopes for Dickinson. What was it like for you to witness this?

SH: It was astonishing. For years and years I went around with my slides endlessly giving lectures, hoping for this day. And now it's here. Perhaps we needed the history of visual art for the last two or three decades to prepare us for this moment. There was a stunning show at The Drawing Center called *3 X Abstraction: Agnes Martin, Hilma af Klint, and Emma Kunz*. And in so many ways their work crosses into the territory of Dickinson's late manuscripts—that is to say, into visual art. *The Gorgeous Nothings* affirms this sense of Dickinson's late works, too.

MW: Martin, af Klint, and Kunz: They were working in the domain of abstractionism, but they were also testing the boundaries of the mystical realm. Do you see that element in Dickinson? Not to make her a precursor of Martin or af Klint, because obviously she's very different in certain ways, but to admit a connection in her work, her writing practice, and a spiritual practice.

SH: Yes. She's living in the age of Turner, she has read *Modern Painters*.[14] And I think she enters a space that's ahead of her time, completely ahead of her time. It was a space then being entered by Turner's late watercolors and in Ruskin's writings about Turner. But like those three early female abstract artists—well, Agnes Martin is contemporary, but like Hilma af Klint and Emma Kunz—Dickinson is operating to a kind of formula established in the mind's eye. And I think that she also enters the space of a kind of solitary, deeply private person who can't throw belief away.

MW: Dickinson's connections to the world were made through words—through reading, writing. But these forms of connection also allowed her to maintain solitude.

SH: Yes, she is an enigma. And she came to that liminal space where nothing matters but you and the look of the words on the page. That's what matters. I think she realized, finally, that she wasn't interested in fame. She started on her way to find it; she wrote to Higginson—and kept writing to him all her life. But after the 1860s, the desire for recognition is suspended and transformed into something else, into the simple happiness of daily practice.

MW: "The Codes of Bliss are few – ." Have you, too, come into that space?

SH: Maybe. Once I finished my essay on Wallace Stevens, I felt—okay, I've done it now. I don't have the physical or mental energy to do anything like that again. And, in a very deep sense, I feel like I have fulfilled what I was called to fulfill. I felt as much for Stevens as I did for Dickinson.

MW: Your early break into scholarship was through Dickinson; your late break into a space—a region—somewhere beyond it has been through Stevens. What is the connection for you between these writers? Is your work on Stevens a departure from, or a fulfillment of, your work on Dickinson?

SH: I suppose the connection is Emerson. Stevens's and Emerson's "poet" is also a scholar and a mystic. And Dickinson certainly knew Emerson's essays. All of these authors are aphorists. To produce aphorisms is to enter the domain of philosophy. Stevens and Dickinson both do this. It's too often a male domain. Dickinson and Gertrude Stein are magnificent aphorists.

MW: You've already spoken of Dickinson's supreme—and affirming—relation to negation. In "The Snow Man," Wallace Stevens gives us the beautifully unembellished last lines,

> For the listener, who listens in the snow,
> And, nothing himself, beholds
> Nothing that is not there and the nothing that is.

Do Dickinson and Stevens enter into the same or into different "nothings"?

---

14. John Ruskin, *Modern Painters* (5 vols.) (London: George Routledge, 1850–1860).

SH: The nothing in the American landscape, in Hawthorne and Henry James' sense of it; also my mother's, I might add. But for me Stevens is comforting in a way Dickinson is not. She's more akin to Edwards, where you are walking at the edge of hell on one side, and on the other side, you get this just spectacular acceptance of nothing as everything, the ultimate beauty. Every word you choose must be perfect. Your sense of surprise, of wonder, must be rendered visually concrete, tangibly audible. This also describes Edwards' sense of affection as the passion of a mind bent on a particular object, but without its actual presence. The word stands in for the object, so the words chosen must be perfect.

MW: Today, when you're writing about Dickinson, do you still wonder whether you're right or wrong about her?

SH: Oh, yes. Always. Now, in 2016, in the Trumpian sense of the term, in relation to Hillary Clinton, she's the ultimate "nasty woman." An inspiration. Volcanic. When I start to write about her, I always feel, "uh-oh."

MW: Does it matter ultimately if you're right or wrong?

SH: Not in the end. It doesn't matter. All that matters is the work. Continuing to work.

❧

SH: Where has my grandfather's book gone?

MW: It's just here...I was looking at the Dickinson chapter.

SH: He calls Emily Dickinson an enigma. He writes about Mabel Loomis Todd's design for the first edition, about Higginson's introduction, and about the editing of those early collections.

MW: But you didn't know about your grandfather's work, you weren't aware of this book until just recently?

SH: No, I wasn't aware of it. I just went downstairs where I keep my Boston books and I looked at it now.

MW: So all your life, it's been right here.

SH: And this is what he wrote:

> ...Some day there should be a truly complete edition of her writing, and—who knows?— perhaps a definitive critical biography which together will establish for all time her pre-eminent place in American letters.[15]

MW: So strange.

SH: But I am always finding grandpa in my research. If only in footnotes. His children were Modernists. Though they loved him they considered his writing to be second-rate. But when I was working on [Charles Sanders] Peirce, there he was.

---

15. M. A. DeWolfe Howe, *Who Lived Here?*, 68.

And here he is again, in 2016, with Dickinson. Our sources are always secrets, even to ourselves.

> If you saw a bullet
> hit a Bird —

We never know when we will hit our mark.

Textual Preface: Transcriptions as "Thin Maps"

Marta Werner

> Like her translated faces –
> Teazing the want – (H 46)
> —*from* "You see I cannot see – your / lifetime"
> Emily Dickinson (H 56)

On three prior occasions, moved by the hope of representing the dynamics of the vulnerable, time-bound manuscript rather than the fixed, timeless text—and, equally, by the desire to see the author in the midst of composition—I have approached transcription as a form of translation.[1] The transcriptions in *The Gorgeous Nothings,* created in intense collaboration with Jen Bervin, represent the most recent and resolute attempt to harness print technology "against itself," that is, against its tendency to regularize and limit the potential meanings of the manuscript. To this end, we not only traced the borders, external and internal, of Dickinson's manuscripts, the disposition of her text across the page, the varying sizes and forms of her alphabet, and her unconventional punctuation; still more ambitiously, we sought to re-immerse the transcriber and the reader alike in the struggle of pursuing the "shifting, floating, ambiguous relations of clause to clause, phrase to phrase" in Dickinson's poems and other writings.[2]

In the end, however, even the most ambitious transcript is still only ever a "thin map" composed from a limited perspective, flat and two-dimensional. It can never quite capture what Philip Larkin called the "magical value" of the manuscript, a

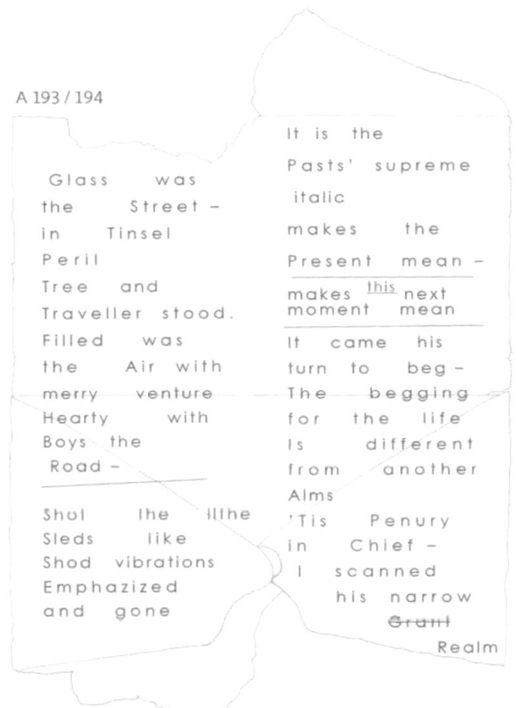

Figure 1: Transcription of MS AC 193/194 as a "graphic equivalent," from *The Gorgeous Nothings*, Jen Bervin and Marta Werner, eds. (New York: New Directions Books / Christine Burgin, 2013).

---

1. For my earlier experimentations with transcription, see *Emily Dickinson's Open Folios: Scenes of Reading, Surfaces of Writing* (Ann Arbor: University of Michigan Press, 1995), *Radical Scatters: An Electronic Archive of Emily Dickinson's Late Fragments and Related Texts*, 1870-1886 (Center for Digital Research in the Humanities, University of Nebraska, Lincoln, 2007-210), and (with Jen Bervin) *The Gorgeous Nothings,* Jan Bervin and Marta Werner, eds. (New York: Granary Books, 2012; New York, New Directions, 2013).

2. Thomas Greene, "Anti-hermeneutics: The Case of Shakespeare's Sonnet 129," in *Poetic Traditions of the English Renaissance*, ed. Maynard Mack and George deForest Lord (New Haven: Yale University Press, 1982), 146.

value linked in some way to the intricate, often conflicting, and almost always unfathomable human experience that gives rise to art.[3] Instead of fostering a genuine encounter with the otherness of the artifact remote in time and place from us, an appointment that, as George Herbert's editor Thomas Greene claimed, results in a true "clarification" of the manuscript's meaning, the transcript inevitably mediates our experience of the manuscript, controlling its meanings in obvious ways as well as in ways of which we are less keenly aware.[4] In the end, the transcript still "teazes the want."

In composing the transcriptions for the Morgan's exhibition of Dickinson's manuscripts, I have taken a "middle way," retreating from the perhaps hubristic attempt to create a "graphic equivalent" of the manuscript page in print and reconciling myself to renderings of the manuscripts that are closest to what François Masai called "diplomatic interpretive" transcriptions.[5] They report, as precisely as possible, the texts Dickinson left us, following her orthography, punctuation, alterations, additions and cancellations, and marking physical line and page breaks. Yet while the transcriptions represent, at least to some degree, the "faces" of the manuscripts, they make no claim to being mirrors of the mind that made them. In part, the decision to provide printed transcripts at all proceeds from my present sense of context: The Morgan's exhibition envisions diverse viewers, some of whom may already be adept at deciphering Dickinson's manuscripts, but others who may be grateful for a little guidance in uncharted territory. But this decision is also an acknowledgment that however far the transcriber goes in an attempt to represent the manuscript, something of its essential nature remains untranslatable.

A further caution attends the transcription in print of Dickinson's work. Since she neither oversaw nor approved the few print publications of her work, nor seemed to imagine her work within a print tradition, it is impossible to know how—or even if—she would have wanted her work presented in this medium. Under these conditions, the distance that separates original from transcription is absolute; and it may even be that by trying to lessen it, we inadvertently risk luring readers into seeing connections, even a passage, between them where in reality a gulf exists. The question Thomas Greene poses to readers of Herbert in his edition resonates deeply for readers of Dickinson: Is it not finally necessary to give up the goal of

---

3. See Philip Larkin, "A Neglected Responsibility: Contemporary Literary MSS," *Encounter,* July 1979, 33–40. Larkin identifies two kinds of value by which manuscripts are assessed: their "magical value," that is, the very paper chosen by the writer and the words "emerging for the first time in particular miraculous combination"; and the "meaningful value," that is, the extent to which the manuscript "can enlarge our knowledge and understanding of a writer's life and work."

4. Thomas Greene, "Anti-hermeneutics: The Case of Shakespeare's Sonnet 129," in *Poetic Traditions of the English Renaissance*, ed. Maynard Mack and George deForest Lord (New Haven: Yale University Press, 1982), 155.

5. François Masai, "Principes et conventions de l'édition diplomatique," *Scriptorium* (4) (1950), 177–193.

The Networked Recluse

fully appropriating the text, to "accept estrangement" and "settle for less than full understanding"?[6]

Among the numerous interpretive challenges posed by Dickinson's manuscripts the following are at once fundamental to an understanding of the manuscript and not completely resolvable in print transcription: the inherently expressive character of her punctuation and alphabetic symbols; her representation of majuscules and minuscules not always as distinct forms but as existing along a continuum; and her aesthetic of what Sharon Cameron has called "choosing not choosing" as it is manifested in her deployment of authorial variants (the word "variant" is itself problematic, implying, perhaps not always correctly, Dickinson's intention to substitute one word or phrase for another) and in her decisions regarding line breaks.

The innumerable variations in the lengths and angles of Dickinson's dashes as well as the evolution of the form of the dash over many years have so far confounded meaningful typographic representation (Figure 2). And yet, despite—or perhaps because of—this quality of elusiveness, the dash cannot easily be dismissed as an "accidental," a mark that contributes nothing to the meaning of the work. Rather, as Jen Bervin's striking six-by-eight-foot embroidered panels collating Dickinson's punctuation marks strongly suggest, this most heterogeneous of semiotic marks does carry meaning, though we have as yet been unsuccessful in fully decoding that meaning.

Similarly, certain letters seem to carry an excess of meaning. While Theodora Ward's early studies of chronological trends in Dickinson's handwriting and Ralph W. Franklin's later refinements to Ward's work certainly guide us, no transcriber—whether from the nineteenth, twentieth, or twenty-first century—can approach Dickinson's letterforms and punctuation solely in a technical way.[7] The experienced transcriber of Dickinson, used to her repertory of letterforms and diacriticals, is uniquely influenced by the myriad of sonic and visual forces at work in her handwriting. That said, no one transcriber has produced a thoroughly consistent rendering of her alphabet. Even one of Dickinson's most comprehensive and methodical editors, Ralph Franklin, falls under the sway of the visual power of her alphabet, translating certain instances of her use of the word conventionally rendered "Upon" as "Opon" in his variorum edition of her poems (Figure 3). In each case, Franklin's rendering seems guided by his interpretation of variations in the graphical formation of the character, nuances of meaning encoded in both the letterforms and the syntactic role of the preposition, and the acoustic force of the

Figure 2: Random dashes from diverse manuscripts, Amherst College Archives and Special Collections, Emily Dickinson Collection, A 80-8; A 84-2; A 88-13; A 106; A 431.

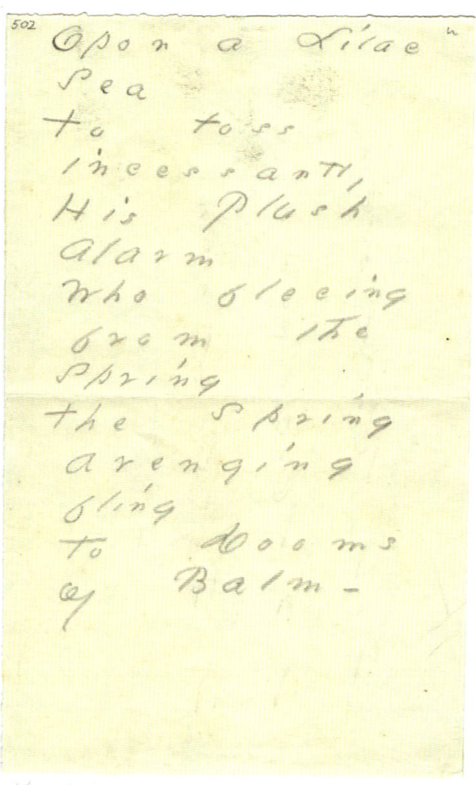

Figure 3: "Opon the Lilac / Sea" (ca. 1875). Amherst College Archives and Special Collections, Emily Dickinson Collection, AC 502.

---

6. Thomas Greene, "Anti-hermeneutics: The Case of Shakespeare's Sonnet 129," 156–57.

7. See especially "Characteristics of the Handwriting," in *The Poems of Emily Dickinson* (3 vols.), Thomas H. Johnson with Theodora Ward, eds. (Cambridge, Mass.: The Belknap Press of Harvard University Press, 1955), xlix–lix. See also Ralph W. Franklin's "Introduction" to *The Poems of Emily Dickinson*, Variorum Edition, 1–43.

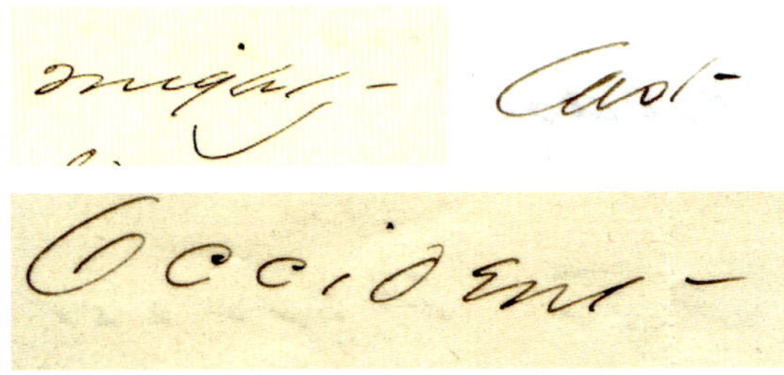

Figure 4: Final and penultimate "t's" perhaps doubling as dashes, Amherst College Archives and Special Collections, Emily Dickinson Collection, AC 83-5; AC 84-2; AC 813a.

Figure 5: Illustrations of elongated crossbars in "A narrow Fellow in / the Grass" (Cat. 5.04), ca. 1865, Amherst College Archives and Special Collections, Emily Dickinson Collection, A 88-13.

phoneme. A single letter away from "Open," the repeating "O's" in "Opon" carry the sound of plenitude or of emptiness, or, more exactly, of some condition in which plenitude and emptiness converge or change places.

While Franklin responded to the visual force of Dickinson's "O's," other letters might move us as well. I cannot, for example, react to Dickinson's "t's" / "T's" in a neutral way. While I believe I can differentiate between upper- and lower-case "T's," a belief no doubt influenced by my absorption of Johnson and Franklin's transcriptions, I am nonetheless struck by the exquisitely elongated crossbars of the letter in its (apparently) lowercase form that, fully detached from the stem, so often appears to perform, at least potentially, as a dash (Figure 4).

Equally, something I wish to convey but cannot fully represent in print is communicated in the sweeping reach of the element, its extension across an entire word or, at times, into the space beyond the word in which it appears (Figure 5).

A related challenge in the transcription of Dickinson's handwriting into print arises from our encounter with the subtle gradations of scale in letterforms. While print distinguishes clearly between majuscules and minuscules, handwriting exists along a continuum on which letters may grow or diminish incrementally. In Dickinson's hand, this tendency is especially marked when the metamorphosis of a letter from lower- to upper-case depends essentially on subtle gradations in size as opposed to significant alterations in shape—e.g., A/a; C/c; J/j; K/k; M/m; N/n; O/o; P/p; S/s; U/u; V/v; Z/z. Given Dickinson's habit at times of enlarging initial letters of all parts of speech—not only nouns, but also pronouns, verbs, adjectives, and even articles—it is at least conceivable that she saw changes in scale as integral to the meaning of her work, and that even in making hard and fast distinctions between upper- and lower-case letters transcribers erase part of this meaning.

The representation of Dickinson's line breaks and her authorial variants remain two of the longest standing and most contested issues touching the transcription of her manuscripts. In both cases it is clear that the transcriber's orientation to Dickinson's prosody—what he or she hears—has great bearing on the rendering of Dickinson's manuscripts in print. In recent years, two contrasting lines of thinking have prevailed.[8] In one, most fully and convincingly articulated by Ralph W. Franklin and Cristanne Miller, Dickinson is apprehended as a poet for whom the stanza, specifically the hymn stanza, as opposed to the line, is the most fundamental poetic

---

8. Ralph Franklin, Cristanne Miller, Susan Howe, and Sharon Cameron have written extensively on Dickinson's prosody. Among the most relevant works are Franklin's critical introductions to *The Manuscript Books of Emily Dickinson*, (2 vols.) ed. Ralph W. Franklin (Cambridge, Mass.: The Belknap Press of Harvard University Press, 1981), *The Master Letters of Emily Dickinson* (Amherst, Mass.: Amherst College Press, 1986), and *The Poems of Emily Dickinson*, Variorum Edition (3 vols.) (Cambridge, Mass.: The Belknap Press of Harvard University Press, 1998); Cristanne Miller's *Emily Dickinson: A Poets Grammar* (Cambridge, Mass.: Harvard University Press, 1989), and *Reading in Time: Emily Dickinson in the Nineteenth Century* (Amherst, Mass.: University of Massachusetts Press, 2012); Susan Howe's *My Emily Dickinson* (New York: New Directions, 2007), and *The Birthmark: Unsettling the Wilderness in American Literary History* (Wesleyan, 1993); and Sharon Cameron's *Lyric Time: Dickinson and the Limits of Genre* (Baltimore: Johns Hopkins University Press, 1981) and *Choosing Not Choosing: Dickinson's Fascicles* (Chicago: University of Chicago Press, 1993).

unit, and for whom authorial variants function as alternatives that may be exclusively correlated with specific words or phrases in a given poem. In the other, first voiced by Susan Howe and soon after by Sharon Cameron, Dickinson is conceived as a poet for whom the line, as opposed to the stanza, stands as the key poetic unit (Howe), and for whom variants do not necessarily stand in a one-to-one relationship to words or phrases they are meant to replace but participate simultaneously in multiple syntactical structures and relationships (Cameron, Howe). From this perspective, Dickinson's authorial variants introduce an antinomian strain into the poem that volatizes it and problematizes its identity, even as it encourages the poems' reverberation in the larger soundscape of the nineteenth century.

In the transcriptions originally prepared for the Morgan exhibition and now reproduced here, two opposing, even contradictory, tendencies are present. In my renderings of Dickinson's dashes and letterforms, I have submitted to the regularizing system of print: all dashes, with the exception of final dashes that are radically elongated, have been represented as en-dashes; all letterforms have been treated as equal and none singled out as unique; and no attempt has been made to render the relative sizes of letters, though at times the spatial positioning of variants and addenda has resulted in slight adjustments of type size.[9] Far from evidence of my belief that these elements as well as others not specifically mentioned are not at times crucial to the environment of the poems or letters, this practice is testimony of my hesitation to propose a singularly "meaningful"—i.e., a way beyond simple replication or mimicry—to indicate in print the range of possible mental associations these features might convey. In these cases it is my hope that the very "flatness" of type will convey my view of the subordinate nature of the transcription and of its role as a companion to—never a proxy for—the manuscript.

In the representation of line breaks and textual variants, however, I have allowed my practice of transcription to be guided by Cameron's and Howe's lines of argument regarding the poem's troubled identity. Instead of assuming that Dickinson invariably imagined her lines rendered metrically, I have marked her physical line breaks in order to allow new, sometimes even strange cadences a heightened audibility. Similarly, in my approach to the representation of Dickinson's experiments with addenda, cancellations, and possible variants, the first question I posed was

---

9. Though not without exceptions, my judgments concerning majuscule and miniscule forms have largely tended to agree with those found in Franklin's 1998 variorum of the poems or in Johnson's 1958 edition of Dickinson's letters. What this agreement signifies, though, is hard to say: I cut my teeth on these editions—especially Johnson's—and how deeply the print editions have influenced my reading of Dickinson' manuscripts cannot be precisely known. In addition to considering Johnson's and Franklin's transcriptions of Dickinson's work, it is critical to consult other scholarly renderings of her work. Given the number of documents in the exhibition and in the Morgan's own collection addressed to Susan Gilbert Dickinson, readers will want to consult Martha Nell Smith and Ellen Hart's scholarly edition *Open Me Carefully: Emily Dickinson's Intimate Letters to Susan Gilbert* (Paris Press, 1998). Cristanne Miller's recent reading edition of Dickinson's poems, *Emily Dickinson's Poems: As She Preserved Them* (Cambridge, Mass: The Belknap Press of Harvard University Press, 2016), offers yet another source.

Figure 6. Transcription of "A little madness," ca. 1875. Amherst College Archives and Special Collections, Emily Dickinson Collection, AC 106.

how to limit the critical presumption of a one-to-one relationship between words and variants so as to invite still richer, less narrowly referential interpretations of her poems. To this end, the transcriptions prepared for this volume maintain as far as possible the more ambiguous, open relations between lines and "variants" by preserving their spatial (as opposed to strictly grammatical) positioning: authorial experimentations, often with a single word or brief phrase, jotted above or below a given line retain this placement on the printed page, while new or expanded experimentations with the same word or phrase—yet appearing on their own lines or in different sectors/quadrants of the manuscript (e.g., the verso)—continue to hold their spatial position and autonomy. What is lost or obscured in this presentation, namely the sequential dimension of the compositional process especially within the variant streams, I have tried to restore in the notes. Even here, though, readers must approach interpretations of the temporal dynamics of the manuscript with caution: the moments of composition—like Dickinson's "numerals of / Eden" (AC 753)—may not be counted in the same manner in which we count the discretely passing seconds or minutes on a clock, even as the order of words on the page may never match the order in which they appeared in the mind. Once again, the transcription is exposed as only a "thin map," for even transcribers who desire to document the array of their interpretative possibilities opened by the manuscript, to signal the several possible relationships of variants to a poem, or to portray the mind's movement in the process of composition, only ever partially capture something of the poem's existence-in-suspension.

The transcription of Dickinson's worksheet draft of "A little madness / in the Spring" (Figure 6) shows the application of these principles. Here Dickinson's striving over the final lines of the poem is especially marked. After concluding the

The Networked Recluse

poem, Dickinson turned to rework its penultimate lines, "This sudden legacy / of Green," initially focusing on the word "sudden," before turning her attention to the word "legacy." The first variant stream provoked by her discontent—or only her restlessness—with the word "sudden" includes the choices "bright," "whole," "swift," and "fair"; a second variant stream adds the possibilities "gay," "<u>quick</u>," "fleet," and its rhyming companion, "sweet"; and in a third variant stream, Dickinson returns once more to weigh the word "whole" in the line's balance. The initial impulse for the second variant stream appears to arise during Dickinson's immersion in the first variant stream. Here, the word "Apocalypse" presents itself as an alternative for "legacy," a change perhaps compelled by the earlier change from the two-syllable word "sudden" to the eight, single-syllable variants proposed to replace it. Abandoning, at least momentarily, the lines "This sudden legacy / of Green," Dickinson begins anew on the verso with the lines, "This whole Apocalypse / of Green – ," then generates four additional candidates for "Apocalypse": "Experience – ," "Astonishment – ," "Periphery – ," and "<u>Experiment</u>." A last alternative, "wild Experiment," is proposed in the final, indented line, presumably an alternate for the phrase "whole Apocalypse."

In this case, two other manuscripts of the poem, both fair copies resolved in identical ways and assigned to the year 1875, are extant: Susan Gilbert Dickinson received one, and Elizabeth Holland the other. Yet it would be misleading to use these gift-poems as templates for deciphering Dickinson's final intentions regarding the wording and form of "A little madness." Nowhere among Dickinson's own papers do we discover a resolved copy of the poem; instead, only the worksheet appears to have been saved, a sign, perhaps, that it is not always the pristine copy Dickinson most prizes, but, instead, the anarchic draft, with its summons to continue to seek the poem's ideal form.[10]

The future state of a poem does not necessarily disclose its past forms, its multiple or subtle transformations: the transcriber must be willing to perceive what appears before her on the page without the dubious gift of an interpretative "second sight." And even so the most rigorous transcription of the unseen processes of composition will always stand as a proposal only, a belated and imperfect witness. In some cases, moreover, there will be blind spots, things the transcriber cannot fully interpret. On this manuscript, for example, the meaning of the graphic marks partly enclosing

---

10. Ralph W. Franklin's account of Dickinson's relationship to her work and of the different states of her manuscripts is essential to an understanding of her archive. Franklin speculates that Dickinson engaged in a "major stocktaking [of her poems] in 1858," or in the "silent" years preceding the fascicles. At this time, she may have sorted through the poems of the pre-fascicle years, saving a few and destroying many more. When Dickinson began copying and binding work into fascicles, Franklin believes, she habitually destroyed earlier working drafts. Among these drafts were both initial drafts, generally executed quickly, and what Franklin calls "intermediate" copies, very few copies of which survive. Later, Franklin maintains, after Dickinson ceased binding her work into fascicles, what most often survives are second or later drafts. While Franklin's account is detailed and nuanced, I would add that many of these second or later drafts frequently exhibit as many features of the worksheets as of the fair copies. See Franklin's "Introduction" to *The Poems of Emily Dickinson*, Variorum Edition, 1–43.

"gay" and surrounding "Green" certainly signified something to Dickinson during the drafting process, but that private meaning is still lost to us. Other details, at first more apparently recognizable, turn out to be ambiguous: Is Dickinson underlining "quick" or canceling "whole"? Most importantly, perhaps, there are different possible renderings of these lines depending on whether one views Dickinson's experiments as variants or addenda.

$\approx$

It would be disingenuous to propose that these issues of temporality and utility are entirely the province of scholarly approaches to Dickinson's works. Beneath all these questions rumbles the critical machinery of scholarly editing and its strict separation of an author's "definitive work" and a critical apparatus that assigns all other words and forms to a "secondary" status (i.e., scribal or authorial variants worthy of note but not as part of the form of the work that the editor has determined to be "final"). This either/or paradigm can be anathema to writers whose experimentations were never finalized, at least in a way that is indicated in their papers and texts. Certainly Dickinson's penchant for allowing multiple and perhaps simultaneous experiments to co-exist and to "pile up" as lexical investigations of the poetic moment, potentially extended across decades and multiple versions, defies the conventional mechanics of the critical edition.

In the end, the transcriber's rendering of a manuscript, while influenced by scholarly tradition, must also be intuitive and may also be changeful. At the same time, the irregularities exhibited in different transcriptions of Dickinson's manuscripts are not necessarily errors to be eradicated, but evidence of the unique—and living— transaction between a transcriber-reader and the poet at a particular moment in time. Thoughtful differences among transcriptions, with transparent explanations of criteria, perhaps somewhat paradoxically affirm the singular beauty of the original artifacts in all their vulnerability and mystery—artifacts that, for Dickinson, were solitary fields of experimentation that would become surfaces of dialogue between the space and time of the very tangible process of her poetic expression.

A Note on the Transcriptions

The following pages present transcriptions prepared by Marta Werner for inclusion in this volume, as well as for the use of readers and scholars everywhere. They are held in copyright by the Trustees of Amherst College, but are made available on an open access basis for the use of researchers, scholars, and students. (For more information on this license, see the copyright page.)

The transcriptions were originally composed in Microsoft Word and then re-formatted in Adobe InDesign. While the Word transcriptions offered a view of the text only, the InDesign transcriptions provide the opportunity for readers to visualize the text in relation to the writing canvas—e.g., the leaf or part-leaf, the bifolium (one sheet folded to make two leaves or four writing surfaces)—and to reconstruct how she utilized her writing materials. For example, readers may notice Dickinson's occasionally profligate use of paper when she copies a brief poem for a recipient onto the recto of a bifolium sheet and then leaves the three remaining writing surfaces blank. Other patterns of paper use—e.g., Dickinson's common practice of composing fair-copy letters only on the rectos of bifolium sheets, or her use, especially in her drafts, of the verso of a leaf to experiment with variants and addenda—may also be made more visible and complement our more developed understanding of her patterns of paper use in the fascicles. Here, a few conventions will help to clarify the views presented in the transcriptions.

- Frames are added to texts composed on single leaves, especially when the borders of the document help to indicate scale (e.g. AC 357, AC 214) or when the borders significantly influence the disposition of the text over the writing surface (e.g., AC 450, AC 868).
- One exception is made to this general directive: texts composed on both sides of a single leaf, part-leaf, or fragment are unframed, though a vertical line separates the obverse (front) and the reverse (back).

- Texts composed on bifolium sheets are framed and the bifolium sheets are displayed as open spreads, with the association of leaves marked in brackets (e.g., [1r]=first recto of a page, or folded sheet; [1v]=first verso of a page, or folded sheet, etc.])

- Fascicle sheets are identified by their place in a given fascicle (e.g., the designation [5r] would mean the recto of the fifth bound page.)

- Disjunct leaves that were once conjunct are indicated by double vertical lines indicating the lost adjoining writing surfaces.

While the external and internal borders of Dickinson's manuscripts often resonate in compelling ways with the texts composed within them, the frames here are used only to indicate the relations of sheets, leaves, and partial sheets or fragments in a given document.

Because any author's handwriting is distinctive—and Dickinson's particularly so—there are necessarily choices that must be made in rendering an author's writing into a clear transcript. As Susan Howe says, in the rendering of transcriptions "there is no solution."[1] The purpose here is to yield in clear type what appears on Dickinson's manuscript pages. That means, inevitably, that the fluid spacing and dynamic flow of her handwriting is necessarily hidden by the uniformity of a typeset page. As a general rule, the designers have sought to render the transcripts plainly as left-justified lines of text. However, in cases in which the specific landscape of the paper that bears the handwritten lines seems important to convey to the reader, an indication has been given of how the shape of the page interacts with the lines of Dickinson's hand. In a few cases, where the visual elements of a manuscript are significant to understanding the work itself, the designers have sought to represent as well as possible in type the interplay of the author's hand and the graphic signifiers of her working process.

The transcriptions presented here are limited to those works written by Dickinson in her own hand, as included in the exhibit. We do not present here transcriptions of works by other hands that also appear. Similarly, with only one exception, markings on Dickinson's manuscripts made by diverse hands—the hands of her interlocutors and editors—are not recorded in the transcriptions. The exception is AC 833 (p. 177ff), where we have shown the work of an unknown transcriber working, at fairly close proximity in time to Dickinson's writing of the manuscript, to reshape Dickinson's poetry along more conventional lines. The point of this illustration is to show the immediacy with which her singular voice was recognized—yet required to conform to contemporary literary tastes.

Most of the works presented here are held by the Archives and Special Collections of Amherst College, and are indicated with Amherst's indexing system (for example, "AC 80"). Materials held in other collections are indicated with the call number assigned to them by those institutions.

---

1. See Susan Howe and Marta Werner, "Transcription and Transgression," above at 130.

Transcriptions of the Manuscripts

<table>
<tr><td>

William A Dickinson

per Mr. Baker

</td><td>

Monday AM

Dear brother Austin

As Mr Baker was going directly to where you are I thought I would write a line to inform you that if it is pleasant day after to morrow we are all coming over to see you, but you must not think too much of our coming as it may rain and spoil all our plans. however if it is not pleasant so that we do not come over

</td></tr>
<tr><td>[2v]</td><td>[1r]</td></tr>
</table>

<table>
<tr><td>

Father says that you may come home on Saturday, and if we do not come he will make some arrangement for you to come and write you what it is.
I attend Singing School. Mr. Woodman has a very fine one Sunday evenings and has quite a large school. I presume you will want to go when you return home. We had a very severe frost here last night and the ground was froz en-hard. We all had our noses nipped a little. The Ladys Society meets at our house tomorrow and I expect we shall have a very pleasant meeting If you was at home it

</td><td>

would be perfectly sure. we wish much to hear from you, and if you have time I wish you would write a line and send by Mr. Baker.
Mother wishes if your stockings are any of them thin, that you should do them up in a little bundle & send them by Mr Baker. Accept much love from us all.

your affectionate sister E

If we don't come Wednesday, we may Thursday if not father will write you.

</td></tr>
<tr><td>[1v]</td><td>[2r]</td></tr>
</table>

Cat. 1.07 | AC550

Autumn 1844. Letter composed in pencil by Dickinson to Austin Dickinson on two leaves (l = 12.3 x 10 cm) of one sheet of off-white, lightly ruled paper folded vertically in half and then horizontally into thirds. In lieu of an envelope, Dickinson addressed the letter on the outer fold to "William A Dickinson / per Mr. Baker." In 1844, Austin Dickinson was pursuing studies in Classics at Williston Seminary, in Easthampton, Massachusetts. Although a penciled note on letter reads, "Probably sent to Easthampton – 1845," Thomas H. Johnson dates the letter earlier based largely on Dickinson's internal reference to the frozen ground. This letter, though neatly executed, exhibits the irregular punctuation and capitalization typical of Dickinson's letters from this early period.

[2v]

Austin Dickinson, Esq.
Amherst.
Mass.

[1r]

tell Father . I am obliged to him much . for his offers of "pecuniary" assistance, but do not need any – We are furnished with an account-book, here & obliged to put down every nickel, which we spend & what we spend it for & show it to Miss. Whitman every Saturday, so you perceive your sister is learning to keep accounts in addition to the other branches of her education. I am getting along nicely in my studies and am happy – quite for me. Wont you ask Father for Aunt Elisabeth's address & give it to me when you write me for I wish to write her & dont know to whose care to send it.

Tuesday noon

My dear Brother . Austin .

I have this moment finished my recitation in History & have a few minutes, which I shall occupy in answering your short, but welcome letter. You probably heard that I was alive & well – yesterday, unless, Mr. E. Dickinson was robbed of a note, whose contents were to that effect. But as robbers are not very plenty now a days, I will have no forebodings on that score, for the present. How you! do you get along without me, now & does "it seem any more like a funeral," than it did before your visit to your <u>humble</u> <u>servant</u> in this place? Answer me!!! I want much to see you all at home & expect to 3. weeks from tomorrow, if nothing unusual, like a famine or pestilence, occurs to prevent my going home. I am anticipating much in seeing you on this week Saturday & you had better not dissappoint me!! for if you do, I will harness the "furies" & pursue you with a "whip of scorpions," which is even worse you will find, than the "long oat" which you may remember. Have you heard from Sarah Pynchen lately & have you found out "those particular reasons" which prevent her corresponding with me, much to her sorrow &

Cat. 2.08 | AC552

November 2, 1847. Letter composed in ink by Dickinson to Austin Dickinson on two leaves (l = 20 x 15.7 cm) of a folded sheet of wove, blue-gray stationery. In 1847, Dickinson was studying at Mary Lyon's Mount Holyoke Female Seminary, in South Hadley, Mass.; she addressed the letter herself, on the fold: "Austin Dickinson, Esq. / Amherst. / Mass." The elaborate folding patterns—the document was folded vertically in thirds, then horizontally in quarters—may have guaranteed the privacy of a letter sent without an envelope. To avoid using a second sheet of paper, Dickinson engaged in a modified form of cross-writing, and the end of her letter appears on the initial page, perpendicular to and partly crossing the text of the opening of the letter. A "Bill of Fare" from the South Hadley Seminary, copied on a separate sheet, is enclosed with this letter.

my inexpressible regret, for having few letters to write, now I am away from home, it would be a pleasant method of employing my leisure time & keep my mind from vain & foolish thoughts in the leisure time before mentioned. How long is Mary . Warner - to be absent from home? I received a long letter from her a few days since & sent her a letter directed to Medford . to day.

I hear often from Abby . & think she has not forgotten me, though absent. She is now my debtor to the amount of one long letter & I wish you would inform her, if you have an opportunity, that I am anxiously waiting to receive it. I received a letter last eve, of an amusing nature & signed by the writer as "John Klima." I read it, but as I found the postage was 10. cts. I concluded it was not intended for me & sent it back to the office. The postmark . was so faint that I could not decipher it & I have not a little curiosity respecting it. If you can give me any clue to the mystery, I will be obliged to you, in due proportion to the amount of information which you are able to give me. How do the plants look now & are they as flourishing as before I went away? I wish much to see them. Some of the girls here, have plants, but it is a cold place & I am very glad that I did not bring any, as I thought of doing.

A young lady by the name of Beach . left here for home this morning. She could not get through her examinations & was very wild beside. Miss Lyon . said she should write her father, if she did not change her course & as she did not, her father came for her last night — He was an interesting man & seemed to feel very badly that his daughter should be obliged to leave, on account of bad conduct.

Perhaps you saw an account some time since, of a carriage, being presented to Henry Clay, by a Mr. Beach. It was the self same. Why dont Sarah Thompson's brother come once to see her, if he has one spark of affection for her? Please tell him, she is very anxious to see him & will not receive him if he dont come soon. You must tell mother that I was delighted to see her hand-writing once more, but that she need not put herself out to write me, for I know just how much she has to do & on that account do not expect to see letters from her very often. Please tell Viny, that if she has any time from the cares of her household, to write a line to me, that I would receive it with all due deference to her age & majesty & honors. I suppose "Cook" occupies most of her time & will therefore excuse her long delay for the past, but not for the future. Cousin Emily. had a letter from Grandmother . . last night and she mentioned in her letter, that Mrs Coleman & Eliza were daily expected in Monson & would probably spend some time at Aunt Flynt's. It seems impossible to me that Mrs - Frink . is dead. How is Jacob . Holt . now? I have not heard a word form him since you were here & feel quite anxious to know how he is. Give much love to him & tell him I will write him as soon as I can find a spare moment for it. Are Thompson . & Newton . going away before I come home?

Give much love to Father . Mother . Viny & Abby, also thank Abby for her note & tell her I consider it only a type of what is forthcoming. Do write a long letter to

Your aff sister . Emily .

<table>
<tr><td>[1v]</td><td>[2r]</td></tr>
</table>

I am really at Mt Holyoke Seminary & this is to be my home for a long year. Your affectionate letter was joyfully received & I wish that this might make you as happy as your's did me. It has been nearly six weeks since I left home & that is a longer time, than I was ever away from home before now. I was very homesick for a few days & it seemed to me I could not live here. But I am now contented & quite happy, if I can be happy when absent from my dear home & friends. You may laugh at the idea, that I cannot be happy when away from home, but you must remember that I have a very dear home & that this is my first trial in the way of absence for any length of time in my life. As you desire it, I will give you a full account of myself since I first left the paternal roof. I came to S. Hadley six weeks ago next Thursday. I was much fatigued with the ride & had a severe cold besides, which prevented me from commencing my examinations until the next day, when I began. I finished them in three days & found them about what I had anticipated, though the old scholars say they are more strict than they ever have been before. As you can easily imagine, I was much delighted to finish without failures & I came to the conclusion then, that I should not be at all homesick, but the reaction left me as homesick a girl as it is not usual to see. I am now quite contented & am very much occupied now in reviewing the Junior studies, as I wish to enter the middle class. The school is very large & though quite a number have left, on account of finding the examinations more difficult than they anticipated, yet

[2v]   [1r]

Cat. 2.09 | Mount Holyoke College Archives and Special Collections

Mt. Holyoke College, November 6, 1847. A letter composed in ink from Dickinson to Abiah Root on two leaves (l = 25.5 x 19.8 cm) of a folded sheet of wove, light blue stationery possibly embossed "E" in the upper left corner. The letter begins a third of the way down the opening leaf and continues on pages 2 and 3. Dickinson then turned the first page 90 degrees and concluded the letter in the upper margin of page 1. A modified form of cross-writing appears on this leaf. The letter was folded into thirds and folded into thirds again to create a packet and sealed with a forest green circular wafer marked "D," about 2/3 of which is still extant. On a panel of the letter-packet, Dickinson added the address, "Miss. Abiah. P. Root. / Care of Miss: Mary. Campbell. / Springfield. / Mass.~". A South Hadley postmark (date not recoverable) remains visible. Another hand, probably Abiah's, has written "Mrs. A. P. Strong" in blue ink diagonally across the upper third of the address panel. Much later, the same hand turned the address panel 90 degrees to the left and wrote in pencil, subsequently erased, "Nov. 6, / My letter, tells / about So. Hadley / Keep." Outside the address panel, several other markings, in another hand, are visible. Numerous tiny (here unrepresented) pointings appear throughout the letter where Dickinson apparently rested her pen.

there are nearly 300. now. Perhaps you know that Miss. Lyon is raising her standard of scholarship a good deal, on account of the number of applicants this year & on account of that she makes the examinations more severe than usual. You cannot imagine how trying they are, because if we cannot go through them all in a specified time, we are sent home. ^again I cannot be too thankful that I got through as soon as I did, & I am sure that I never would endure the suspense which I endured during those three days for all the treasures of the world. I room with my Cousin Emily, who is a Senior. She is an excellent room-mate & does all in her power to make me happy. You can imagine how pleasant a good room-mate is, for you have been away to school so much. Everything is pleasant & happy here & I think I could be no happier at any other school away from home. Things seem much more like home than I anticipated & the teachers are all very kind & affectionate to us. They call on us frequently & urge us to return their calls & when we do, we always receive a cordial welcome from them. I will tell you my order of time for the day, as you were so kind as to give me your's. At 6. oclock, we all rise. We breakfast at 7. Our study hours begin at 8. At 9. we all meet in Seminary Hall, for devotions. At 10 ¼. I recite a review of Ancient History, in connection with which we read Goldsmith & Grimshaw. At .11. I recite a lesson in "Pope's Essay on Man" which is merely transposition. At .12. I practice Calisthenics & at 12 ¼ read until dinner, which is at 12 ½ & after dinner, from 1 ½ until 2 . I sing in Seminary Hall. From 2 ¾ until 3 ¾ . I practise upon the Piano. At 3 ¾ I go to Sections, where we give in all our accounts for the day, including, Absence – Tardiness – Communications – Breaking Silent Study hours – Receiving Company in our rooms & ten thousand other things, which I will not take time or place to mention. At 4 ½ . we go into Seminary Hall, & receive advice from Miss. Lyon in the form of a lecture. We have Supper at 6. & silent-study hours from then until the retiring bell, which rings at 8 ¾, but the tardy bell does not ring until 9 ¾, so that we dont often obey the first warning to retire. Unless we have a good & reasonable excuse for failure upon any of the items, that

I mentioned above, they are recorded & a <u>black</u> <u>mark</u> stands against our names: As you can easily imagine, we do not like very well to get "exceptions" as they are called scientifically here. My domestic work is not difficult & consists in carrying the Knives from the 1st tier of tables at morning & noon & at night washing & wiping the same quantity of Knives. I am quite well & hope to be able to spend the year here, free from sickness. You have probably heard many reports of the food here & if so I can tell you, that I have yet seen nothing corresponding to my ideas on that point from what I have heard. Everything is wholesome & abundant & much nicer than I should imagine could be provided for almost 300. girls. We have also a great variety upon our tables & frequent changes. One thing is certain & that is, that Miss. Lyon, & all the teachers, seem to consult our comfort & happiness in everything they do & you know that is pleasant. When I left home, I did not think I should find a companion or a dear friend in all the multitude. I expected to find rough & uncultivated manners, & to be sure, I have found some of that stamp, but on the whole, there is an ease & grace a desire to make one another happy, which delights & at the same time, surprises me very much. I find no Abby. or Abiah. or Mary. but I love many of the girls. Austin came to see me when I had been here about two weeks & brought Viny . & Abby. I need not tell you how delighted I was to see them all, nor how happy it made me to hear them say that "they were <u>so</u> <u>lonely</u>." It is a sweet feeling to know that you are missed & that your memory is precious at home. This week, on Wednesday, I was at my window, when I happened to look towards the hotel & saw Father & Mother, walking over here as dignified as you please. I need not tell you that I danced & clapped my hands, & flew to meet them for you can imagine how I felt. I will only ask you do you love your parents? They wanted to surprise me & for that reason did not let me know they were coming. I could not bear to have them go, but go they must & so I submitted in sadness. Only to think Abiah, that in 2 ½ weeks I shall be at my own dear home again. You will probably go home at Thanksgiving time & we can rejoice with each other.

Early 1850. Letter composed in ink by Dickinson to Emily Ellsworth
Fowler. To create this letter, Dickinson took a sheet of wove, light
blue wove stationery and tore out a portion (8.8 x 17.5 cm) from one
corner. She then folded the torn portion into an almost perfect square
of two leaves (l=8.8 x 8.7 cm). Upon finishing the letter, Dickinson
then folded it in half by turning the upper half down and addressed it
(upside down to the text of the letter), "Miss Emily E Fowler. / Austin."
Dickinson then flipped it again vertically and folded the right corner
down.

Austin.

Miss Emily E. Fowler.

~ ~

    I wanted to write, and just tell you
that <u>me</u> and <u>my spirit</u> were fighting
this morning. It is'nt known generally, and
you mustn't tell anybody.
I dreamed about you last night, and waked
up putting my shawl, and hood on to go and
see you, but this wicked snow-storm looked in

[2v]   [1r]

at my window, and told me I could'nt.
I hope God will forgive me, but I am very
unwilling to have it storm – he is mer-
ciful to the sinning, is'nt he?
I cannot wait to be with you – Oh ugly
time, and space, and uglier snow-storm
than all! Were you happy in Northampton?
I was very lonely without you, and wanted
to write you a letter <u>many</u> times, but Kate
was there too, and I was afraid you would
both laugh. I should be stronger if I could

[1v]

see you oftener – I am very puny alone.
You make me so happy, and glad, life seems
worth living for, no mater for all the trials.
When I see you I shall tell you more – for
I know you are busy this morning.
That is'nt an <u>empty</u> blank where I began –
It is so full of affection that you cant
See any – that's all. Will you love, and
remember me when you have time from
 worthier ones? God keep you till I have seen
you again! Very earnestly yrs – Emily.

[2r]

About 1876. Poem draft, with variants or addenda, composed by Dickinson in pencil on the verso of one leaf (l = 15.9 x 10.1 cm) of wove, cream stationery embossed BATH in a decorative surround. No other manuscript of this poem is known to be extant. On the recto of this leaf is an 1850 invitation from George Gould to a candy pulling. The original invitation was folded horizontally in half; sometime after that, the document was folded one more time, again horizontally. In the poem draft, the "b" of "booming" appears to have been reformed or written over another letter. The dashes in the text appear more like downward trending slashes. Stanza breaks may or may not be indicated by the spacing of the text.

I   suppose   the   time   will
come
Aid   it   in   the   coming
When   the   Bird   will   crowd
the Tree
And   the   Bee   be   **b**ooming   –

I   suppose   the   time   will
come
Hinder   it   a   little
When   the   Corn   in   Silk
will   dress   Gilt
And   in   Chintz   the
Apple   Red   –   Pink   –

I   believe   the   Day   will
be
When   the   Jay   will
  giggle
  At   his   new   white
  House   the   Earth
That,   too,   halt   a
little –

[Reverse]

Spring 1858. Letter draft composed in ink by Dickinson to an unidentified recipient ("Master") on two leaves (l = 18.7 x 12.3 cm) of a folded sheet of cream, very lightly blue-ruled stationery. Although the manuscript has been cross-folded as if in preparation for mailing, this copy remained among Dickinson's papers. On the verso of the opening leaf, Dickinson appears to have reformed the second "e" of "indeed." On the second leaf, Dickinson made notes for two potential revisions. Above the passage first formulated as "and /whether the hills will / look as blue as the / Sailors say −", Dickinson wrote "will the," tentatively reimagining the lines to read "and / will the hills / look as blue as the / Sailors say − ." At this juncture the fair copy MS turned into a draft, and several lines later, Dickinson made a second, more definitive revision, canceling the words "talk," "more," and "now" in favor of "stay," "longer," and "tonight." Thus the line originally reading "I cannot talk any more tonight" is first reimagined as "I cannot stay any longer now," and then as "I cannot stay any longer tonight."

[2v]

tell me, please to tell
me, soon as you are
well −

[1r]

Dear Master

    I am ill −
but grieving more
that you are ill, I
make my stronger hand
work long eno' to tell
you − I thought perhaps
you were in Heaven,
and when you spoke
again, it seemed
quite sweet, and
wonderful, and surprised
me so − I wish that
you were well.
I would that all I

[1v]

love, should be weak no
more. The Violets are
by my side − the Robin
very near − and "Spring" −
they say, Who is she −
going by the door −
Indeed it is God's house −
and these are gates
of Heaven, and to
and fro, the angels
go, with their sweet
postilions − I wish that
I were great, like Mr −
Michael Angelo, and
could paint for you.
You ask me what
my flowers said −
then they were
disobedient − I gave
them messages −

[2r]

They said what the
lips in the West, say,
when the sun goes
down, and so says
the Dawn −
Listen again, Master −
I did not tell you that
today had been the
Sabbath Day.
Each Sabbath on the
Sea, makes me count
the Sabbaths, till we
          will the
meet on shore − and
whether the hills will
look as blue as the
Sailors say −
         stay longer
I cannot ~~talk~~ any ~~more~~
~~now~~
tonight, for this pain
denies me −
How strong when weak
to recollect, and easy
quite, to love. Will you

---

156   **The Networked Recluse**

I   kissed   the   little
blank   —   you   made   it
on   the   second   page
you   may   have   for
gotten —
I   will   not   wash
my   arm   —   +   the   one
you   gave   the   scarf   —
it   is   brown   as   an
Almond   —   'twill   take
      your   touch   away —

I   try   to   think   when
I   wake in   the   night
what   the   chapter
would   be   for   the
chapter   would   be
in   the night
would 'nt it   —   but
    I   can not   decide —
It   is   strange   that
I   miss   you   at   night
so much when
I was never with
you — but the
punctual love
invokes you soon
as my eyes are
shut — and I
wake warm with
the want sleep
  had almost filled —
I dreamed last
week that you
had died — and
one had carved
a statue of you
and I was asked
to unvail it —
and I said what
I had not done
in Life I would
  not in death

for you tonight now

[Obverse]

when   your   loved
eyes   could   not
forgive —
The   length   of   the
hour was beautiful —
The   length   of   the
heavenly   hour
how   sweetly   you
counted   it
The   numerals   of
Eden   do not
oppress   the   student
long   our   Eden
ebbs   away   to   di
viner   Edens   —
Therefore   Love   is
  so
speechless —
seem to   withhold
Darling
I   never   seemed
toward you
Lest I   had   been
too   frank   was
often   my   fear —
How could   I   long
to   give   who never
saw   your   natures
  Face —

[Reverse]

Cat. 2.17 | AC 753

About 1880. Letter draft composed in pencil by Dickinson to Otis P. Lord on a partial sheet of laid, cream, blue-ruled stationery measuring 25 x 10.3 cm and folded horizontally in quarters. Dickinson's writing is composed against the rule of the paper. Along the torn left edge of the draft, and partly cut off, it is possible to make out the following words: "… [illegible] for you tonight now [illegible]." Although large parts of the draft appear to have been cancelled, the vertical cancellation marks are far apart, allowing Dickinson to see the text behind them. If she made a copy of the draft, she may have been canceling drafts of passages used in the fair copy. This manuscript was found among Dickinson's papers after her death.

Cat. 2.19 | MA 1488

About 1860. Poem composed or copied by Dickinson in pencil on the recto of one leaf (l = 18.5 x 12.3 cm) of a folded sheet of cream stationery embossed with a cornucopia or horn (?) in a decorative surround. The remaining three writing canvases are blank. The manuscript was folded horizontally into thirds and sent to Susan Gilbert Dickinson. A variant version of the poem was copied into Fascicle 8 around the same time, where it appears on the fascicle's opening sheet following the poem "A <u>Wounded</u> Deer – leaps highest –" and preceding the final poem on the sheet, "I met a King this afternoon!"

[2v]   [1r]

[1v]   [2r]

Cat. 2.20 | MA 1641

About early 1864. Poem composed or copied in ink by Dickinson on a partial leaf (12.6 x 11.3 cm) of wove, white note-paper. Dickinson appears to have turned the leaf 90 degrees just before composing the text. The fold in the sheet, now appearing as a horizontal, rather than a vertical fold, thus serves to "close" the manuscript in preparation for sending to Susan Gilbert Dickinson. The punctuation in the final line is ambiguous, as Dickinson seems to have added both an angled dash and a period, perhaps indicating an exclamation point (as transcribed here). A second, variant copy of this poem was bound into Fascicle 38 around the same time; it is the final poem on the leaf containing three other poems: "It was a Grave – yet / bore no Stone – ," "She staked Her Feathers – ," and "Despair's advantage is / achieved."

The sun kept stooping – stooping – low –
The Hills to meet him – rose –
On his part – what Transaction!
On their part – what Repose!

Deeper and deeper grew the stain
Opon the window pane –
Thicker and thicker stood the feet
Until the Tyrian.

Was Crowded dense with Armies –
So gay – so Brigadier –
That <u>I</u> felt martial stirrings –
Who once the Cockade wore –

Charged – from my Chimney Corner –
But nobody was there!

Emily –

[2v]   [1r]

Two – were immortal –
twice –
The privilege of few –
Eternity – obtained – in
Time –
Reversed – Divinity –
That Our ignoble
Eyes
The   Quality   perceive
Of   Paradise   Superlative –
Thro' Their – Comparative !

[Obverse]

Distance – is not
the Realm of Fox
Nor by Relay of
Bird
Abated – Distance is
Until thyself, Beloved.
        Emily –

[2v]   [1r]

Cat. 2.21 | MA 1357

About 1866. Poem composed or copied by Dickinson in pencil on the recto of one leaf (l = 15.5 x 9.9 cm) of a folded sheet of wove, cream stationery embossed PARIS in a decorative surround. The remaining three writing canvases are blank. The manuscript, folded horizontally into thirds, was sent to Susan Gilbert Dickinson. No record copy of the poem is extant, compelling us to wonder if Dickinson sent away her only text of the poem.

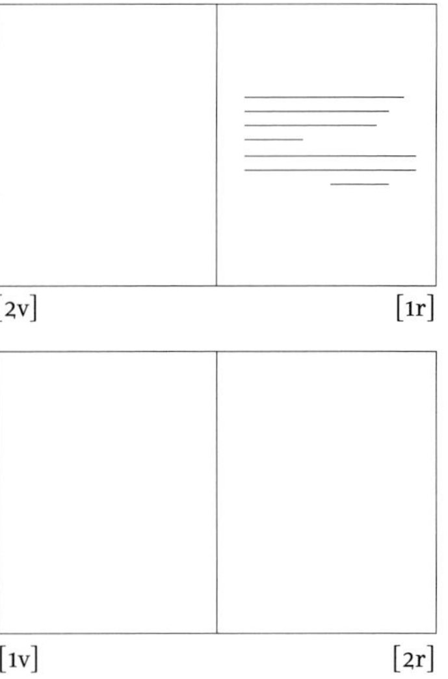

[2v]   [1r]

[1v]   [2r]

Dear Girls –
        I hope you
are having superb
times, and am
sure you are,
for I hear your
voices – mad and
sweet – as a Mob
of Bobolinks –
I send you my
love – which is
always new for
Rascals like you,
and ask instead
a little apartment
in your Pink Hearts –

call it Endor's
    Closet –
If ever the World
should frown on
you – he is old –
you know – give
him a Kiss, and
that will disarm
him – if it dont –
tell him from me,
Who has not found
the Heaven – below –
Will fail of it above –
For Angels rent
the House next our's,
Wherever we remove –
    Lovingly, Emily –

[Obverse]   [Reverse]

Cat. 2.22 | MA 1556

About 1883. Letter composed in pencil by Dickinson to her niece, Martha Dickinson, and Martha's friend, Sally Jenkins, on two formerly conjunct leaves (l = 20.3 x 12.6 cm) of one sheet of wove, off-white stationery watermarked WESTON'S LINEN 1876 and folded horizontally into thirds in preparation for mailing. When the leaves were conjunct, the text of the letter would have appeared on the recto of the opening leaf and the recto of the second leaf. The final six lines of the letter comprise a poem, Dickinson's record copy of which has not survived, if indeed one ever existed.

Cat. 2.23 | AC 814

About 1864. Poem composed or copied by Dickinson in ink on two leaves (l = 15.1 x 10 cm) of a folded sheet of cream, wove stationery embossed PARIS in a decorative surround. Signed "Emily," the manuscript was folded in uneven quarters to fit into an envelope and sent to Josiah and Elizabeth Holland. Between 1864 and 1873, Dickinson seems to have returned to a record copy of the poem, now missing or no longer extant, on several occasions, generating at least four other variant copies: one, produced in 1866, was sent to Susan Gilbert Dickinson; another, revised in 1873, remained among Dickinson's papers; still another (now lost) was sent to T. W. Higginson also in 1873; and one, composed in 1883, was enclosed in a letter to Thomas Niles. The copy to Niles is also featured in this exhibit (see Cat. 5.11, AC 833).

<table>
<tr><td>

That held the
Dams – had parted
hold –
The Waters Wrecked
the Sky –
But overlooked
my Father's House –
Just quartering
a Tree –

      Emily –

</td><td>

The Wind begun
to knead the
Grass –
As Women do a
Dough –
He flung a
Hand full at the
Plain –
A Hand full at
the Sky –
The Leaves unhooked

</td></tr>
<tr><td>[2v]</td><td>[1r]</td></tr>
</table>

<table>
<tr><td>

themselves from Trees –
And started all
abroad –
The Dust did
scoop itself like
Hands –
And throw away
the Road –
The Wagons quick-
ened on the Street –
The Thunders gossiped
low –

</td><td>

The Lightning showed
a Yellow Head –
And then a livid
Toe –
The Birds put up
the Bars to Nests –
The Cattle flung
to Barns –
Then came one
drop of Giant Rain –
And then, as if
the Hands

</td></tr>
<tr><td>[1v]</td><td>[2r]</td></tr>
</table>

[2v]

The Day undressed –
Herself –
Her Garter – was of
Gold –
Her Petticoat – of
Purple plain –
Her Dimities – as old

Exactly – as the
World –
And yet the newest
Star –

[1r]

[1v]

Enrolled opon the
Hemisphere
Be wrinkled – much
as Her –
Too near to God –
to pray –
Too near to Heaven –
to fear –
The Lady of the
Occident
Retired without a
care –

[2r]

Her Candle so
expire
The flickering be seen
On Ball of Mast
in Bosporus –
And Dome –
and Window Pane –

Emily –

Cat. 2.25 | AC 813

About 1862. Poem composed or copied in ink by Dickinson on two leaves (l = 15.1 x 10 cm) of a folded sheet of wove, cream stationery embossed PARIS in a decorative surround. The manuscript has been folded into uneven quarters to fit into an envelope. Not formally addressed, but signed, this poem was sent to Josiah and Elizabeth Holland. A triangular cut appears at the top-center of both leaves. One other manuscript carrying a variant copy of the poem was bound into Fascicle 23 at around the same time; in this context, it is the opening poem of the sixth and final sheet of the fascicle and shares the sheet with three other poems: "The Beggar Lad – dies early – ," "One and One – are One – ," and "I lived on Dread – ."

Cat. 2.26 | Houghton MS 1118.2 (17a)

About spring 1859. Poem composed or copied in ink by Dickinson on one leaf (l = 16 x 10.1 cm) of a folded sheet of wove, cream paper embossed PARIS in a decorative surround. The remaining three writing canvases are blank. Dickinson affixed a rose bud to the leaf with a piece of green ribbon threaded through document. Signed and folded to fit into an envelope, the poem was sent to Elizabeth Holland. At some point before the document reached the Houghton Library, the rosebud fell off and was reattached with pressure-sensitive tape. A variant copy of this poem was bound into Fascicle 2 around the same time; it is the final poem of the fascicle.

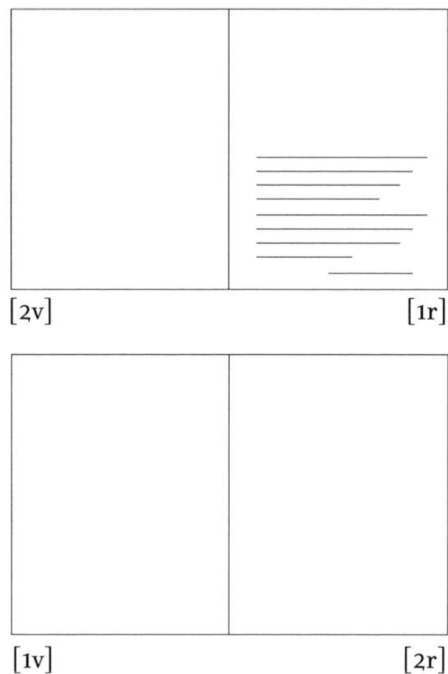

[2v] [1r]

[1v] [2r]

Baffled for just a day or two –
Embarrassed – not afraid –
Encounter in my garden
An unexpected Maid!
She beckons, and the Woods start –
She nods, and all begin –
Surely – such a country
I was never in!

Emilie

[1r]

Cat. 3.05 | AC 793

About December 1849. An early message composed in ink by Dickinson to Elbridge G. Bowdoin on one leaf (l = 15.8 x 10 cm) of a folded sheet of wove, cream paper possibly embossed with a wreath. Dickinson folded the manuscript horizontally into thirds and addressed the message on the outer fold: "Mr. Bowdoin." Two penciled notes by Bowdoin—"Miss E Dickinson, Dec 49" and "on returning *Jane Eyre* – The leaves mentioned were Box Leaves, sent to me in a little Bouquet"— confirm both the date and the occasion.

Mr. Bowdoin.

Mr. Bowdoin.

    If all these leaves were altars, and on every one a prayer that Currer Bell might be saved – and you were God – would you answer it?

[2v] [1r]

Dear friend –
No "Sonnet"
had George Eliot –
The sweet
Acclamation of
Death is forever
bounded –
There is no
Trumpet like
the Tomb –
The Immortality
she gave,
We borrowed
at her Grave –
For just one
Plaudit famishing –

[2v]

[1r]

Cat. 3.06 | AC 810

Undated; Probably late April 1886. Letter draft composed in pencil by Dickinson to Thomas Wentworth Higginson on two leaves (l = 25 x 13 cm) of a folded sheet of laid, cream stationery bearing the watermark Pure Irish Linen F. H. D. & Co. This unsigned draft remained with Dickinson's papers, perhaps because it is incomplete, or perhaps because it contained the only record copy (variant in punctuation and capitalization) of the poem "The Immortality / she gave" mailed to T. W. Higginson in the final draft of the letter.

The might of
Human Love –

Beautiful as
it is it's
criminal shortness
maims it –

[1v]

[2r]

Cat. 3.07 | AC 129

About 1870. Poem draft, with addenda, variants, and corrections, composed by Dickinson in pencil on both sides of one leaf (17.8 x 11.2 cm) of wove, off-white, faintly blue-ruled stationery embossed with a right-facing head, possibly representing Athena, in full profile. The manuscript has been folded horizontally into thirds. No other manuscript of the poem is known to be extant. Before composing the poem draft, Dickinson affixed a three-cent stamp (1869 issue) and two clippings from *Harper's Magazine* (May 1870) to the paper: the name "George Sand" and the title of Sand's novel "Mauprat." Here, variants and addenda seem to have occurred to Dickinson during the initial drafting process.

Alone and in a Circumstance
    of
Reluctant to be told
A Spider on my reticence
Assiduously   crawled
  deliberately
  determinately
  impertinently
And so much more at
Home than   I
Immediately   grew
I   felt   myself a
       the
visitor
And hurriedly withdrew –
  hastily

Revisiting my late abode
with Articles of Claim
I found it quietly assumed
as a Gymnasium
for
where Tax asleep and
Title off
    peasants
The inmates of the Air
Perpetual presumption took
  complacence

       lawful
As each were special
      only
Heir –
A If any strike me on
the street
I can return the Blow,
If any take my property
  seize
According to the Law
The Statute is my Learned
friend
But what redress can be
      nor
For an offence not here
      anywhere
nor e there
So not in   Equity –
That Larceny of time
and mind
The marrow of the
Day
By spider, or forbid
it Lord
That I should specify –

[Obverse]   [Reverse]

Cat. 3.08 | AC 851

Last decade. Lines, with variants, composed in pencil by Dickinson on a remnant (16.9 x 11 cm) of brown wrapping paper. No other manuscript of this draft is known to be extant, although the passage "A something overtakes the Mind –" appears in another brief draft (AC 879) belonging to the same period but reflecting on the effects of Nature, rather than of poetry: "We must Travel / Abreast with / Nature if we / want to know / her, but where / shall be obtained / the Horse – / a something / over takes the / mind – we do / not hear it / coming ."

Did you ever
read one of
her Poems back –
ward, because
the plunge from
the front over –
turned you?
I sometimes
     often have –
      many times have –
A something
overtakes the
Mind –

[Obverse]

Dear friend –
    To the Oriole
you suggested
I add a Humming
Bird and hope
they are not untrue –

A Route of
Evanescence
With a revolving
Wheel
A Resonance of
Emerald
A Rush of
Cochineal

[2v]   [1r]

And every
Blossom on the
Bush
Adjusts it's
tumbled Head –
The Mail from
Tunis, probably,
An easy Morning's
Ride –

[1v]   [2r]

Cat. 3.09 │ AC 816

About 1879. Letter (unsigned) composed in pencil by Dickinson to Helen Hunt Jackson on two leaves (l = 24 x 12.8 cm) of a folded sheet of wove, white or off-white paper folded horizontally into thirds for mailing. "A Route of / Evanescence," inscribed in the body of the letter, is among the few poems Dickinson circulated among a wide range of correspondents: Frances and Louise Norcross (1879, original MS destroyed); Helen Hunt Jackson (1879, left); Sarah Tuckerman (1880); T. W. Higginson (1880); Mabel Loomis Todd (1882); and Thomas Niles (1883). In addition to the six copies sent to others, Dickinson retained one variant record copy. The copy sent to Mabel Loomis Todd is included in this exhibit (Cat. 5.15, p. 78).

Cat. 3.11 | AC 857

About late 1885. Letter draft or fragment, with addenda or variants,
composed by Dickinson in pencil on two mailing wrappers, each
measuring 14.5 x 11.3 cm and folded into uneven quarters. The lines,
written in Dickinson's late and most disordered handwriting, were
jotted down in the wake of Helen Hunt Jackson's death in
San Francisco on August 12, 1885. No other manuscript of this draft is
known to be extant.

I never saw
Mrs Jackson
but twice, but
those twice are
indelible, and
one Day more
I am deified
was the only
impression she
ever left on
any House
    Heart
she entered —

Helen of Troy
will die, but
Helen of Colorado
never
Dear friend, can
you walk
were the last
words that
I wrote her —
Dear friend I
can fly — her
immortal
  soaring reply —

[Obverse]

[Reverse]

Cat. 4.04 │ AC 680

Late March, 1862. Letter (unsigned) composed in ink by Dickinson to Samuel Bowels on two leaves (l = 17.7 x 11.1 cm) of a folded sheet of wove, cream stationery embossed with a queen's head in full profile in a decorative surround. The manuscript has been cross-folded for mailing.

that She – was trying
to find out – if you
had a little 'Drinking
Flask" – to take abroad
with you – I would
like to serve – Sue –
And if you will tell
me – by Monday's mail –
whether you have one –
And promise me – for her
sake – not to get one –
if you hav'nt – I can
fix the telling her –
Mary sent beautiful flowers –
Did she tell – you?
Austin hopes his Errand
Will not tire you –

[2v]

Dear friend –
        Will you be
kind to Austin – again?
And would you be kinder
than sometimes – and
put the name – on – too –
He tells me to tell
you – Austin is disap –
pointed – He expected to
see you – Today –
He is sure you wont
go to Sea – without
first speaking to Him –
I presume if Emily and

[1r]

Vinnie knew of his
writing – they would
entreat Him to ask
you – not –
Austin is chilled – by
Frazer's murder –
He says – his Brain
keeps saying over
"Frazer is killed" –
Frazer is killed", just
as Father told it – to
Him – Two or three
words of lead – that
dropped so deep, they
keep weighing –
Tell Austin – how to
get over them!

[1v]

He is very sorry you
are not better –
He cares for you – when
at the Office – and
afterwards – too – at Home –
and sometimes – wakes
at night, with a
worry for you – he did'nt
finish – quite – by Day –
He would not like
it – that I betrayed
Him – so you'll never
tell – And I must
betray Sue – too –
Do not think it
dishonorable –
I found out – accidentally –

[2r]

Cat. 4.05 | AC 106

About 1875. Poem draft, with variants and/or addenda, composed in pencil by Dickinson on both sides of a partial leaf (12.7 x 11.4 cm) of off-white, lightly ruled stationery later cross-folded. Two other manuscripts of the poem, both fair copies assigned to the year 1875, are extant: Susan Gilbert Dickinson received one, and Elizabeth Holland received the other. In these copies, the variant readings are resolved. Since Dickinson retained the worksheet draft among her papers, however, it is entirely possible that she had not settled on a final version. Here Dickinson's striving over the final lines of the poem is especially marked. After concluding the poem, Dickinson began to rework its penultimate lines, "This sudden legacy / of Green," initially focusing on the word "sudden," before turning her attention to the word "legacy." The first variant stream provoked by her discontent—or simply restlessness—with the word "sudden" includes the alternates (or addenda) "bright," "whole," "swift," and "fair"; a second variant stream adds the possibilities "gay," "quick," "fleet," and its rhyming companion, "sweet"; and in a third variant stream, Dickinson returns to once more weigh the word "whole." The initial impulse for second variant stream appears to arise during Dickinson's immersion in the first variant stream. Here, the word "Apocalypse" presents itself as an alternative for "legacy," a change perhaps compelled by the earlier change from the two-syllable word "sudden" to the eight single syllable variants proposed to replace it. Abandoning, at least momentarily, the lines "This sudden legacy / of Green," Dickinson begins anew on the verso with the lines, "This whole Apocalypse / of Green –"; then generates four additional candidates for "Apocalypse": "Experience – ," "Astonishment – ," "Periphery – ," and "Experiment." A last alternative, "wild Experiment", is proposed in the final, indented line, presumably an alternate for the phrase "whole Apocalypse." The initial "A" in the manuscript has been reformed. The significance of the authorial brackets surrounding "gay" and "Green" on the recto, though they may have had a private meaning for Dickinson, is unknown. For another account of the unfolding of this poem, see Ralph W. Franklin's notes for F1356.

A   little   madness

in   the   Spring

Is   wholesome

even   for the King

But God be with

the   Clown

who ponders this

Tremendous scene

This sudden legacy

of   Green

As if it were

his own – bright   \gay

quick

whole – swift – fleet

fair   Apocalypse _ of   sweet

|Green – whole

[Obverse]

This   whole   Apocalypse

of Green –

Experience – Astonishment –

Periphery –   Experiment

wild   Experiment

[Reverse]

Of   our   deepest   delights
there   is   a   solemn   shyness
—PROGRAMME—

                        The   appetite
                        for   silence
        PART I
                        is   seldom

                        an   acquired
1. 1st and 2nd movements from 1st Organ Sonata,   .   .   *Mendelsohn.*
        MR. PARKHURST.   taste

[Obverse]

Cat. 4.06 | AC 868

About 1873 or last decade.. Lines composed by Dickinson in pencil on a remnant (5.7 x 12 cm) of a concert program. No other manuscript of this draft is known to be extant. The concert, performed on 27 June 1873, featured organist Howard Elmore Parkhurst, a graduate of Amherst College's class of 1873. The resonance of the textual fragment with its material substrate may be evidence that Dickinson penciled these lines down soon after the concert; on the other hand, it is highly unlikely that she attended the concert, and she may have jotted them down on another occasion. Parkhurst, in addition to becoming a distinguished musician, was, like Dickinson, fascinated by birdsong. From 1884 until his death in 1916, he taught music and published books about birds and ecology, including *The Birds' Calendar*, *Song Birds and Waterfowl*, and *Trees, Shrubs, and Vines of the Northeastern United States*.

Light is sufficient
to itself —
If others want to
see
It can be had on
Window panes
Some Hours of the Day —

But not for Com —
pensation —
It holds as large

[2v]   [1r]

a Glow
To Squirrel in the
Himmaleh
Precisely — as to Me —

[1v]   [2r]

Cat. 4.07 | AC 274

About 1863. Poem composed or copied in ink by Dickinson on two leaves (l = 15.2 x 9.9 cm) of a folded sheet of wove, cream stationery embossed PARIS in a decorative surround. A variant manuscript of this poem was copied by Dickinson in early 1865 onto a sheet of wove, cream, lightly ruled stationery also carrying the poems "A Doubt if it be Us", "Absence disembodies —," "Split the Lark and / you'll find the Music — ," and "That Distance was between / Us." In this later sequence "Light is sufficient" appears fourth, just before "That Distance was between / Us."

Cat. 4.08b | AC 84–1 / 2

About 1863. Poem composed or copied in ink by Dickinson on one leaf
(l = 22 x 12.4 cm) of a folded sheet of laid, cream, faintly ruled
stationery embossed WM above a shield with a double-headed eagle.
No other manuscript of this poem is known to be extant. Three further
poems are inscribed on the same sheet: "They called me to the /
Window, for"; "No Romance sold unto"; and "The Soul that hath a /
Guest." "I heard a Fly buzz – when / I died –" appears third in this
sequence of four. These poems, along with an additional seventeen
poems on five sheets, were originally stab-bound into Fascicle 26, itself
fastened with a white string. Binding holes appear 6.5 cm from the top
edge and 6.3 cm from the bottom edge of the folded sheet. In this view
of "I heard a Fly buzz – when" we can also see the ending of
"They called me to the / Window, for" and the third poem in the fascicle,
"No Romance sold unto."

This – too – the Showman
rubbed away –
And when I looked again –
Nor Farm – nor Opal Herd –
was there –
Nor Mediterranean –
   + an Amber
+ stead –

—————————

No Romance sold unto
Could so enthrall a Man –
As the perusal of
His individual One –

        + contract
'Tis Fiction's – to + dilute to
+plausibility +credibility
Our –$^+$ Novel – When tis small eno'
  To$^+$credit – 'Tis'nt true –
 + Romance —————————
+compass –

I heard a Fly buzz – when
I died –
The Stillness in the Room
Was like the Stillness in the Air –
Between the Heaves of Storm –

The Eyes around – had wrung them
dry –
And Breaths were gathering firm
For that last Onset – when the King
Be witnessed – in the Room –

I willed my Keepsakes – Signed away
What portion of me be
Assignable – and then it was
There interposed a Fly –

With Blue – Uncertain – stumbling Buzz –
Between the light – and me –
And then the Windows failed – and then
I could not see to see –

[1v]   [2r]

Bless God, he went as soldiers −
His musket on his breast −
Grant God, he charge the bravest
Of all the martial blest!

Please God, might I behold him
In epauletted white −
I should not fear the foe then −
I should not fear the fight!

———————————————

[4r]

Cat. 4.09 | AC 80−8

About 1859. Poem composed or copied in ink by Dickinson on a separated and torn leaf (l = 20.4 x 12.3 cm) of laid, greenish-white, lightly ruled stationery embossed SUPERFINE above a shield. The leaf has been torn in such a way as to disconnect "Bless God, he went as soldiers −" from the poem directly below it, "If I should cease to bring a Rose." No other manuscript of this poem is known to be extant. On the verso of the torn leaf is the beginning of "One Sister have I in the house," which has been entirely inked over presumably in an attempt by someone—most likely Mabel Loomis Todd—to blot out references to Susan Gilbert Dickinson. Since the left edge of this leaf appears to have been trimmed, perhaps by the same person who obliterated the poem, the original binding holes are no longer visible. The three poems on this leaf, however, along with an additional twenty-one poems on seven leaves, were originally stab-bound into Fascicle 2, itself fastened with a white string.

Cat. 4.10 | AC 83−4

About summer 1859. Poem composed or copied in ink by Dickinson on part of one leaf (l = 19.5 x 12.9 cm) of a folded sheet of wove, cream, lightly ruled stationery. No other manuscript of this poem is known to be extant. Dickinson inscribed six other poems on the same sheet: "'Good night,' because we must!"; "South winds jostle them − "; "Low at my problem bending"; "What Inn is this"; "I had some things that I called mine − "; and "In rags mysterious as these." "My friend attacks my friend!" completes this seven-poem sequence. These poems, along with an additional eighteen on three sheets of stationery, were originally stab-bound into Fascicle 5, itself fastened with a white string. Binding holes appear 6.8 cm from the top edge and 7.7 cm from the bottom edge of the folded sheet.

In rags mysterious as these
The shining Courtiers go,
Vailing the purple, and the plumes −
Vailing the ermine so −

Smiling, as they request an alms
At some imposing door −
Smiling when we walk barefoot
Opon their golden floor!

———————————————

My friend attacks my friend!
Oh Battle picturesque!
Then I turn Soldier too,
And he turns Satirist!
How martial is this place!
Had I a mighty gun
I think I'd shoot the human race
And then to glory run!

———————————————

"Good night," because we must!
How intricate the Dust!
I would go to know −
Oh Incognito!

Saucy, saucy Seraph,
To elude me so!
Father! They wont tell me!
Wont you tell them to?

———————————————

South winds jostle them −
Bumblebees come −
Hover − hesitate −
Drink, and are gone −

Butterflies pause
On their passage Cashmere −
I − softly plucking,
Present them here!

———————————————

[4v]   [3r]

Low at my problem bending,
Another problem comes −
Larger than mine − serener −
Involving statelier sums.

I check my busy pencil −
My fingers file away −
Wherefore, my baffled fingers
Thy perplexity?

———————————————

What Inn is this
Where for the night
Peculiar Traveller comes?
Who is the Landlord?
Where the maids?
Behold, what curious rooms?
No ruddy fires on the hearth −
No brimming tankards flow −
Necromancer! Landlord!
Who are these below?

———————————————

I had some things that I called mine −
And God, that he called his −
Till recently a rival claim
Disturbed these amities −

The property, my garden,
Which having sown with care −
He claims the pretty acre −
And sends a Bailiff there −

The station of the parties
Forbids publicity,
But Justice is sublime
Than Arms, or pedigree −

I'll institute an "Action −"
I'll vindicate the law −
Jove! Choose your counsel −
I retain "Shaw " !

———————————————

[3v]   [4r]

Cat. 4.11 | Houghton MS Am 1118.3 (35a)

About late 1861. Poems, one with variants or addenda, one continued on the verso, composed or copied in ink by Dickinson on a leaf (l = 20.7 x 12.9 cm) of wove, cream, blue-ruled stationery embossed with a queen's head above the letter L and enclosed in a decorative surround. The poem beginning "I held a Jewel in my fingers −" concludes on the verso (not pictured here): "And now, an Amethyst / remembrance / Is all I own − ." This leaf was originally bound into Fascicle 11.

I'm Nobody! Who are you?
Are you − Nobody − too?
Then there's a pair of us!
Don't tell!   they'd banish
us − you know!   advertise

How dreary − to be − Somebody!
How public − like a Frog −
To tell your name − the livelong
June −
To an admiring Bog!

───────────────

I held a Jewel in my fingers −
And went to sleep −
The day was warm, and winds
were prosy −
I said " 'Twill keep" −

I woke − and chid my honest
fingers,
The Gem was gone −

[5r]

Soul, take thy risk − s −,
          chance
with Death to be

were better than be not

with thee

[Obverse]

Cat. 4.12 | AC 357

About 1867. Poem draft, with variants or addenda, composed by Dickinson in pencil on a tiny remnant (4.5 x 9.8 cm) of cream paper embossed with flowers. On the verso is a drawing of a tombstone. No other manuscript of this poem is known to be extant.

        The way
    Hope   builds   his
  House
It   is   not   with   a   sill −
              +
nor   Rafter   −   has   that
Edifice   mars − knows
But   only   Pinnacle −
────── ────── ──────

Abode   in   as   supreme
This   superficies
As   if   it   were   of
Ledges   smit
Or   mortised   with   the
And
Laws −

[Obverse]

Cat. 4.13 | AC 450

About 1879. Poem draft, with addenda or variants, composed by Dickinson in pencil on the inside of a partial envelope originally containing a wedding invitation to the Dickinson family. Unfolded the slit-open envelope measures 13.5 x 14.4 cm. No other manuscript of this poem is known to be extant.

About late 1865. Poem composed or copied in ink by Dickinson on two leaves (l = 20.3 x 12.5 cm) of a folded sheet of wove, cream, blue-ruled stationery. One other manuscript carrying a variant version of this poem is extant: it was sent to Susan Gilbert Dickinson late in 1872. Another variant manuscript of the poem, now lost, was printed in *The Springfield Daily Republican* on February 14, 1866, and titled "The Snake." Dickinson inscribed two further poems on the same sheet as the poem above: "Ashes denote that Fire / was –" and "The Leaves like Women, / interchange"; both follow "A Narrow Fellow in / the Grass."

The Leaves like Women,
interchange
Sagacious Confidence –
Somewhat of Nods
and somewhat
Portentous inference –

The Parties in both
cases
Enjoining secrecy –
Inviolable compact
To notoriety.

[2v]

A narrow Fellow in
the Grass
Occasionally rides –
You may have met Him –
did you not
His notice sudden is –

The Grass divides as
with a Comb –
A spotted shaft is
seen –
And then it closes
at your feet
And opens further on –

He likes a Boggy
Acre
A Floor too cool
for Corn
Yet when a Boy, and
Barefoot –

[1r]

I more than once at
Noon
Have passed, I thought,
A Whip lash
Unbraiding in the Sun
When stooping to secure
it
It wrinkled, and was
gone –

Several of Nature's
People
I know, and they know
me –
I feel for them a
transport
Of cordiality –

But never met this
Fellow
Attended, or alone

[1v]

Without a tighter
breathing
And Zero at the Bone –

———————

Ashes denote that Fire
was –
⁺Revere the Grayest Pile
For the Departed Creature's
sake
That hovered there awhile –

Fire exists the first in
light
And then consolidates
Only the Chemist can
disclose
Into what Carbonates –

+ Respect

[2r]

my slowness goad
you, you knew before
myself that
Except the smaller
size
No lives are round –
These – hurry to a
sphere
And show and end –
The larger – slower
grow
And later hang –
The Summers of
Hesperides
Are long.
                Dickinson

[2v]

                          Amherst
Dear friend
                Whom
my Dog understood
could not elude
others.
I should be glad
to see you, but
think it an
apparitional pleasure –
not to be fulfilled.
I am uncertain of
Boston.
I had promised
to visit my Physician

[1r]

for a few days in
May, but Father
objects because he
is in the habit
of me.
Is it more far
to Amherst?
You would find
a minute Host
but a spacious
Welcome –
Lest you meet
my Snake and
suppose I deceive
it was robbed
of me – defeated

[1v]

too of the third line
by the punctuation.
The third and
fourth were one –
I had told you
I did not print –
I feared you might
think me ostensible.
If I still entreat
you to teach me,
Are you much
displeased?
I will be patient –
constant, never
reject your knife
and should my

[2r]

Cat. 5.05 | Boston Public Library, MS. Am. 1093 (23)

Early 1866. Letter from Dickinson to Thomas W. Higginson composed in ink on both sides of two leaves (l = 17.9 x 11.35 cm) of a sheet of wove, off-white stationery folded horizontally into thirds for mailing. The letter was at one time attached to a scrapbook, and remnants of a hinge are still visible on the document. The poem beginning "Except the smaller / size" and inscribed in the body of this letter exists in three variant forms: the earliest extant version was copied into Fascicle 26 about summer 1863; a second copy containing only the opening two stanzas and variant in punctuation was sent to Susan Gilbert Dickinson in 1863; and, finally, this version was sent to Higginson in 1866. The letter is accompanied by an envelope, also addressed in ink by Dickinson, to "Col. T. W. Higginson / Newport / Rhode Island." A three-cent stamp is affixed and marked "paid" and the envelope was postmarked in South Hadley on March 17.

Cat. 5.06 | AC 654

About autumn 1859. Poem composed or copied by Dickinson in pencil on one leaf (l = 16.8 x 10.6 cm) of a folded sheet of cream, faintly ruled stationery embossed FINE NOTE PAPER in a decorated surround. The other three writing surfaces are blank. The manuscript has been folded horizontally in thirds, perhaps in preparation for mailing. Although no trace of a legible address is visible even under magnification, Ralph W. Franklin notes that the manuscript may have been sent to Susan Gilbert Dickinson. Of the original five variant manuscripts of this poem, three are known to be extant. Of these, two manuscripts, including the one represented here and another bound into Fascicle 6, were composed about 1859; the final manuscript, also featured in this exhibition (see below at Cat. 5.07, A 465), was revised twenty-four years later in 1883.

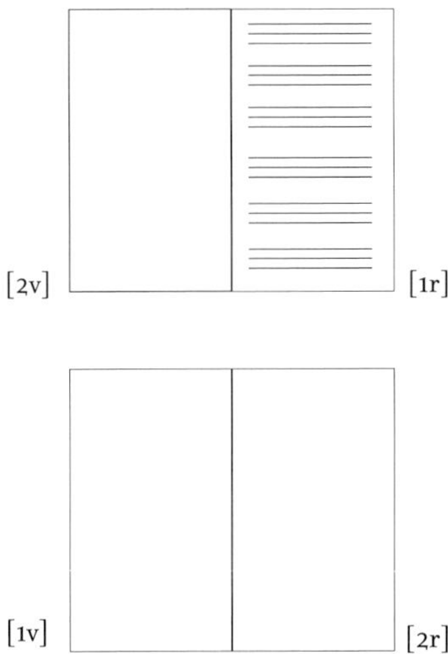

Cat. 5.07 | AC 465

About 1883. Poem composed or copied in pencil by Dickinson on a leaf (l = 22 x 12.5 cm) of wove, cream stationery later cross-folded. On the holograph, a line drawn below "Mistake" but not rendered in the transcription may suggest an emphasis on the poem's final word or only mark its ending. Of the five variant manuscripts of this poem, three are known to be extant: an 1859 copy bound into Fascicle 6; an 1859 copy sent to Susan Gilbert Dickinson; and the late 1883 copy reproduced here and found among Dickinson's papers at her death. Containing only two of the original six stanzas, Dickinson's final version of the poem distills it to its essence.

These are the days when Birds come back –
A very few – a Bird or two,
To take a final look –

These are the days when skies resume
The old – old sophistries of June –
A blue and gold mistake.

Oh fraud that cannot cheat the Bee,
Almost thy plausibility
Induces my belief,

Till ranks of seeds their witness bear,
And swiftly thro' the altered air
Hurries a timid leaf –

Oh Sacrament of summer days!
Oh last Communion in the Haze –
Permit a Child to join –

Thy sacred emblems to partake –
Thy consecrated bread to take
And thine immortal wine –

[1r]

These are the
Days when Birds
come back –
A very few – a
Bird or two –
To take a
parting look –

These are the
Days when Skies
resume
The old – old
sophistries of June –
A Blue and
Gold Mistake –

———————

[Obverse]

The Networked Recluse

Dear friend –
Thank
you for the
Kindness –
I am glad
if the Bird
seemed true
to you –
Please efface
the others and
receive these
three, which are
more like him –
a Thunder –
Storm – a Humming
Bird, and a

[2v]   [1r]

Marian Evans
Her losses make our gains ashamed –
She bore life's empty Pack
As gallantly as if the East
Were swinging at her back

Life's empty pack is heaviest,
As every porter knows
In vain to punish honey
It only sweeter grows –

Country Burial –
The Life of
Marian Evans
had much
I never knew –
A Doom of
Fruit without the
Bloom, like the
Niger Fig –
Her Losses make
our Gains ashamed –
She bore Life's
empty Pack
As gallantly as
if the East
Were swinging
at her Back –
Life's empty

[1v]   [2r]

Cat. 5.11 | AC 833

About April 1883. Letter composed in pencil by Dickinson to Thomas
Niles on six partial sheets (1 sheet [2 leaves]; 1 leaf; 1 sheet [2 leaves];
1 leaf; 1 sheet [2 leaves]; 1 sheet [2 leaves]) of laid, cream stationery
watermarked PURE IRISH LINEN F. H .D. & CO. and cross-folded
for mailing. Unfolded the sheets measure 20.5 x 26.4 cm; individual
leaves measure 20.5 x 13.2 cm. The poem titles and regularized
transcriptions inscribed directly on the manuscript may be the work
of Niles. It is difficult to identify precisely where the letter veers into
poetry: Is it with the lines "A Doom of / Fruit without the / Bloom…",
or later, with the lines, "Her Losses make / our Gains ashamed – "?
The later lines have links to two other manuscripts by Dickinson, both
belonging to the year 1883: a poem fragment found among Dickinson's
papers after her death (AC 207); and a variant fair copy sent to Susan
Gilbert Dickinson (H266). Two of the three other poems enclosed
in the letter, "The Wind begun / to rock the Grass" and "A Route / of
Evanescence" and are among the few poems Dickinson sent to a wide
range of recipients. At least five variant copies of "The Wind begun,"
four of which are known to be extant, originally existed: the earliest
surviving fair copy (c. 1864) was sent to Josiah and Elizabeth Holland;
a second, later copy (c. 1866) was sent to Susan Gilbert Dickinson; a
third, substantially revised copy was composed in 1873 and remained
among Dickinson's papers; a fourth copy, also assigned to 1873 and
since lost, was sent to Thomas W. Higginson; and a last copy (see
above) was sent to Thomas Niles in 1883. The 1864 manuscript of the
poem sent to the Hollands is included in this exhibition (see Cat. 2.23,
AC 814). Similarly, six variant copies of "A Route" originally existed:
the earliest surviving copies were sent to Frances and Louise Norcross
(1879, original MS destroyed) and Helen Hunt Jackson (1879); two
years later, Dickinson sent variant copies to Sarah Tuckerman (1880)
and Higginson (1880); next, she gave a copy to Mabel Loomis Todd
(1882); and, finally, she sent the copy transcribed above to Thomas
Niles in 1883. In addition to the six copies of this poem sent to others,
Dickinson retained one (variant) copy. The variant copies sent to
Mabel Loomis Todd and Helen Hunt Jackson are included in this
exhibition (see Cat. 5.15, AC 766, and Cat. 3.09, AC 816). Finally, in
addition to the copy of "Ample make / this Bed – " enclosed in this
1883 letter to Thomas Niles, there are at least three variant manuscripts
of the poem. The earliest copy, bearing neither address nor signature,
may have been sent to Susan Gilbert Dickinson or Samuel and Mary
Bowles in 1864; a second variant copy set down in 1865 served as a new
record copy; and a third variant copy was mailed to Higginson in 1866.
An older record copy, since destroyed or lost, was presumably used as
the base text for the 1864 version.

Note: In this transcription, the work of another transcriber is shown
in gray italic type as it appears in the manuscript itself. At some point
soon after Dickinson wrote this letter, another hand—perhaps that of
the recipient—transcribed four of the poems contained in the missive,
forcing them into more conventional spelling, capitalization, and line
structure. The contrast between Dickinson's unique voice and the
effort of the transcriber to reconcile her originality with the literary
tastes of the day is dramatically evident.

<table>
<tr><td>

Pack is heaviest,
As every Porter
knows —
In vain to
punish Honey —
It only sweeter
grows —

———

</td><td>

</td></tr>
</table>

[Obverse 3]   [Reverse 3]

<table>
<tr><td>

</td><td>

A Thunder Storm

The Wind begun
to rock the Grass
With threatening
Tunes and low —
He threw a Menace
at the Earth —
Another — at the
Sky —
The Leaves
unhooked themselves
from Trees
And started
all abroad —
The Dust did
scoop itself like
Hands

</td></tr>
</table>

[5v]   [4r]

<table>
<tr><td>

A Thunder Storm

The Wind begun to rock the grass
With threatening tunes and low —
He threw a menace at the Earth —
Another at the sky.
The leaves unhooked themselves from trees
And started all abroad;
The Dust did scoop itself like hands
And throw away the road.

The wagons quickened on the streets,
The thunder hurried slow;
The lightning showed a yellow beak,
And then a livid claw.

The birds put up the bars to nests,
The cattle clung to barns,
Then came one drop of giant rain,
And then as if the hands

That held the Dams, had parted hold —
The Waters wrecked the sky,
But overlooked my father's house,
Just quartering a tree.

</td><td>

And throw away
the Road —
The Wagons
quickened on the
Streets
The Thunder
hurried slow —
The Lightning
showed a yellow
Beak
And then a
livid Claw —
The Birds put
up the Bars
to Nests —
The Cattle
clung to Barns —

</td></tr>
</table>

[4v]   [5r]

      The Networked Recluse

Then came one
Drop of Giant
Rain
And then as
if the Hands
That held the
Dams, had
parted hold –
The Waters
wrecked the Sky –
But overlooked
My Father's House –
Just quartering
a Tree ——

[Obverse 6]

[Reverse 6]

A Route
of Evanescence,
With a revolving
Wheel –
A Resonance
of Emerald
A Rush of
Cochineal –
And Every
Blossom on the
Bush
Adjusts it's
tumbled Head –
The Mail
from Tunis – prob –
ably –

[8v]

[7r]

An easy
Morning's Ride –

[7v]

[8r]

A Country Burial

Ample make
this Bed —
Make this
Bed with Awe —
In it wait till
Judgment break
Excellent and Fair —

Be it's Mattrass
straight —
Be it's Pillow
round —
Let no Sunrise —
yellow Noise
Interrupt this
Ground ______

[10v]

[9r]

A Country Burial
Ample make this Bed,
Make this Bed with Awe ,
In it wait till Judgment break,
Excellent and fair.

Be its Mattrass straight,
Be its Pillow round;
Let no sunrise' yellow noise
Interrupt this ground.

[9v]

[10r]

'Tis whiter than an
Indian Pipe –
'Tis dimmer – than a
Lace –
No Stature has it, like
a Fog
when you approach
the place –
Not any voice
+imply it here
Or intimate it there –
A spirit – how doth
it accost –
What +function hath the Air?

This + limitless Hyperbole
Each one of us
shall be –
~~This~~ 'Tis Drama –
if Hypothesis
It be not Tragedy –
+ denote –   + designate –

+ What customs –
+ And this – this
unsurmised thing –
Apocalyptic thing –

Cat. 5.12 | AC 483

About 1879. Poem draft, with variants or addenda and cancelations,
composed by Dickinson in pencil on both sides of a partial leaf (13.3
x 12.6 cm) of cream, blue-ruled stationery, embossed with a right-
facing female head in full profile and folded horizontally in half. No
other manuscript of this poem is known to be extant. The "T" of the
initial "'Tis" appears to have been reformed. This document offers
a fine example of the way Dickinson often used the verso of a leaf to
continue her experimentation with variants and addenda. In this case,
the relationships among the variants, though spatially distant, are easily
discernible: "+imply" / "+ denote – "; "intimate" / "+ designate – ";
"What +function" / "+What customs"; "This + limitless Hyperbole" /
"+ And this – this / unsurmised thing –" / "Apocalyptic thing – ."
Dickinson drew several lines through the word "This," when she
canceled it in favor of the word "'Tis."

Dear   friend   —
          That without
suspecting   it
you   should
send   me   the
preferred   flower
of   life,   seems
almost   supernat —
ural,   and   the
sweet   glee   that
I   felt   at   meeting
it,   I   could
confide   to   none   —
I   still   cherish
the   clutch   with
which   I   bore

[2v]

[1r]

it   from   the   ground
when   a   wondering
Child,   an   un —
earthly   booty,   and
maturity   only
enhances   Mystery,
never   decreases
it   —   To   du —
plicate   the   Vision
is   almost   more
amazing,   for
God's   unique
capacity   is   too
surprising   to
surprise —
I   know   not
how   to   thank
you   —   We   do   not

[1v]

[2r]

thank   the
Rainbow ,   al —
though   it's   Trophy
is   a   snare —
To   give   delight
is   hallowed   —
perhaps   the   toil
of   Angels,   whose
avocations   are
concealed —
I   trust   that   you
are   well,   and
the   quaint   little
Girl   with   the
deep   Eyes,   every
day   more   fathom —
less —
          With joy,
          E. Dickinson —

[Obverse 3]

Cat. 5.14 | AC 765

September 1882. Letter composed in pencil by Dickinson to Mabel
Loomis Todd on 3 leaves (1 sheet [2 leaves]; 1 leaf) (l = 19.8 x 12.4 cm)
of wove, cream stationery watermarked IRISH LINEN FABRIC and
folded horizontally into thirds for mailing. The envelope accompanying
the letter survives. Addressed in ink by George Montague—"Mrs.
Todd / #1413 College Hill Terrace / Washington / D.C."—Dickinson's
message was mailed on September 30 and reached Washington, D.C.,
on the morning of October 2.

Dear friend,
I cannot
make an
Indian Pipe
but please
accept a
Humming Bird –

A Route of
Evanescence
With a revolving
Wheel –
A Resonance
Of Emerald –

[1r]

[2v]

A Rush of
Cochineal –
And every
Blossom on
the Bush
Adjusts it's
tumbled Head –
The mail
from Tunis
probably –
An easy
Morning's Ride –

E. Dickinson –

[2r]

[1v]

Cat. 5.15 | AC 766

October 1882. Letter composed in pencil by Dickinson to Mabel Loomis Todd on two leaves (l = 20.3 x 12.7 cm) of a folded sheet of wove, cream stationery watermarked WESTON'S LINEN RECORD 1881 and folded horizontally into thirds for mailing. Dickinson wrote only on the rectos of each leaf, leaving the versos blank. She addressed the envelope, also in pencil, "Mrs Todd – ." On the second leaf, the "A" in the line "A Rush of" has been reformed. The poem inscribed in the body of the letter, "A Route of / Evanescence," is one of the few poems Dickinson sent to a wide range of correspondents: Helen Hunt Jackson (1879); Frances and Louise Norcross (1879, original MS destroyed); Sarah Tuckerman (1880), Thomas W. Higginson (1880), Mabel Loomis Todd (MS above); and Thomas Niles (1883). In addition to the six copies sent to others, Dickinson retained one variant copy. The copies sent to Helen Hunt Jackson and Thomas Niles are included in this exhibition (see Cat. 3.09, AC 816 and Cat. 5.11, AC 833).

Cat. 5.18 | AC 214

Last decade. Lines, with variants or addenda, composed by Dickinson in pencil on the torn bottom of a notebook page measuring 1.7 x 11.6 cm. No other manuscript of this fragment is known to be extant.

Cat. 5.21 | AC 85–7

About summer 1862. Poem composed or copied by Dickinson in ink and pencil on one leaf (l = 20.5 x 12.7 cm) of a folded sheet of laid, cream, blue-ruled stationery embossed with a flower in a decorative oval surround. In the opening stanza, the "o" of "for" has been reformed or written over. The variant word choices, "Knees" and "two," as well as the associated "+" marks, are in pencil and appear to have been added later, though how much later is not known. The sheet, carrying only one other poem, "If you were coming in the Fall," was originally stab-bound along with thirteen additional poems on five sheets into Fascicle 17. Binding holes are 8.3 cm from the top edge and 6.3 cm from the bottom edge of the leaf.

Honey grows every where
valor
but iron on a

seldom Bush –

[Obverse]

I'd toss it yonder, like a
Rind,   +taste
And +take Eternity –

But, now, uncertain of the
length
Of this, that is between,
It goads me, like the
Goblin Bee –
That will not state –
its' sting –

———————

[8v]

It was not Death, for
I stood up,
And all the Dead, lie down –
It was not Night, for
All the Bells
Put out their Tongues, for Noon –

It was not Frost, for on
my + Flesh   + Knees
I felt Siroccos – crawl –
Nor Fire – for just my +
marble feet   +two
Could keep a Chancel, cool –

And yet, it tasted, like
them all,
The Figures I have seen
Set orderly, for Burial,
Reminded me, of mine –

[7r]

As if my life were shaven,
And fitted to a frame,
And could not breathe
without a key,
And 'twas like Midnight,
some –

When Everything that ticked –
has stopped –
And Space stares – all around –
Or Grisly frosts – first Au –
tumn morns,
Repeal the Beating Ground –

But, most, like Chaos –
Stopless – cool –
Without a Chance, or spar –
Or even a Report of Land –
To justify – Despair .

[7v]

If you were coming in the Fall,
I'd brush the Summer by
With half a smile, and
half a spurn,
As Housewives do, a Fly.

If I could see you in a
year,
I'd wind the months in balls –
And put them each in
separate Drawers,
For fear the numbers fuse –

If only Centuries, delayed,
I'd count them on my Hand,
Subtracting, till my fingers
dropped
Into Van Dieman's Land –

If certain, when this life was out –
That your's and mine, should be –

[8r]

A   Pang   is   more
conspicuous   in   Spring
    In   contrast   with   the
    things   that   those –
                                   sing
Not   Birds   entirely   –   but
Minds   –   Minute   Effulgen –
                             –cies
    And   winds   –
    When   what   they   sung

for   is   undone
    who   cares   about
    a   Blue   Bird's   Tune   –
why,   Resurrection
    had   to   wait
Till   they   had   moved
         a   Stone   –

[Obverse]

Cat. 5.23 | AC 109

About 1881. Poem draft, with variants, composed by Dickinson in pencil on the inside of a partial, slit-open envelope originally addressed "Vinnie." Having reached the far edge of the envelope, Dickinson hyphenated the word "Effulgen – /– cies," writing the last four letters, preceded by a dash, directly below the first eight letters. The final lines, beginning with the line "When what they sung," appear again on the inside of a second envelope, this one addressed by Louise Norcross to Dickinson. In this variant manuscript, the final lines become the opening lines of a new, variant draft.